A SOWER WENT OUT

Reverend Dr. Eugene C. Bay

Portrait by William Benson, 2004

A SOWER WENT OUT

Selected Sermons

by

Eugene C. Bay

For

my grandchildren

Annelise, Cooper, Ian, Matthew,

Michael, Robbie, and Timmy

Contents

PART FOUR:
SERMONS ON THE ISSUES OF THE DAY

Preface

This is a collection of sermons, a representative sample of my preaching in the Bryn Mawr Presbyterian Church over a period of more than seventeen years. They are printed as they were preached. They are arranged in four categories: sermons for Advent and Christmas, sermons for Lent and Easter, sermons for "Ordinary Time," and sermons that were preached in response to societal issues or events in the world.

I wish to acknowledge my indebtedness to the theologians and Biblical scholars who, over many years, have informed my preaching, to my colleagues at Bryn Mawr and elsewhere who have both supported and challenged me, and to the members of a congregation who have listened attentively, been willing to think about what they have heard and, above all, by their faith and actions, have encouraged this preacher to believe that his labor has not been in vain.

I am especially grateful to two others: my wife, Jean, who has been at one and the same time a lifelong cheerleader and an honest and helpful critic of my homiletical efforts, and my Assistant, Marguerite Hanna, not only for her skillful preparation of this manuscript, but for her devoted helpfulness for the entire time of my ministry at Bryn Mawr.

It has been my goal in preaching to relate the good news of the gospel to the world as it is and to persons where and as they are. Whether these sermons meet that test the reader will be the judge. Insofar as any of them kindle faith, encourage hope, or prompt loving behavior, their author will rejoice and give thanks to God.

Eugene C. Bay

PART ONE

Sermons for
Advent and Christmas

~

The Truth Is . . .

Readings: **Micah 5:2-5a**   **December 19, 1999**
              Hebrews 1-1-4
              John 1:1-18

And the Word became flesh and lived among us, and we have seen his glory, the glory as of a father's only son, full of grace and truth.

— John 1:14

Raymond Brown, who died earlier this year, was widely acknowledged as the Dean of New Testament scholars, appreciated both for his scholarly work and his reverent spirit. His book, *The Birth of the Messiah,* is easily the definitive commentary on the infancy narratives in Matthew and Luke. Such was Brown's renown that even newspaper reporters would turn to him on those occasions when they sought an authoritative word on something having to do with the Bible. He said once that every Christmas reporters would call him to ask, "What really happened?" He would reply, one imagines with some impatience, that they would do well to ask instead what the real message of the stories was . . . and is![1]

That is good advice, wise counsel, not only for skeptical reporters, but also for you who have found your way to worship this morning. We are nearing the time when we will listen once more to the stories we know so well and love so much, when we will sing again of "angels bending near the earth, to touch their harps of gold," to that time when a few of you will even don costumes and pretend that you are shepherds minding sheep or wise men bearing gifts. One or two may even masquerade as angels — which is pretty funny, when you stop to think about it! What a shame it

2

would be to do all these things and not to ponder the important question — not the matter of fact — what really happened? — but the matter of meaning — what is the real message?

That is what you should care about. It is all that the Fourth Gospel cares about. In what is called the Prologue to John's Gospel there is nothing at all about angels or shepherds, no reference to magi or manger, not even a mention of Mary and Joseph — or, for that matter, of Jesus, by name! John cares nothing at all about who was or was not there, and what was or was not said and done. For him, all that matters is the question of meaning. So, unlike Matthew, who introduces his version of the Christmas story by saying, "Now the birth of Jesus . . . took place in this way," unlike Luke, whose account is set in the days when "a decree went out from the Emperor Augustus," and in contrast with Mark, who omits any reference to Jesus' origins, John's narrative has for its context the region of the celestial. He opens his Gospel by saying: "In the beginning was the Word, and the Word was with God, and the Word was God." According to no less a personage than Saint Augustine, the verses that follow must have been divinely inspired, for, Augustine maintained, it would be impossible for a mere mortal to manufacture speech of such elegance and eloquence.[2]

In those verses, we are told of God's gift of life, and of a divinely-initiated light that shines in the darkness. There is a reference to the witness of John the Baptist, and the suggestion that while some are happy to receive God's Word, others may not even recognize it for what it is, or refuse it even if they do. Those who do receive it, John says, experience something like a second birth and know themselves to be "children of God." All of which leads to what has been described as "the audacious claim of the Christian gospel" — the assertion that God chose both to reveal himself, and to accomplish the work of salvation, in the person of Jesus. "And the Word became flesh and dwelt among us," is the way John puts it, "and we have seen his glory, the glory of a father's only son, full of grace and truth."

* * *

Recently I came across the story of a man from a small southern town whose father had died when the man was an infant. While other boys would play catch or go fishing with their fathers, this man had no father, not even any memories of his father. As he grew older, he became obsessed by the desire to learn about his dad. Whenever he met someone who may have known his father — a school teacher in the town where his father had grown up, a retired minister who had once served in his father's home church, an aging cousin of his father — he would ask, "What can you tell me about my father?" It is said the man spent a lifetime piecing together shards of recollection, pieces of anecdotes, trying to get a picture of his father, the one who, with his mother, had given him life.[3]

In a much more profound way, the author of the Fourth Gospel knows that we human beings long to know the One from whom we came and in whom we live and move and have our very being. We yearn to meet someone who can inform us about our divine parent. What we desire to know, says John, God wants us to know, and has gone to extraordinary lengths to tell us. The theological word for it is "incarnation": the revelation of God in human flesh and blood. The claim is not that this is the sole disclosure of the divine. The law was given through Moses, John declares. The Book of Hebrews says: "Long ago God spoke to our ancestors in many and various ways by the prophets. . . ." But the meaning of Christmas is that all other means of divine communication have been forever superceded by that which began in Bethlehem. "In these last days," says the author of Hebrews, God "has spoken to us by a Son. . . ." And John says: "No one has ever seen God. It is God the only Son, who is close to the Father's heart, who has made him known."

*   *   *

"The truth is," we sometimes begin a sentence, when for one reason or another what is true is in question — when there is a falsehood to be corrected, say, or when there is some misunderstanding to be cleared up, or when perhaps there are contradictory claims of truth, or when there is ambiguity or mystery. "The truth is . . . ," we say. John says when it comes to God, "the truth is a person."[4] Not an abstract idea, not a proposition, a person.

There are two other places in the Fourth Gospel where this claim is highlighted. One is at the Last Supper when Jesus informs his disciples that he will soon be leaving them. "You know the way to the place I am going," he tells them. Thomas says, "Lord, we do not know where you are going. How can we know the way?" That's when Jesus says: "I am the way, and the truth and the life."

A bit later, after his arrest, there is the conversation between Jesus and Pontius Pilate. Pilate asks Jesus if he is a king, and Jesus replies that he "came into the world, to testify to the truth." Pilate responds, whether as a cynic or out of curiosity, I do not know: "What is truth?" There is no reply. Jesus doesn't say anything. In John's mind, he doesn't need to say anything. The answer to Pilate's question is standing there, right in front of him. The truth is a Person.

Even we Christians sometimes forget where to begin when we want to know the truth about God. "It is astonishing," Donald Baillie has written, "how many people assume they know what the word 'God' means. But it is even more astonishing that (those who) profess Christian belief . . . are apt to start with some conception of God, picked up we know not where . . . , which is different from the Christian conception, and then (they) attempt the impossible task of understanding how such a God could (be) incarnate in Jesus."[5] If and when you get the real message of Christmas, you won't make that mistake. You won't start with ideas about God and try to make them fit Jesus. Once you understand what Christmas means, you will start with Jesus and let him tell you the truth about God — and not just by what he says, mind you, but by what he does, and even more by who he is — the one "who is close to the Father's heart."

*   *   *

What if you were to let this Son tell you the truth about his Father? What would it mean? What is the nature of the One who came to us in Jesus? That's a question I long for you to think about and answer for yourself. You may see things I do not. But here is a little of what I see.

When I look at "the Word made flesh" I see almost the opposite of what many people assume is the nature of God: not almighty power, but lowliness, humility. John says of him who came from God and lived among us, "we have seen his glory." But it is, you must admit, a strange glory. It is, as another put it, "the majesty that had no where to lay its head; the grandeur that was meek and lowly; the beauty that had neither form nor comeliness that anyone should desire him; (his is) the splendor of a lonely Wanderer, weary and footsore, with nails through his hands and feet. . . ."[6] A strange kind of glory, indeed.

When I look at "the Word made flesh" — the God who came to us in Jesus — I see a vulnerable God, one who comes to us as goodness unguarded, who, out of respect for our freedom, never coerces, but always seeks to persuade. At the same time, I see One who is nothing if not persistent. The English poet Francis Thompson called him, "the Hound of

Heaven." "I fled Him down the nights and down the days," he writes. "I fled Him down the arches of the years." And he goes on to describe the "strong feet that followed, followed after," until at last Thompson abandons his flight and hears a voice saying: "All which thy child's mistake fancies as lost, I have stored for thee at home: Rise, clasp my hand and come!"[7]

Ann Lamott has a different, yet similar image. Her book, *Traveling Mercies,* is the story of her rescue, her redemption, from a life of drunkenness and debauchery. In it, she tells of the night she first experienced the presence of Christ. "This experience spooked me badly," she writes, "but I thought it was just an apparition, born of fear and self-loathing and booze. But then everywhere I went, I had the feeling that a little cat was following me, wanting me to reach down and pick it up, wanting me to open the door and let it in. But I knew what would happen," she says: "you let a cat in one time, give it a little milk, and then it stays forever. So I tried to keep one step ahead of it, slamming my houseboat door [which is where she lived] when I entered or left."

The next Sunday Lamott went to church. She says: "I began to cry and left before the benediction and I raced home and felt a little cat running along my heels, and I walked down the dock past dozens of potted flowers, under a sky as blue as one of God's own dreams, and I opened the door to my houseboat, and I stood there a minute, and then I hung my head and said, '. . . I quit.' I took a long deep breath and said out loud, 'All right. You can come in.'" It was, she says, "My beautiful moment of conversion."[8] The truth about God, she had finally realized, is a Person: lowly, vulnerable, not the least bit coercive, but, as Thompson had found before her, persistently following after.

What it comes down to, I believe, is this: in the person called Jesus, and especially in the miracle of the incarnation, God's commitment to this world becomes the astonishing certainty. "The Word became flesh and lived among us." Lived among us not in some Garden of Eden untouched by evil or tragedy, but in this world with all its grime and crime, with its wars and rumors of wars. In this world where some children are abandoned and other children run away. In this world of sin and sorrow, of sickness and death. "The Word became flesh and lived among us." Not only lived among us, but died for us and rose for us. So the truth is, there is nowhere God in Christ cannot get to, no place beyond the reach of His grace and mercy. Not the divorce court. Not the hospital waiting room.

Not the home that is filled with squabbling and bickering, even at Christmas time. Not even the cemetery. The truth about this God who came to us in Jesus is, not only is there no place so dark his light can't shine in it, there is no life so lost he cannot touch and transform with his "grace and truth." Why, it could happen to you, right here, right now. The One who came into the world at Bethlehem, would like nothing more than to enter that little world which is you. "Listen!," he is saying. "I am standing at the door, knocking; if you hear my voice and open the door, I will come into you and eat with you, and you with me."

*   *   *

What really happened? I don't know, and I don't much care. It's not that the facts about the shepherds and the star, the angels and the magi don't matter. "It's just that they don't matter as much as the stories do, and stories can be true whether they happen or not."[9] And, as George Buttrick said once, the stories of Christmas don't prove Jesus; he proves them.[10] What matters about the Christmas stories is their meaning. What they all want us to know is, when it comes to God, the truth is — a Person!

> Word of the Father,
> Now in flesh appearing!
> O come, let us adore Him
> Christ, the Lord!

1. Reported by Fleming Rutledge in *The Christian Century*, December 8, 1999, p. 1195.
2. Raymond Brown, *The Gospel According to John,* The Anchor Bible, Vol. I (Garden City, NY: Doubleday & Co., 1966), p. 18.
3. Thomas G. Long, *Hebrews*, Interpretation (Louisville: John Knox Press, 1997), p. 15.
4. A statement attributed to Theologian Thomas Torrance.
5. Donald Baillie, *God Was In Christ,* as quoted in *The Living Pulpit,* Vol. 3, No. 1, p. 38.
6. Paul Scherer, *Love Is a Spendthrift* (New York: Harper, 1961), p. 14.
7. *The World's Great Religious Poetry*, Caroline Miles Hill, editor (New York: The MacMillan Co. 1954), p. 45.
8. Anne Lamott, *Traveling Mercies* (New York: Partheon Books, 1999), p. 50.
9. Barbara Brown Taylor, *Home By Another Way* (Cambridge, Boston: Cowley Publication, 1999), p. 28.
10. Quoted from memory.

~

Imagine That!

Readings: **Isaiah 11:1-9**   **December 9, 2001**
                  Romans 15:4-13
                  Matthew 3:1-12

The wolf shall live with the lamb, the leopard shall lie down with the kid, the calf and the lion and the fatling together, and a little child shall lead them.

                                                    — Isaiah 11:6

This was the text that inspired the painting by the 18th century Quaker painter-philosopher, Edward Hicks, to which he gave the title, "The Peaceable Kingdom." The painting is in the possession of our own Art Museum. But, at the moment, as I learned the other day, it is not on display; it is in storage. I don't know why. Perhaps because, in our current climate, it seems so unreal, so idealistic.

Isaiah envisions a time when "they shall not hurt or destroy on all my holy mountain." But in our time newspaper headlines shout a different message: "U.S. Planes Pound Taliban Positions Around Kandahar"; "Israel Begins 'War on Terror'"; "Americans Killed and Wounded by Friendly Fire." Last Sunday we heard another of Isaiah's prophecies: "They shall beat their swords into plowshares, and their spears into pruning hooks; nation shall not lift up sword against nation, neither shall they learn war any more." These prophetic texts do not represent what we call "reality." They are mocked by current events. They are completely at odds with the world we know and experience. Which, I believe, is precisely why they insist on being heard in this Advent season. By the mercy of God, we are not permitted to rest comfortably in this world as it is. We are

8

summoned to believe that what has always been, and now is, is *not* what must, or will, forever be. We are invited and encouraged to imagine a world different from the one with which we are familiar, and to which we have for so long acquiesced.

*   *   *

Isaiah's envisioning of a new and different reality, as we have it in the 11th chapter of his prophecy, consists of two parts. In part one the prophet imagines the emergence of an unusual leader. In part two he describes how the world will be changed as a consequence of this leader's coming.

Isaiah tells of one who comes from God, but who emerges from a strange place. "A shoot shall come out from the stump of Jesse . . . ," he says. The image is that of a forest that has been cut down, all the trees leveled, nothing left but stumps. Scholars think Isaiah may have had in mind the end of the dynasty of King David. It was all but wiped out. Nothing left of it but a few distant relatives — "stumps." But then, in the mind's eye of the prophet, "the spirit of the Lord" begins to blow, and from one stump a tender shoot emerges. There comes forth one with "the spirit of wisdom and understanding . . . ," one whose "delight is in the fear of the Lord." This one is able to probe deeply into the human condition, to see far beyond what the eye can discern, and to know far more than what the ear alone can hear. This unusual leader has a particular empathy for "the poor," for "the meek of the earth." He seems instinctively to know that before there can be peace, there must be justice. Inequities must be dealt with; "righteousness" must become a reality. Such, Isaiah says, is the one who comes forth like a tender shoot "from the stump of Jesse."

Hearing all this, we think of Jesus. Not merely because it is said of him that he descended from the house of David. We think of him because he arose from such an unlikely place, a stump-like place. He came from Nazareth, of which it was said, "Can anything good come out of Nazareth?" We think of Jesus because "the spirit of the Lord did rest upon him, because he did not "judge by what his eyes (saw)," because his delight was "in the fear of the Lord," and because "righteousness" was "the belt around his waist, and faithfulness the belt around his loins." Perhaps we think of Jesus, as well, because we sense that if we ever did really listen to him, if we ever did really do as he says, if ever we were not satisfied just to worship him but really and truly began to follow him, then maybe it would be as Isaiah imagines, and the wolf and the lamb would be able to lie down together . . . and the Israelis and the Palestinians, the Christians and the Muslims, the Democrats and the Republicans, even the conservative Presbyterians and the liberal Presbyterians! . . . and "they (would) not hurt or destroy" anywhere on God's good earth.

*   *   *

Such, in any case is the world the prophet dares to imagine. And, in this season of Advent, Isaiah summons us to join in. "The wolf shall live with the lamb . . ."— imagine that!, says the prophet. "The cow and the bear shall graze" — imagine that! "The nursing child shall play over the hole of the asp" — imagine that! "They will not hurt or destroy in all my holy mountain" — imagine that!

I must tell you, I cannot, in good conscience, hide it from you: these Sundays of Advent are subversive. Their intent is to contradict what we think of as "reality." All week long we read the *Wall Street Journal, The New York Times, Newsweek.* We listen to Katie Couric and Peter Jennings. This is the way it is, they tell us. This is the way the world works. Get used to it. You can't change it. All week long we hear of a world of human autonomy, a world where we are in charge, where God is not present and God is not real. Then, on these Advent Sundays, we come to church, and we encounter these strange texts, announcing what Stanley Hauerwas of Duke calls "the triumph of God against the deadening of (the human) imagination. . . ."[1] These texts suggest that we are not autonomous, after all. There is something like a wind blowing through our world, something called "the spirit of the Lord." What it means is, maybe things do not have to be the way they are, after all.

"A shoot shall come out from the stump. . . ." Advent invites us to imagine, with Isaiah, a future not held hostage to the past, and not in bondage to the present. Advent invites a new orientation toward the future. It's what crabby, crusty old John the Baptist is doing when he says, "Repent, for the kingdom of God is at hand." When John says, "Repent," perhaps what you hear is "Be remorseful, feel guilty." John could care less about that. He is not interested in guilt or remorse. He wants us to prepare for a future that will be different from the past or the present. He wants you and me to re-orient ourselves around the coming of the reign of God. To start now to live the way it will be when that kingdom you and I keep praying for really comes. Imagine what that will be like, John is saying, and get with the program. "Repent, for the kingdom of God is at hand."

*   *   *

Advent summons us to see a world in which "the spirit of the Lord" is at work, to look beyond what our eyes see and imagine a world different from the one that is. "The first thing we must do," writes my friend Joanna Adams, "is turn toward the vision God gives us of a world made right and say, 'Aha! I see it. This is what God intends, these great reversals to the way we have always assumed things have to be.'"[2] To those who say, "what always has been, and is now, will always be," the prophet answers, you have not factored in "the dreams dreamed by God and by the agents of God, ordinary people like you and me in whose minds and hearts God has planted God's own dream."[3]

Examples come readily to mind. The long-suffering people of South Africa to whom "the spirit of the Lord" gave a vision of a time when apartheid would be no more. The mothers in Northern Ireland — Catholic and Protestant — who imagined a land free from violence and began to insist that their men folk join them in making it a reality. And, then there is the one who, not so many years ago, stood at the Lincoln Memorial and stirred our own land with a dream of racial reconciliation.

Our own Kenwyn Smith has given us a story of another imagining prompted by "the spirit of the Lord," an imagining that transformed what he calls "the wilderness of AIDS" into a community of hospitality, compassion, and conversion. The reality was people all around dying from AIDS. Many of them were going hungry and most of them were alone. A few Presbyterians began to imagine a different possibility: what they might do "to ensure that in the Philadelphia region, no man, woman, or child who was homebound and ill with HIV/AIDS ever went hungry again." Imagine that!, a handful of Christian people said, and what ultimately became MANNA was born: some 650 volunteers, using the financial contributions of 3,000 people, to prepare and deliver 2,500 meals a day, and to discover that in their giving was a great and unexpected receiving. Kenwyn's book — available from our book center in the Ministries Center — tells of the transformation that occurred, in the lives of those who were being helped, and in the lives of the helpers. On the next-to-last page of his book, Kenwyn says that what came into being was one of those "possibilities previously only imaginable in the dream world."[4]

"They will not hurt or destroy on all my holy mountain. . . ." Imagine that!, says Isaiah. Imagine the world as a hospitable place. Imagine a world safe for children. Imagine communities where there is rejoicing with those who rejoice, and weeping with those who weep, where love is genuine and people out-do one another in showing honor. Imagine that! It's what Advent summons us to do. And I want to say to you: do not fail to do some imagining closer to home. Is there a dark, seemingly hopeless place in your own life, where you work, perhaps, or in your neighborhood, or even in your own family, where you have come to accept as unchangeable what, with "the spirit of the Lord" and you at work, might be changed? How might it be different? Imagine that!, and who knows?, it may become different.

*   *   *

"The wolf shall live with the lamb, the leopard shall lie down with the kid, the calf and the lion and the fatling together, and a little child shall lead them." Imagine that! Foolish old Isaiah, to imagine all that he did. But it's precisely what people of faith always do. "Faith is the assurance of things hoped for," says the Letter to the Hebrews, "the conviction of things not seen."

"The church on Sunday morning," writes Walter Brueggemann, "may be the last place left in our society for imaginative speech that permits people to enter into new worlds of faith and to participate in joyous, obedient life."[5] In any case, it's what we do here. It's what Advent insists we do. Listen to people like foolish Isaiah, and crazy old John the Baptist, and dare to believe that what is not yet may, "the spirit of the Lord" and the likes of us cooperating, come to be. "They will not hurt or destroy on all my holy mountain. . . ." Imagine that!, and who knows?, somehow, somewhere, God may use you to help bring the day when it is no longer just a dream.

Prayer:

By your spirit, O God, give us grace to imagine what no eye has seen, nor ear heard, nor the human heart conceived, but what you have prepared for those who love you. And having imagined, grant us strength, courage, and perseverance to serve as your agents in helping to make it so, through Jesus Christ our Lord. Amen.

1. William H. Willimon and Stanley Hauerwas, *Preaching To Strangers* (Louisville, KY: Westminster/John Knox Press, 1992), p. 121.

2. Joanna Adams, "It Takes Imagination," Trinity Presbyterian Church, December 10, 2000.

3. Ibid.

4. Kenwyn K. Smith, *Manna In the Wilderness of AIDS* (Cleveland, Ohio: The Pilgrim Press, 2002), p. 209.

5. Walter Brueggemann, *Finally Comes the Poet* (Minneapolis: Fortress Press, 1989), p. 3.

~

The Advent Question

Readings: Isaiah 35:1-10   December 16, 2001
               James 5:7-11
               Matthew 11:2-11

When John heard in prison what the Messiah was doing, he sent word by his disciples and said to him, "Are you the one who is to come, or are we to wait for another?" Jesus answered them, "Go and tell John what you hear and see: the blind receive their sight, the lame walk, the lepers are cleansed, the deaf hear, the dead are raised, and the poor have good news brought to them. And blessed is anyone who takes no offense at me."

— Matthew 11:2-6

I am guessing you are not exactly thrilled by yet one more appearance of John the Baptist in this Advent season. By the time you get this close to Christmas you are wanting to hear the angels sing. You are ready for the company of shepherds and wise men. You are anxious to make your way to the manger. But, first, we have to deal with John. It seems we are not permitted to go to Bethlehem and see the baby until, first, we have considered that honest and haunting question John puts to Jesus: "Are you the one who is to come, or are we to wait for another?"

* * *

We come upon John in a different place from where he was when we heard from him a week ago, and he himself appears different. Out there in the wilderness he seemed austere, judgmental, and down right uncouth with his denunciation of the religious big wigs as "a brood of vipers."

Today, however, he is a more subdued and sympathetic figure, locked up, as he is, in a hellhole of a prison somewhere near the Dead Sea. He is there, not because of any criminal activity, not because he is a threat to society. He is there because he is a threat to the tyrannical Herod, because he has had the courage of his convictions, because he has spoken truth to power.

Being in prison, John has had lots of time to think. Mostly he has been thinking about Jesus, and he had begun to wonder if perhaps he was wrong about him. Earlier, John has been sure that Jesus was the promised Messiah. He was the one who would bring the day of the Lord. The one who would seize the ax and cut down all those trees that were bearing no fruit. The one who would pick up the winnowing fork and separate the wheat from the chaff. But, according to the rumors that had come to John in prison, nothing of that sort was happening. What John expected and what Jesus was doing were worlds apart. John had to know. He had invested himself heavily in the cause of God's righteousness. It was about to cost him his life. He had to know: Was Jesus the one who had been promised? Or, had John thrown his life away on a mistake? John had to know. And so he sent his disciples to Jesus to ask, "Are you the one who is to come, or are we to wait for another?"

It's a question that echoes down the centuries, a question most of us find an occasion to ask now and again. The reason is that, like John, we have put our faith in Jesus. We have our expectations of Jesus. When he doesn't perform as we think he ought, when we are disappointed because of what does, or does not happen, we too, begin to wonder, Is he really the one?

Maybe, for example, you turn on the evening news, and what you see is a scene of a fire burning, smoke rising, and dead bodies lying all around, some of them children, the result of one more bombing of Israelis by Palestinians or vice versa. You sit there wondering, Why, if Jesus is the Christ, isn't the world a better place? If he is the Prince of Peace, when does he begin to reign?

Or you answer the phone and are told that your best friend has just died of a heart attack at age 50. And you want to say what Mary and Martha did say when Lazarus died: "Lord, if you had been here, it wouldn't have happened." Or you read in the newspaper how a mother of five, suffering from postpartum depression, has drowned her children, one by one, in a bathtub full of water. And you ask yourself, where in the world was the one who said, "Let the children come to me"? Or maybe you have been trying for a long time to get pregnant, praying to get pregnant, and finally it has happened; and then in the fourth month there is a miscarriage. You are devastated, and you may well feel like asking, Jesus, why did you set me up for such a disappointment? Are you the one?

Personally, I think it is next to impossible to live in this world as it is, and not ask John's question from time to time. And it's all right to do so. It's something I especially want the youth who are with us today to know: it's all right to ask such questions. It's part of what it means to be a human being. It is evidence of your stature as a creature bearing the image of God. It's a testimony to your nobility, to your capacity for transcendence. You have the ability not only to experience life, but to ponder its meaning, to reflect on its mystery. And, as you do, questions are bound to arise, including the Advent question: "Are you the one who is to come, or are we to wait for another?"

*   *   *

What John does with this question is to send it directly to Jesus. He tells his disciples, "Go and find Jesus and ask him: 'Are you the one who is to come, or are we to wait for another?' " When they do find Jesus, and ask him, what does he do? He doesn't scold John for asking, doesn't rebuke John's disciples for bringing the question. Jesus honors the question, just as immediately afterwards, he honors John himself, saying of him, "I tell you among those born of women no one has arisen greater than John the Baptist. . . ."

Jesus honors the question but, as you must have noticed, he does not answer it directly. He doesn't say, "Yes, I am," or, "No, I am not." What Jesus does is point to what is happening as a result of his ministry. "Go and tell John what you hear and see: the blind receive their sight, the lame walk, the lepers are cleansed, the deaf hear, the dead are raised, and the poor have good news preached to them."

Part of John's problem seems to be that he has read, or taken to heart anyway, only a portion of the Hebrew Bible, our Old Testament. He knows the parts of it that tell of God's wrath, of the coming day of judgment. With his answer, Jesus seems to be telling John that he needs to familiarize himself with other parts. He should re-read the prophecies of Isaiah, for example, those prophecies that say that, when God comes, it will be as a shepherd feeding his flock, gathering the lambs in his arms, and gently leading the mother sheep. He will come with good news for the poor. He will bind up the broken-hearted. At his coming, the blind will see, the deaf will hear, the lame will leap like a deer, and where the souls of people have become desert-like, wilderness places, they will blossom and rejoice with joy and singing.

Still, Jesus' answer to John's question is enigmatic, much like Jesus himself, if you ask me. Jesus reminds John of the prophecies of Isaiah, suggests that what Isaiah had promised would happen is happening, but in the end, Jesus leaves it to John to answer his own question, saying, "Blessed is anyone who takes no offense at me."

There are, in our day, as perhaps there have always been, those who claim to know exactly who Jesus is. Not only are they certain in their beliefs, but they are insisting that everybody else should believe just as they do. It seems a strange way to honor the one who himself refused to spoon-feed John with an answer, but batted the theological ball back into John's court. What John did with it, we are not told. We never learn whether or not John's question was answered to his satisfaction. We don't know if, when his disciples reported back to him with Jesus' answer, John said, "Oh, now I get it." We are not told what John's response was. The reason, I think, is because Matthew knows that we all have to arrive at our own response. John's question is one we all have to answer for ourselves.

But, what does it mean when Jesus says, "And blessed is anyone who takes no offense at me"? Is it a recognition by Jesus that he is not the kind of Messiah some people so desperately want? Somebody who will fix everything. Somebody who will wave a magic wand and make everything all right. Somebody who will make it unnecessary for you and me to have to do the hard work of peacemaking, say, or the work of racial reconciliation.

Does it mean, perhaps, that Jesus well understood the offense some would take when they heard things like: "Blessed are the meek," "Blessed are the merciful." Did Jesus realize how hard it would be even for some of us today to deal with a saying like: "You have heard that it was said, 'You shall love your neighbor and hate your enemy.' But I say to you, love your enemies and pray for those who persecute you. . . ."? Did Jesus know that many would turn away upon hearing: "If any want to become my followers, let them deny themselves and take up their cross and follow me"?

Did he understand how hard he was making it for would-be followers, believers? A college student taking an introductory New Testament course was heard to say: "You know, all that 'What Would Jesus Do?' stuff they taught us in youth group sure seemed more helpful before I actually read the Bible. You know, Jesus is just really, really strange."[1] It sounds to me as if Jesus knew how strange he must seem to a world in love with power and pleasure and self-seeking.

"Blessed is anyone who takes no offense at me." I wonder if Jesus knew, or could foresee, what was coming. He must have known that some were already offended by the seemingly boundless generosity of his love? He must have known that some were already threatened by the extravagance of his grace, at the ease with which he sat down to eat with sinners, at his seeming carelessness about the company he kept. I wonder if, off in the distance, he could also see a cross looming, and knew the offense it would be to many: a Messiah who, instead of destroying evil, would allow himself to become its victim. I don't know: maybe that's why he said, "And blessed is anyone who takes no offense at me."

*   *   *

"Are you the one who is to come, or are we to wait for another?" It's a question we all ask from time to time. Yes, the preacher, too. And, it's a question each of us has to answer for him or herself. You cannot answer for me, and I cannot answer for you.

But if you are wondering about my answer, I can tell you this: when I have trusted that he is the one, it has been a blessing. When I have taken my grief to him, and trusted him with my beloved dead, it has been a blessing. When I have not taken offense at his hard sayings, and the difficult or dangerous things he asks of me, I have been blessed. When I really stop to look at him on that cross of his and realize it is for the likes of me that he hung there, I know myself to be blessed. I haven't always done so, but looking back over the years, I know that it is when I have yielded my life to him, that I have been at my best. When I have allowed him to have his way, when, now and then, I have managed to lose a little of my life for his sake, when I have sought first his kingdom and his righteousness, it has been a blessing.

And here, this morning, I find myself identifying with a character in one of George MacDonald's novels, a minister named Thomas Wingfold, as he describes the years he has spent in the service of Christ. "Whatever energies I may or may not have," he says, "I know one thing for certain: that I could not devote them to anything else I should think entirely worth doing. Indeed nothing else seems interesting enough . . . but the telling . . . about the one man who is the truth, and to know whom is the life.[2] "Even," Wingfold goes on, "if there be no hereafter, I would rather live my time believing in a grand thing that ought to be true if it is not. No facts can take the place of truths; and if these be not truths," — that is, the things Jesus says and does and the person he is — "then is the loftiest part of our nature a waste." That's what I would say, as well.

*   *   *

John was the first to ask the Advent question, but not the last. Indeed, his question echoes down the centuries. "Are you the one who is to come, or are we to wait for another?" The response of Jesus has not changed: "Go and tell John what you hear and see . . . and blessed is anyone who takes no offense at me." Blessed is he. Blessed is she. Blessed are they! Blessed! Blessed! Blessed!

Prayer:

> Be as patient with us, O Christ, as you were with John when we come to you with our questions. You are mysterious. You say and do such strange things. Forgive us when we are offended. And help us to trust your promise of blessedness — in this world and in the one to come. Amen.

---

1. Patrick J. Willson in *Lectionary Homiletics,* December 2001, p. 21.
2. In Frederick Buechner, *Telling Secrets* (San Francisco: Harper, 1991), pp. 103-104.

~

The Everlasting Light

Readings: Isaiah 9:2-7   December 23, 2001
             Titus 2:11-14
             John 1:1-14

**The light shines in the darkness, and the darkness did not
overcome it.**
                                                        — John 1:5

I know that for some of you one of the delights of the season is sitting
down to re-read a favorite Christmas story: VanDyke's *The Other Wise
Man*, perhaps, or Dicken's *A Christmas Carol*, or Truman Capote's *A
Christmas Memory*. This year, as I have often done in Christmases past, I
reached for Dietrich Bonhoeffer's *Letters and Papers from Prison*, so as
to read once again the letter he wrote to his parents just prior to Christmas
in 1943. Much of the world was at war. Bonhoeffer, a German Protestant
pastor, was in prison, the consequence of his opposition to Hitler. In the
letter, Bonhoeffer thanks his parents for having taught him the proper way
to keep Christmas. "In times like these," he tells them, "we learn as never
before what it means to possess . . . a spiritual heritage untrammeled by
the changes and chances of the present." Bonhoeffer writes that, for him,
being in prison will actually enhance the meaning of Christmas. "That
misery, suffering, poverty, loneliness, helplessness and guilt look very different to . . . God from what they do to (human beings), that God should
come down to the very place which (humans) usually abhor, that Christ
was born in a stable because there was no room for him in the inn — these
are things which a prisoner can understand better than anyone else."
Bonhoeffer ends his letter this way: "It will certainly be a quiet Christmas

for everybody. . . . But for the first time, perhaps, many will learn the true meaning of Christmas."[1]

As I read those concluding words, it occurred to me that they might well apply to us this year. I have heard some of you say that you've not had much enthusiasm or energy for shopping. I am told that a number of companies either cancelled or curtailed their traditional office parties. Many of the cards that have come to our house contain sober reflections on the events of recent months. There are signs pointing to a quiet Christmas.

And perhaps it will be one where we are more susceptible than usual to the true meaning of Christmas, one in which there is less fascination with the frills and the fluff, and more focus on the substance. That possibility has influenced my choice of a text for today. It has led me away from the birth narratives of either Matthew or Luke and to the Prologue of John's Gospel.

John does not tell of Jesus' birth — perhaps because he was well aware that Matthew and Luke had already done so. John tries, instead, to get at the meaning — and not just of the birth of Jesus, but at the meaning of the life that came after. John thinks of Jesus as "the light of the world." Reflecting on all that took place in, through and because of Jesus, John says: "The light shines in the darkness, and the darkness did not overcome it," or, as the New English Bible has it, "the darkness has never quenched it."

*   *   *

The words "light" and "darkness" are metaphors, of course, both deeply embedded in the Bible. There are lots of references there to "darkness," most of them suggestive of the realities we know as evil, sin, suffering, distress, of one kind or another, and death. All of which, of course, we have seen much evidence of, and some of us have experienced personally in recent weeks. We have had powerful reminders of how far we are from the kind of world Isaiah foresees when "all the boots of the trampling warriors and all the garments rolled in blood shall be burned as fuel for the fire."

As Christians the presence and power of the darkness should not be a surprise. Even without Osama bin Laden, we know how dark the world can get. We know the darkness of our own hearts, too: Do we not confess our sins every Sunday morning? Do we not ask, each time we pray the

Lord's Prayer, to avoid temptation and to be delivered from evil? Darkness we know about.

What we may forget, or overlook, in the midst of the usual Christmas festivities, with all their emphasis on joy and good will, what we may fail to appreciate, is the darkness that was a part of that first Christmas. It's there. Not just in John, but in the other Gospels, too. Matthew, for instance, tells of the tyrannical and paranoid Herod, of his massacre of the children, and of Mary and Joseph having to pack up the baby and run for their lives. The context in Luke's Christmas story is that of an emperor issuing his decrees, caring little or nothing about the consequences or difficulties he is causing — especially for the poorest of the people.

The truth is that every Christmas, from the very first one to this one, has been observed in the presence of "darkness." "Every Christmas," as another has put it, "there are wars being fought; if not world wars, then local wars; and if not wars on battlefields, wars going on in families, in political factions, in neighborhood feuds."[2] Every Christmas there are hospitals and hospices filled with the sick and the dying. Every Christmas there are homes broken or breaking. Every Christmas there are refugees roaming the earth, children who are abandoned or abused, and elderly persons and others who have been forgotten and are alone.

*   *   *

There is a sense in which you have to acknowledge the "darkness" that surrounds Christmas before you can begin to understand the meaning of Christmas. The whole point of it, John says, is the coming of God's light in the midst of the darkness. "Light" is another metaphor that occurs often in the Bible, suggesting the presence of God, the manifestation of God, the approach of God's grace, mercy, and peace. The miracle and mystery of Christmas has to do with the light that came into the world in the person of Christ. And the meaning of Christmas today, the reason for continuing to celebrate it, is that "the light shines in the darkness and the darkness did not overcome it." Which is why, in the hymn of Phillips Brooks with which we will conclude our worship, he speaks of Christ as "the everlasting light," the light that shines even now in our "dark streets," upon our world with all its anguish and alienation, with all its grief and gloom.

What must be said is that the light is not now, and never was, a blazing light. It entered the world, not as lightning streaking across the sky, but as a candle flickering in a drafty stable. The sound it made was not the noise of thunder, but the cry of a baby. Only a very few noticed and journeyed toward the light, just a handful came to the stable in Bethlehem, and none that might have been considered among the movers and shakers of that time and place.

It was, from beginning to end, a gentle, modest light that shone in the darkness. As George Buttrick once described it: It came in "a lowly man who lived in a fractious little country on the turbulent edge of empire, who made yokes for oxen and mended children's toys, and raised no money and formed no party and fought no war and built no shrine, and walked around a little lake eleven miles long, and spoke to a few people, and made his protest against the repressive laws of the temple where he worshipped, and almost engaged in banter about the alleged power of the Roman Empire where the great ones lorded it over them — "but it shall not be so among you" — and he paid the price and they bumped him off. Three days later he appeared on a beach in Galilee."[3] It was all done so modestly, as if God was taking the greatest care not to overwhelm, not to coerce.

Such is the conclusion the poet and novelist Wendell Berry came to when he was pondering, not the crib of Jesus but the cross of Jesus. In a recent novel, Berry has the protagonist, a small-town barber with the strange name of Jayber Crow, pondering the fact that "Christ did not descend from the cross except into the grave. And why not otherwise?" he asks. "Wouldn't it have put fine comical expressions on the faces of the scribes and chief priests and the soldiers if at that moment He had come down in power and glory? Why didn't He do it? Why hasn't He done it at any one of a thousand good times between then and now?"

Berry, speaking in the voice of the barber, says: "I knew the answer. I knew it a long time before I could admit it, for all the suffering of the world is in it. He didn't (come down). He hasn't, because from the moment He did, He would be the absolute tyrant of the world and we would be His slaves. Even those who hated Him and hated one another and hated their own souls would have to believe in Him then. From that moment the possibility that we might be bound to Him and He to us and us to one another by love forever would be ended."[4]

From its beginning in Bethlehem, all the way to the hill called Golgotha, and all down the twenty centuries since, it has been a gentle light that has shown in the darkness. Which is why, John says, many in the beginning missed it: "He was in the world, . . . yet the world knew him not." I suppose it is why many do not know him even now. Such a gentle light!

Yet it has proven to be a tough and tenacious light. "The darkness did not overcome it," as John says, and has not to this day. God knows, it was not and is not for lack of trying. Beginning with Herod, the powers of darkness have sought to snuff out the light. One after another, they have tried and failed. Herod couldn't do it despite his massacre of the children. Pontius Pilate could not do it with the crucifixion he arranged for. Imperial Rome could not do it with its program of feeding Christians to the lions. For twenty long centuries the darkness has tried to overcome the light, right up to our own time, but without success. There is a strength and resilience to the light of Christ that astonishes his enemies and often surprises those of us who think of ourselves as his friends.

"The light shines in the darkness, and the darkness did not overcome it." But neither, we must admit, has the light chased away the darkness. The darkness is still around. Very much so. There is not, in John's Prologue, or anywhere else in the New Testament that I can think of, any promise that the darkness will soon disappear, or that you and I will be protected from its destructive power. The promise of Christmas, the meaning of Christmas, is that the light of God's good and gracious love which came into the dark world of Bethlehem continues to shine, and that, because of it, no matter what form the darkness takes, it will be powerless, as Paul says, to separate you and me "from the love of God in Christ Jesus our Lord."

What it also means is that you may approach that light with whatever darkness is in you. Be it the darkness of sin or suffering, the darkness of pain or perplexity, the darkness of alienation or anxiety, the darkness of bereavement or bitterness — whatever your darkness, you may come with it into the presence of Christ and his light will shine upon it. The invitation to do so is not from me; it's from him. "Come to me," he says, "all who are heavily-burdened, and I will give you rest."

If and when you allow that to happen, if, when you welcome the light that is Christ into your own darkness, there is one request Christ makes, and that is that you try to reflect his light in your life so that others may see his light and be drawn to it. If that seems too much to ask, more than you are capable of, if you think of yourself as, at best, little more than a flickering candle, let me say this. The expectation is not that you have to do it all by yourself. I have come to believe that what Christ expects of us may be symbolized by what happens here at the conclusion of our afternoon and evening services on Christmas Eve. We dim the lights, and each person holds a lighted candle, and we sing Silent Night. The light from each of the single candles is not very great. But when we all lift the candles together and hold them up high, the whole place if filled with light. It strikes me as a symbolic expression of what Christ might mean when he tells his disciples, tells us: "You are the light of the world." Don't try to do it all alone. Join your light to the light of others, and there will be a warm and wonderful glow.

*   *   *

I began this sermon with a quote from a letter written by Dietrich Bonhoeffer in 1943. "It will be a quiet Christmas for everybody. . . . But for the first time, perhaps, many will learn the true meaning of Christmas." About a year later, around the time of another Christmas, Bonhoeffer was still in prison and would, in fact, be executed within a few weeks time. Once again, he wrote his parents. He included in the letter a prayer, the concluding portion of which went like this:

> Today, let candles shed their radiant greeting.
> Lo, on our darkness are they not Thy light
> Leading us, haply, to our longed-for meeting?
> Thou canst illumine even our darkest night.[5]

May you find it so this Christmas.

1. Dietrich Bonhoeffer, *Prisoner for God, Letters and Papers from Prison*, edited by Eberhard Bethge (New York: The MacMillan Co., 1959), pp. 58-59.
2. Theodore Parker Ferris, *This Is The Day* (Dublin, New Hampshire: Yankee, Inc., 1976), p. 365.
3. The words are Buttrick's, but I have lost track of the specific source.
4. Wendell Berry, *Jayber Crow* (Washington, D.C.: Counterpoint, 2000), p. 295.
5. Bonhoeffer, *Prisoner for God,* p. 187.

~

A Promise of Newness

Readings: Luke 1:5-25   December 7, 2003
          Luke 1:57-80

Then there appeared to him an angel of the Lord, standing at the right side of the altar of incense. When Zechariah saw him, he was terrified; and fear overwhelmed him. But the angel said to him, "Do not be afraid, Zechariah, for your prayer has been heard. Your wife Elizabeth will bear you a son, and you will name him John."
                                                    — Luke 1:11-13

One of the many things that pleases me about the years we have been together as pastor and people is that we have learned how to observe Advent. With everybody else rushing to Christmas, it is not an easy thing to do, but we do it.

Outside these walls there is nothing of Advent. Stores and streets are ablaze with lights. Santa is busy taking requests from children. Strains of *O Little Town of Bethlehem* are blaring forth from loud speakers. Outside these walls it is already Christmas and has been so since before Thanksgiving. We, on the other hand, are taking our time getting to Christmas. Each Sunday we light one more candle on the Advent wreath: the second of a total of four, this morning. We know, in other words, that today we are only half way to Bethlehem.

One thing about which all four of the Gospels agree: the road to Bethlehem runs through the wilderness where John the Baptist is holding forth, urging repentance, and conducting baptisms. Next Sunday that is where we will be going. But today we have before us the story involving

26

John's parents and the Angel Gabriel. I am confident it is a story about which the world outside knows little or nothing. It is one with which even you may not have had much familiarity prior to this morning's Scripture readings. Yet it is one of the treasures of the season, and is well worth our pondering.

*   *   *

The story opens this way: "In the days of King Herod of Judea, there was a priest named Zechariah. . . . His wife . . . was Elizabeth."

Herod, Zechariah, Elizabeth. Of those three the one that would seem to matter is Herod. His was the name everyone knew. His power, often exercised in cruel and ruthless fashion, was what everybody feared. His plans and policies would have been a prime subject of conversation wherever people gathered.

Zechariah and Elizabeth, on the other hand, would have been of little interest beyond a very small circle. Zechariah was a priest up in the hill country — an inconspicuous rural pastor, if you will. Elizabeth is identified as his wife, as being of priestly lineage, and consistent with the male chauvinism of the Bible, she alone is blamed for the couple's infertility.

Had you been there at the time you would have assumed Herod was the one to watch. And you would have been wrong! The future was not with Herod, but with that ordinary priest and his spouse through whom God was doing a new thing. Luke puts Herod in the story only to provide a date for the really important goings on.

Luke describes Zechariah and Elizabeth as "righteous before God." I take him to mean that they participated in their faith community, did their best to keep the commandments, and tried to live with honesty and integrity. There was nothing exceptional about them.

Oh, Zechariah was a priest, and once a year he went up to Jerusalem to serve in the temple for a week or two. But mostly what he did, and what Elizabeth no doubt helped him do, was to keep alive the flame of faith in his own community: offering prayers, telling the stories, reminding the people of the promises of God, urging them to do justly, love kindness, and walk humbly with their God, and doing all this day in and day out, week after week, year after year.

Of all the Gospel writers, Luke is the one who is keen to emphasize how God works in and through the community of faith and by means of faithful people within that community. It is Luke's conviction that being a member of the believing community "puts one in a position to be used for God's purpose."[1] Such are Zechariah and Elizabeth. Such is what they represent.

You must know that in our time there are those who believe that religion and religious institutions, rather than helping, are hindering God's agenda. These critics of religion are no doubt responding to the arrogance of some who claim that they alone possess the truth, that they alone represent righteousness. These naysayers are aware, as we are, too, how religious fanaticism serves to spawn hatred and undergird violence and warfare. They have concluded "that the less religion we have, the better off we will be."[2]

Our own theological heritage — what we call "the Reformed Tradition" — is not and never has been guilty of a starry eyed idealism when it comes to religion and other religious institutions. We know, and so does Luke, by the way, that churches and other faith communities can and do become distorted and corrupted. Christians can get it wrong and have done so on more than one occasion. At our best we Presbyterians understand that, and so we insist that reformation is an on-going necessity: "the church Reformed and always to be reformed."

On the other hand, here are Zechariah and Elizabeth, reminding us — reminding me, anyway — of all the other ordinary people in all the ordinary communities of faith — churches, synagogues, mosques, temples — whose quiet faithfulness contributes far more to the common good than is often appreciated. No religious institution — including our own — is without its imperfections. Yet, here we are today, continuing the work that this congregation began 130 years ago: conducting worship, celebrating the sacraments, providing pastoral care, teaching the children, guiding the youth, feeding the hungry, sheltering the homeless, partnering with others near and far to work for reconciliation and renewal, for justice and peace — making a difference in individual lives, in our community, and in the world beyond.

Zechariah and Elizabeth remind me — and I hope they will remind you — of how God uses the ordinary lives of ordinary people, their steadfast, unsung faithfulness, to bless the world far more than the world itself is likely to recognize or appreciate, or remember.

*   *   *

There is in Luke's story, however, a figure of greater prominence than any we have so far spoken of. We are told that as Zechariah was going about his priestly duties, "There appeared to him an angel of the Lord. . . ." A little later we learn his identity: Gabriel. "When Zechariah saw him, he was terrified," Luke says; "and fear overwhelmed him."

I don't know if you can understand Zechariah's reaction or not. It is hard to think of angels as terrifying when in our Christmas pageants, they appear as cuddly little children dressed in white with a halo over their heads, or when in the movies they are represented by George Burns, smoking a cigar. Yet, not only in our lesson today, but everywhere in the Bible that angels appear, the initial reaction to them is one of terror. And why not? For the angels are messengers from God. That's what the word "angel" means: "messenger." And what they represent is a dimension far above and beyond ourselves. What they bring is a message from on high.

Come to think of it, it is what is supposed to happen in some fashion in our own worship services, though according to the poet Annie Dillard no one would ever guess it by looking at the likes of us. "Why," she asks, "do we people in churches seem like cheerful, brainless tourists on a package tour of the Absolute? On the whole," she says, "I do not find Christians outside the catacombs, sufficiently sensible of conditions." Dillard asks, "Does anyone have the foggiest idea what sort of power we so blithely invoke? Or, as I suspect, does not one believe a word of it? The churches," says the poet, "are like children playing on the floor with their chemistry sets, mixing up a batch of TNT to kill a Sunday morning. It is madness," she says, "to wear ladies' straw hats and velvet hats to church; we should all be wearing crash helmets. Ushers should issue life preservers and signal flares; they should lash us to our pews."[3] Dillard suspects we are far from ready from any honest to goodness encounter with God, or with one of God's messengers.

Zechariah wasn't prepared for his encounter either, it seems. Nor was he able to believe what Gabriel told him: "Your wife Elizabeth will bear you a son, and you will name him John. You will have joy and gladness, and many will rejoice at his birth, for he will be great in the sight of the Lord."

Zechariah's response to this announcement? Not, "Praise God! It's what we have prayed for and longed for all these years." No, Zechariah is incredulous. He asks: "How will I know that this is so?"

Why is he and why are we so hesitant to trust God's promises? Why are we so much more ready to believe bad news than good news? Bad news comes and we resign ourselves. Sometimes we even say:

"I knew it would come to this. I just knew things were going too well and I would have to pay for it." When good news comes we are apt to say: "This cannot be. This is too good to be true." If you want an example from our own time, take the plan for peace put on the table by the Israeli and the Palestinian working together unofficially, "the Geneva Accords" — to which the official reaction has been, "How can this be?"

In his commentary on the Gospel of Luke, Eduard Schweizer writes: Zechariah's response reveals "how little human lives are ready for God's new act, even the lives of those who live not for themselves . . . but in openness to God. The coming of the real God, not as expected, strikes dumb even the upright and devout, who suddenly discover their lack of faith and see that with all their sincerely held beliefs they did not really reckon on a transforming eruption of God."[4]

Carol Zaleski, a Smith College religion professor, thinks that many believers today suffer from what she calls "imagination fatigue."[5] We cannot imagine how things can be different, or what we ourselves might contribute to make them different. When the angels appear, it is to enlarge our imaginations as to what is possible and to enliven our spirits so that we can welcome and participate in new realities. The angels bid us to prepare ourselves for living, not as we have been, but in anticipation of a new day. Gabriel comes to Zechariah with a promise of newness. He brings an alternative to a world ruled by the likes of Herod. Of the child whose conception and birth he has announced, the angel says: "He will turn many of the people . . . to the Lord their God." And then, foreshadowing John's role as the forerunner to Jesus, Gabriel predicts: "With the spirit and power of Elijah he will go before him, to turn the hearts of parents to their children, and the disobedient to the wisdom of the righteous, to make ready a people prepared for the Lord."

Well, perhaps neither the incredulity of Zechariah, nor our own "imagination fatigue" is other than what should be expected. "Nothing is more surprising," said Paul Tillich in one of his sermons, "than the rise of the new within ourselves. . . . the new is born in us, just when we least believe in it. It appears in remote corners of our souls which we have neglected for a long time. . . . We cannot force it, and we cannot calculate it. . . . All we can do is to be ready for it."[6]

*   *   *

Advent is the season devoted to readiness. We are given these days so that we may be "a people prepared for the Lord." Not merely prepared for Christmas, but prepared for what God may be doing. The difference between those who keep Advent and those who do not is this: those who keep Advent believe God has something better in mind for us. And so we have our ears open to hear the promise of newness whenever and wherever it may be spoken.

What, you may wonder, does such a promise sound like? I believe it sounds very much like the song Zechariah sang after John was born, and when Zechariah had got his voice back. "By the tender mercy of our God," Zechariah said, "the dawn from on high will break upon us, to give light to those who sit in darkness and in the shadow of death, to guide our feet into the way of peace."

Something like that, I believe, is what God's promise of newness sounds like. Advent wants you to anticipate it, to listen for it, to get ready to receive it, rejoice in it, and, even now to let your life begin to be shaped by it.

Prayer:

O God, who has prepared for them that love Thee such good things as pass our understanding, pour into our hearts such love towards Thee that we, loving Thee above all things, may obtain Thy promises, which exceed all that we can imagine or desire."

1. Fred Craddock, *Interpretation, Luke* (Louisville: John Knox Press, 1990), p. 26.
2. Miroslav Volf's characterization of "many intellectuals" in *Context*, July 15, 2003.
3. In Eugene Peterson, *The Contemplative Pastor* (Grand Rapids, MI: Wm. B. Eerdmans Publishing Co., 1989), p. 83.
4. Eduard Schweizer, *The Good News According to Luke* (Atlanta: John Knox Press, 1984), p. 24.
5. In *Christian Century*, June 14, 2003.
6. Paul Tillich, *The Shaking of the Foundations* (New York: Charles Scribners Sons, 1948), pp. 182-83.

~

What Shall We Do?

Readings: Isaiah 12:2-6   December 14, 2003
             Philippians 4:4-7
             Luke 3:1-20

In the fifteenth year of the reign of Emperor Tiberius, when Pontius Pilate was governor of Judea, and Herod was ruler of Galilee, and his brother Philip ruler of the region of Ituraea and Trachonitis, and Lysanias ruler of Abilene, during the high priesthood of Annas and Caiaphas, the word of God came to John son of Zechariah in the wilderness. He went into all the region around the Jordan, proclaiming a baptism of repentance for the forgiveness of sins. . . . And the crowds asked him, "What then should we do?"

— Luke 3:1-3,10

You can't say I didn't warn you. I said last Sunday that, on our way to Bethlehem to see the baby, we would have to go down along the Jordan River where John the Baptist is holding revival services.

I know how odd this must seem to you. Everywhere else the cultural celebration is shifting into high gear. The holiday mood is taking over. Yet here in church we are met by this brusque and bristly figure who has just emerged from the wilderness. He is with us today, courtesy of Luke's Gospel, doing exactly what we heard Gabriel say, last Sunday, he would do. "With the spirit and power of Elijah," the angel promised, "he will . . . make ready a people prepared for the Lord." That's John's role. His job description says he is to "prepare the way of the Lord," get everything and everybody ready so that nobody will miss out on God's gift of salvation. It strikes me as important work. Don't you think so?

*   *   *

The first thing I would like you to notice about John's ministry is when and where Luke says it takes place. "In the fifteenth year of the reign of Emperor Tiberius, when Pontius Pilate was governor of Judea, and Herod was ruler of Galilee, and his brother Philip ruler of the region of Ituraea and Trachonitis, and Lysanias ruler of Abilene, during the high priesthood of Annas and Caiaphas, the word of God came to John son of Zechariah in the wilderness."

John undertakes his work right smack in the middle of the political, social and cultural world of his time. John is a preacher, but his sermons are not about timeless truths or eternal spiritual principles. John's preaching relates to worldly realities and takes place in the immediacy of the moment. That is to say: in the third year of the Presidency of George W. Bush, when Edward Rendell serves as Governor of Pennsylvania and Ruth Ann Minner is the Governor of Delaware, and John Street sits in the Mayor's office in Philadelphia, during the papacy of John Paul II, and when Gene Bay is still the pastor of the Bryn Mawr Presbyterian Church — and yes, on the very day we heard about the capture of Saddam Hussein — the word of God comes to John — and, now, by way of John, comes to us — a word for our time, our situation.

I want you to see the importance of this. One of the temptations of good, Christian people, is to spiritualize the gospel, keep it from ever touching down next to political, economic or social conditions. Some preachers are especially good at doing so. Believing that people come to church, not to hear the truth, but to have their prejudices and preconceptions confirmed, and not wanting to offend, these preachers preach soft and soothing generalities. Following a service I led this past July in a summer chapel, a man came up to me and said: "Mostly what we get here are sermons of the 'I'm okay, you're okay, we're all okay' variety." He thanked me for having brought a different kind.

The night before he was murdered, Martin Luther King, Jr. spoke at a rally in support of the garbage workers of Memphis. "It's all right," he said, "to talk about 'long white robes over yonder'. . . . But ultimately people want some suits and dresses and shoes to wear down here. It's all right to talk about 'streets flowing with milk and honey,' but God has commanded us to be concerned about the slums down here, and his children who can't eat three square meals a day. It's all right,' King went on, 'to talk about the new Jerusalem, but one day, God's preacher must talk about the new New York, the new Atlanta, the new Philadelphia, the new Los Angeles, the new Memphis, Tennessee.' "[1]

Nobody understands that any better than John. That's the kind of preaching he does. How do I know? Because, as Luke tells us, as soon as John's preaching comes to the attention of Herod, he has John arrested and imprisoned, and soon thereafter severs his head from his neck. That doesn't happen to preachers of soft, soothing sermons.

*   *   *

John's preaching is down to earth, practical. Now, I will admit: John could benefit from a good seminary course in homiletics. He could learn to start out a little more gently. Tell a joke to get us all relaxed and in a good mood. Or give us a sentimental story to pluck at our heartstrings. John has not learned how to do that, it seems.

A recent translation of Luke's text has John beginning his sermon this way: "Brood of snakes! What do you think you're doing slithering down here to the river? Do you think a little water on your snakeskins is gong to deflect God's judgment? It's your *life* that must change, not your skin. . . . What counts is your life. Is it green and blossoming? Because if it's dead wood, it goes on the fire."[2] You know, if John is going to preach like that all that time, I'm not sure we want to invite him back!

Yet, Luke says — did you catch it in the earlier reading of the Gospel lesson? — Luke summarizes John's preaching by saying: "So, with many other exhortations, he proclaimed the good news to the people."

Good news? How can that be? Can it be? Yes, and I will tell you why. The sum and substance of John's preaching is a call to repent, an invitation to repent. Luke says: John "went into all the region around the Jordan, proclaiming a baptism of repentance. . . ." Now, I think I know what clicks into your mind as soon as you hear the words "repent" or "repentance." Immediately, you think guilt, shame, being sorry. The kind of things some churches are very good at getting you to feel. But that's not it. That is *not* what repentance is about. Repentance is concerned very little with how you feel, and is much concerned about what you do. Repentance is about change. Repentance has to do with turning your back on those attitudes or behaviors that spoil life, wreck relationships, make it hard for us to be friends with God. Turning away is half of it. The other half has to do with turning toward — toward a way of believing and behaving that makes it possible for us to become the people God means for us to be.

John's preaching is "good news" because he is telling us: change is possible. John comes to us with what may well be the most wonderful and the most outrageous claim of the Christian faith: the claim that God comes to us with an offer of newness of life. God opens the door to transformation and gives us the courage to walk through it. It doesn't get any better than that.

You may think you are trapped in your circumstances, but you are not. You may consider yourself a victim — "my parents were so heavy-handed"; "my husband's death has left me inconsolable"; "my boss will never recognize my talents" — you may think, "I am one of life's victims," but you are not. You may think you are stuck with habits that are stealing all the joy from your life, but you are not. The door to change is open, and you can walk through it. That's what repentance is all about. And Luke is right: when that's what the preacher says, it is good news.

Now, I know that John sounds a note of judgment in his preaching. But let me tell you: If the sound of judgment gets your attention, convicts you, and you know that repentance and forgiveness are available — you know what? — then, even judgment can be good news.

*   *   *

You recall what Luke says happened with the people back there at the Jordan who were listening to John. They understood immediately what repentance is all about. They got it. "The crowds asked him, 'What should we do?'" They did not come out of church saying, "Nice sermon, today, John." Nobody said: "How I wish old So-and-So would have been here today; he needed to hear that." And nobody said anything like what George Buttrick was told once: "Your sermon was like water to a drowning man." There was none of that.

"The crowds asked him, 'What should we *do*?'" Share, John says. "Whoever has two coats must share with anyone who has none; and whoever has food must do likewise." It is something we should have learned as early as nursery school or in kindergarten, at the latest. But some did not learn it then and still have not learned. Some have never learned the correct answer to the question Cain asks in the first pages of the Bible: "Am I my brother's keeper?" John says the answer is yes. Share what you have with those who have not.

John is pretty specific about it, isn't he? You have two coats? Give one away. You have plenty of food? Give some to somebody who doesn't have any.

John's specificity reminds me of the time Bert was telling Harry about the virtues of socialism. Harry is not sure he understands. "Do you mean that if you have two tractors, and I have none, that you are to give me one of yours?" Bert says: "That's what it means." "If you have two cars and I have none, you would give me the extra one?" Bert replies: "That's right." "And if you have two hogs, and I don't have any, I could have one of yours?" "Damn you, Harry," says Bert, "you know I have two hogs."

Well, John knows that many of us have two coats, or maybe even three or four or five. I wonder if he would not like the suggestion Anna Quindlen makes in the most recent Newsweek Magazine. She says that she has "too much stuff," and she thinks most of the rest of us probably do, too, that this Christmas many of us do not really need to get more. She is asking her family, instead of adding to her "stuff," to make a contribution to one of her favorite charities.[3] Oh, by the way, the Alternative Gift Market is still open for business!

"Even tax collectors came to be baptized," Luke says, "and they asked him, 'Teacher, what should we do?' " Tax collectors were notorious for lining their own pockets. John tells them: "Collect no more than the amount prescribed for you." In other words, do your necessary work with integrity. Even if you are part of a system that invites corruption, you do not participate. My guess is he is saying much the same to today's mutual fund managers, to the accountants, to all those CEO's who profited so handsomely at the expense of their employees and stockholders. But now I have gone to meddling!

"Soldiers also asked him, 'And we, what should we do?' " John said: "Do not extort money from anyone by threats or false accusations, and be satisfied with your wages." One wonders if, this morning, he is not also saying: And please remember there may be children in the way of your guided missiles.

I see the soldiers as representing all of us who hold positions of public trust: ministers, judges, teachers, government workers, politicians, the police. John's word to us is: Do not use your position to exploit others. Do not misuse the power your position gives you.

The crowd, the tax collectors, the soldiers all ask: "What should we do?" And there is a common thread running through each of John's answers. None of the ones who come to John, and none of us, is told to abandon the world, leave where we are, become a hermit, or enter a convent. What John encourages is that we live as redeemed people in an unredeemed world. Live with integrity — and do so even if the system we are part of is corrupt. Take responsibility for ourselves and for our world. Take inventory of our own lives and identify the things we wish would be different. John understands that doing these things may not change the world but it can change us: which is where it must begin if this tired old world is ever to be different from what it is now.[4]

*   *   *

John is such a powerful preacher. He does not entertain people. What he does is usher them into the presence of God. He is so authentic. What he does matches what he says. And so the question inevitably arises: Is John the Messiah, perhaps? Is *he* the savior? John's response is firm: "I baptize you with water; but one who is more powerful than I is coming, I am not worthy to untie the thong of his sandals."

In his commentary on Luke's Gospel, Fred Craddock says: "Persons whose work it is to point others to Jesus can themselves become the objects and centers of the attention, affection, and loyalty of many."[5] It is so much to John's credit that he knows: it is not about him. His job is to prepare the way for and to point to the one who is coming.

In this, John is the model for all of us who are pastors. It is not about us. It is all about the gospel. Our job is the same as John's: to prepare the way for and to point to Jesus Christ as the bringer of salvation and the bearer of God's love.

Come to think of it, that's the job of the whole church, of every Christian, every one of you: to tell the world about Jesus, and to try to live your lives in ways that reflect his love and kindness, his justice and peace, his grace and glory. And you know what? If you and I can do that, then perhaps "all flesh" will begin to glimpse "the salvation of God," and they will know immediately that what they are seeing is "good news." As a matter of fact, they may begin to sense it is the best possible news there is — or ever can be!

1. Martin Luther King, Jr., *A Testament of Hope* (San Francisco: Harper & Row, 1986), p. 282.
2. Eugene H. Peterson, *The Message* (Colorado Spring, CO: NAV Press, 1993), p. 122.
3. Newsweek, December 15, 2003, p. 76.
4. Peter S. Gomes, *What We Forgot To Tell You* (Cambridge, MA: The Memorial Church, Harvard University, 2003), p. 327.
5. Fred C. Craddock, *Interpretation, Luke* (Louisville: John Knox Press, 1990), p. 32.

~

Emmanuel

Readings: Isaiah 7:10-17   December 21, 2003
           I Timothy 1:12-17
           Matthew 1:18-25

**All this took place to fulfill what had been spoken by the Lord
through the prophet: "Look, the virgin shall conceive and
bear a son, and they shall name him Emmanuel," which
means, "God is with us."**

                                        — Matthew 1:22-23

At long last we are approaching the little town of Bethlehem. You can
see it up ahead, just a little way down the road. It has taken us a while to
get here. Our journey began on the last day of November with an invitation to "come in out of the dark." We were next in the temple in Jerusalem
where we heard the angel Gabriel speaking "a promise of newness." Last
Sunday, as the snow was falling, we went out to the Jordan River valley,
listened to John's passionate preaching on the theme of repentance, and,
in response, along with the crowds who were there, and the tax collectors
and soldiers, we asked John, "What should we do?" He told us to share
what we have with those who have not, to live with integrity, to avoid
taking advantage of others, and most of all, to get ready to receive God's
gift of salvation. Having been to those places and done all those things,
perhaps now, today we can see the baby.

Well, no, not just yet. Remember, I began by saying that we are
approaching Bethlehem. We have reached only the outskirts of the village.
We will have to wait a little longer, until Christmas Eve, to go, by way of
Luke's narrative, to actually see the baby. Luke is the one who tells about

the trek Mary and Joseph had to make from Nazareth to Bethlehem, about how their search for shelter led to the stable, and how the baby was born there. On Christmas Eve we will hear all about that. We will listen to the angels singing above "the Shepherds' Field," as it is known today, and we will go with the shepherds to the manger. All that we will do on Christmas Eve.

What we have before us, this morning, is Matthew's version of Christmas. While he gives us a bit of the story, a few of the details, Matthew is not so much concerned with what happened as he is with what it all means. And you know something? Maybe, before we come to the Christmas Eve service, hear all the glorious music and sing all the familiar carols, maybe it's not a bad idea to think about the meaning of what we are celebrating. Matthew can help us do that.

*   *   *

I should call your attention to one difference between the two versions of the Christmas story. In Luke, Mary plays a significant role. Gabriel tells her that she is the favored one, the "God-bearer," as she will come to be called. Luke tells of her giving birth, and how she wrapped the child in bands of cloth and laid him in a manger. Joseph, on the other hand, like many would-be fathers — certainly those of my generation — appears to do little or nothing. He just stands there, the proverbial potted plant.

But in Matthew's account, Joseph does do something. Not what he intended to do when he first learned of Mary's pregnancy. Joseph was "a righteous man," Matthew tells us. He means a man who reads his Bible and does what it says to do. Joseph's Bible — our Old Testament — says that a man in Joseph's predicament should divorce the woman, or even have her put to death. Joseph is not ready for the latter, but he is about to head for the divorce court. Until, that is, he has his dream and changes his mind. It is a moment of great consequence. As one commentator writes: Joseph "learns that being truly righteous does not mean looking up a rule in a book" and obeying it unthinkingly. "Joseph learns that doing the right thing "means wrestling with the complexities of a problem, listening for God's voice and then doing God's thing."[1] He provides an example one wishes the biblical literalists, "the Bible says" people of our time, might take more note of.

*   *   *

Matthew makes more of the so-called "virgin birth" — what might better be referred to as "a miraculous conception" — than does Luke. The point being made is that this is no ordinary child who is being born, that God is involved in this birth, that the child is being sent by God to do what only God can do: "save his people from their sins."

Does faith in Jesus as Lord and Savior depend on the "virgin birth"? I don't think so. Neither the Apostle Paul or the Gospel of John seems to know anything of it. Yet Paul and John, of all the authors of the New Testament literature have the loftiest views of Jesus.

I like the response William Willimon, the chaplain at Duke University, gave to the student who asked if she had to believe in the virgin birth in order to be a Christian. "No," said Willimon, "you don't." But, he went on, "if we can get you to swallow that without choking, then there's no telling what (we) can get you to believe." Come back next week and we'll try to persuade you that the meek will inherit the earth, that it is better to give than to receive, that your life does not consist in the abundance of possessions, that it's not nations, or empires, not even the United States, but God who rules the world. Willimon says: "We start you out with something fairly small, like the virgin birth, then work you up to even more outrageous assertions."[2]

*   *   *

Speaking of "outrageous assertions," we come to Matthew's claim as to the meaning of Christmas. He says the birth of Jesus is the fulfillment of Isaiah's prophecy that there will come a child whose name is "Emmanuel — meaning God is with us." It's what theologians of long ago used to call "the scandal of incarnation." The assertion being not just that God is, or even that God is with us, but that God came to be with us as Jesus. That claim is not Matthew's alone. John makes it as well when he says: "No one has ever seen God. It is the Father's only Son, who is close to the Father's heart, who has made him known." And Paul says much the same. In Colossians, for example, where he writes: ". . . In him (that is, in Jesus) all the fullness of God was pleased to dwell, and through him God was pleased to reconcile to himself all things. . . ." The assertion, that God was in Christ is, as a matter of fact, the central claim of the Christian faith.

I do not wish to argue the point, this morning. I will not try to prove the incarnation. What I want to do, instead, is to ask you to consider the nature of the God who comes to be with us as Jesus. There are all sorts of notions about God floating around. But let's just say that Matthew is right, and the meaning of Christmas is Jesus as "Emmanuel," the very best disclosure of who and how God is that anybody will ever have. What does that do to our picture, our image, of God, our notions of God?

There are many things that might be said. I have time to say only two or three.

Perhaps the first thing to say is that the God who is with us as Jesus is one who takes the initiative. In most religions, the effort comes from the human side. God is the distant mystery to be sought by fervent prayer. God is the eternal enigma whose ways we have to try to discern as best we can. But the God who comes as Jesus doesn't wait for us to discover him; he wants to discover us. What is more, he doesn't come only to the good people — whoever they might be. He comes, as Matthew puts it, "to save his people from their sins." He comes, as Paul tells us in our Epistle lesson, "to save sinners."

The God who comes as Jesus takes the initiative. It doesn't mean that we stop our own seeking. But it does mean that our experience is likely to be similar to that described in the old hymn I used to sing in the church of my childhood:

> I sought the Lord and afterward I knew
> He moved my soul to seek him, seeking me;
> It was not I that found, O Savior true;
> No, I was found of Thee.

The God who comes to us as Jesus is one who takes the initiative.

What else? I would say that the God who comes to us as Jesus is a humble God. Here is the way the Lutheran Carl Braaten puts it: "Jesus gave us a new and paradoxical definition of God, a definition of the humility of God. Many people were offended. They wanted a God of glory, not entering the world at the bottom, not from a despised place like Nazareth in Galilee, but he must come in from the top. He must be properly introduced, by the right people, and with the appropriate protocol. But instead the people got the Man from Nazareth, and he was only prepared to give them a message of the humility of God, of the identification of God with the people and things that don't count for very much in this world. He carried his message of God to the extreme, driving the humility of God all the way to the cross."[3]

What a strange and mysterious God who comes to us as Jesus. And the oddness of it, the mystery of it, gets even deeper. As Bill Coffin puts it: "We want God to be like God. God, on the other hand, wants to be human."[4] And in Jesus, born of Mary, he is. The God who comes as Jesus enters fully into the human condition: shares our fears and anxieties, our sadness and worry, our pain and suffering. The defining moment took place on the hill outside Jerusalem when he was crucified. But there was a hint of it in the very beginning. My friend Susan Andrews puts it like this: "The two ends of the Christian story are what set our spiritual saga apart from all other world religions. God as a tiny, helpless baby. God as a crumbled, bleeding corpse. God as utterly vulnerable. . . . God as one who embraces the fullness of human experience in order to sanctify it all."[5]

There is a story told about a little girl who was afraid to sleep at night. She often cried and made such a fuss about it that the parents came to dread the nightly ritual of tucking her in. They would read to her, she would say her prayers, and they would talk for a while with the lights off, and she would go to sleep, but eventually, she would wake up and come to her parents' bed. One night when she did so, her mother asked her of what she was afraid. "I hear sounds and they scare me," she said. "Well don't you know that God is here and it's all right, and that God will protect you?" her mother asked. The child thought about this for a minute or so and then said, "But I want somebody with skin on."[6] What God has done in Jesus is put skin on. That's the meaning of Christmas, according to Matthew. God has come to be with us as Jesus, and that is why he is called Emmanuel.

*   *   *

I have thought long and hard about what to say to you on the eve of this Christmas. Not only because it's the last one when I will be in this pulpit. But also because of the difficult and dangerous age in which we live. Life is a precarious business, and more than a few of you are going through tough and trying times. I have nothing to say that will make the world a safer, more peaceful place. I have nothing to say that will "fix" the things in your lives that need fixing, mend the broken places. What I have to tell you is: God is with you, and the God who is with you looks like Jesus, his grace and mercy are like that of Jesus. His peace, his gentleness, his love are that of Jesus.

Matthew says the baby's name is Emmanuel — "God with us." He makes that astonishing and wonderful claim in the very beginning of his Gospel. I wonder if you recall what, in Matthew's gospel, Jesus himself says at the very end. "Remember," he tells us, "I am with you always, to the end of the age."

Trusting, as I do, what Matthew says about Jesus in the beginning of his Gospel, and what Jesus himself says at its end, my word to you this Christmas is "God is with you. You who are in mourning because of the empty chair at your table: God is with you. You who are struggling for health, undergoing chemo treatments five days a week, perhaps, or waiting, waiting, waiting for the kidney you need and wondering, maybe, if the waiting is worth it: God is with you. You who are about to send a son or daughter off to Iraq: God is with you. You young people, adolescents, trying to figure out who you are exactly and what you will do with your life: God is with you. You who feel unworthy, perhaps because your very own church has said that you are: God is with you. You who are worried about a child, or watching as a loved one with ALS slowly but surely loses the use of one part of the body after another: God is with you. And you whose shoulders are weighed down with heavy responsibilities, you who go to work early and come home late, who feel much of the time that nobody can possibly understand the burdens you bear: God is with you.

That is my word to you, to each of you. I cannot force it upon you, I can only offer it to you in the hope that you will receive it, believe it, trust it. Here is something else I hope, as well: that, as you come to Christmas, your prayer might be something like that of Phillips Brooks:

> O holy Child of Bethlehem,
> Descend to us, we pray;
> Cast out our sin and enter in,
> Be born in us today.
> We hear the Christmas angels
> The great glad tidings tell;
> O come to us, abide with us,
> Our Lord Emmanuel!

1. Thomas G. Long, *Matthew* (Louisville, KY: Westminster Bible Companion, Westminster John Knox Press, 1997), p. 14.

2. William Willimon, *Pulpit Resource*, December 21, 2003, p. 51.

3. Carl E. Braaten, *Stewards of the Mysteries* (Minneapolis: Augsburg Press, 1983), pp. 27-28.

4. In "Emmanuel," *Sermons from Riverside*, December 9, 1979, p. 3.

5. In "Vital Vulnerability," published in a periodical of unknown name and date.

6. Thanks to Jon Walton for reminding me of this story in *"Face-off at the Palace,"* First Presbyterian Church, New York City, November 23, 2003.

PART TWO

Sermons for
Lent and Easter

~

A Rumor of Resurrection

Readings: Isaiah 25:6-9   April 16, 1995
           I Corinthians 15:1-11
           Luke 23:50-24:10

**Now, it was Mary Magdalene, Joanna, Mary the mother of James,
and the other women with them who told this to the apostles.
— Luke 24:10**

A rumor. That's what it was, at first. That's all it was: a rumor that,
somehow, Jesus remained at large — not because he had survived, but
because he had surmounted, death.

He had died on Friday. Not peacefully in his bed, not accidentally, or
as the result of a tragic mistake. He had been put to death. It's called capital punishment. We do it by way of an electric chair, or with a lethal injec-
tion. At the time, Rome preferred crucifixion. The idea was to make it as
painful and as public as possible. Not only because the guilty deserved it,
but because it might serve to deter other would-be criminals, revolution-
aries, traitors, and trouble-makers. Sound familiar?

Typically the crucified were left to hang on their crosses long after
death had ended their agony. The deterrence factor again: let the example
sink in. But, in the case of Jesus, Joseph of Arimathea is said to have persuaded Pilate, the Roman official in charge of such things, to permit a
swift and decent burial. Two Marys, Joanna, and some other women constituted the funeral procession. They saw where the body was entombed.
Then they left in order to prepare the spices and ointments with which
they planned to anoint the dead Jesus. On the Sabbath, faithful Jews that
they were, they rested and consoled one another.

48

At dawn's early light the women returned to discover the stone rolled away from the entrance and an empty tomb. There was not, as is often supposed, an immediate leap to the conclusion that Jesus had risen from the dead. Luke says simply that "they were perplexed." Whereupon, two mysterious strangers appeared, gently asking, "Why do you look for the living among the dead?" and then announcing, "He is not here, but has risen." Soon after, the women hurried off to tell other friends of Jesus what they had seen and heard. "But," says Luke, "these words seemed to them an idle tale, and they did not believe them."

*   *   *

Easter began as a rumor, and was responded to, we should note, not with a joyful celebration, but with skepticism, doubt, unbelief. The problem was, you understand, that there were no witnesses. In this regard, Easter was — and still is! — so very different from Good Friday.

The events of Good Friday had been public — were intended to be public. Had it happened today, you can rest assured that it would have all been televised, with on-site interviews of spectators, and next day guest appearances on *The Today Show* by the likes of Caiaphais and Pilate. As it was, all the sordid details had been witnessed: the betrayal, the arrest, the trial, the mocking and scourging, the procession to Calvary, the hammering of the nails through the hands, the crown of thorns, the cry of dereliction, "My God, my God, why have you forsaken me?" and the agonizing process of dying. It was all public, and is so familiar. As Barbara Taylor has written: "Good Friday is verifiable, then and now. It is where we live, in the land of betrayal, corruption, violence and death."[1]

Compared to Good Friday, Easter retains the status of a rumor. Whatever happened happened in private. No one was invited to be present. No one was there to observe. The women reported the empty tomb and what they had been told about it. Later, it was said that some people had seen Jesus, only it didn't look like him exactly, and before anybody could do much in the way of verification, he was gone.

Why such reticence on the part of God? It's not the way we would have done it is it? I mean, if you had been the one doing it, wouldn't you have had Jesus march right back to Pilate's headquarters, or show up for services in the temple on the next Sabbath? The way it happened was a public relations disaster — which is precisely the point of a poem someone has addressed to the risen Christ.

Any good Communications Expert would
      have told you it was a mistake
If there's going to be a resurrection
It should be on a mountain top
With saturation coverage, advance publicity
A stand nearby to sell souvenirs
And, up near the tomb, a special reserved
      section for VIPs
Roped off from the pushing, noisy, eager crowd
      You can't just walk out of death,
Come back to life in an empty garden
      early on a Sunday morning
When the world is sleeping in. . . .[2]

It isn't the way we would have arranged for Easter to happen. And, come to think of it, if we were going to fabricate a story about resurrection, this is not the way we would do that either. Nothing to go on except an empty tomb and some linen cloths lying around — that and the dream-like accounts of those who saw him later? Surely, we could think of something more impressive, more persuasive.

Yet, there is something about the reticence of Easter, the quietness and understated quality of it, that is so like God. It corresponds, anyway, with the Biblical record of God's gentle graciousness. To be sure, here and there signs are given which compel people to stop, look, and listen. Moses sees a burning bush in the desert, or the walls around Jericho come crashing down, or a leper is healed, or a blind Bartimaeus gets his sight back, or Paul gets knocked off his feet on the Damascus Road. There are such exceptional episodes. But they are exceptional. For the most part, we are given glimpses and glimmers of what Sam Terrien calls an "elusive Presence."[3] God knocks at the door, but never breaks it down or comes crashing through. There is no coercion. And there is always the possibility that we won't hear the knock or notice anything unusual. Easter is more of the same: an all but hidden triumph of life over death, of love over hatred, of hope over despair. Just a rumor of resurrection.

*   *   *

Now, there are rumors, and there are rumors. False ones, and true ones. Which is it with regard to the Easter rumor? Can we trust it? In other words, is all this fanfare of an Easter morning justified, or not?

In responding to such questions preachers like myself are tempted in one of two directions: either to suggest that the rumor of resurrection has to be accepted on faith, or to roll up our sleeves and go to work trying to prove it. I myself cannot do the former — just accept it all on faith. I'm not built that way. Some people are, but I'm not, and I don't think many of you are, either. But, I also know that I cannot prove the truth of Easter. No one can. When you get right down to it, there is precious little that really matters which we can prove. We can't prove love, or free will, or forgiveness, to say nothing of God. And we can't prove the rumor that is Easter, either. Interesting enough, the New Testament doesn't try. It simply announces: "He is risen!"

What I can do is to suggest why it is that I trust the rumor that got started on the first Easter morning.

When, for instance, I read the resurrection narratives in the Gospels, and the accounts of Paul and others, and I recognize that there are inconsistencies among them and legendary aspects to them. But I also realize that the manner in which an event is described — the way it is expressed — is not the same as the event itself. What strikes me as important is not any one version of the story, but the way in which references to the resurrection sparkle like pieces of shining metal, all through the New Testament. It is apparent to me that, apart from Easter, there would be no interest at all in the person of Jesus. And, like another, "it seems to me more and more as I grow older that the picture is blurred by the brightness of it, and I, for one, would not have it otherwise."[4]

What makes no sense to me at all is the notion that behind the rumor is nothing but wish projection or a desire for a happy ending. If the first Christians wanted a happy ending, it's hardly what they got, ridiculed and persecuted as most of them were, and murdered, as more than a few were. And why would the apostles have fabricated a story in which they come off so poorly, "capable at best of occasional insight and occasional loyalty"?[5] And what changed them from the cowering cowards they were into the courageous witnesses they became? As the Jewish theologian Pinchas Lapide puts it: "If the defeated and depressed group of disciples overnight could change into a victorious movement of faith, based on auto-suggestion or self-deception — without a fundamental faith experience — then this would be a much greater miracle than the resurrection itself."[6]

There is, as I see it, a good deal more behind the rumor than the Biblical witness. There is the simple fact that the rumor has survived for nearly twenty centuries — despite the sometimes sorry record of the church which has been its custodian. The rumor lives despite a Christian community that has been scandalously divided, despite quarreling congregations, and unworthy pastors, priests and popes, despite our inept testimony and our timid witness, despite all our betrayals, denials, and desertions. Despite the unfaithfulness of Christians past and present, the rumor survives. Moreover, through the Holy Spirit, the grace of our Lord Jesus Christ continues to meet us when we gather to worship, when we work together, when we care for one another.

The rumor survives, and Christ keeps rising from the dead. The world has never been able to rid itself of him. God knows, it's not for lack of trying. The world has ignored him, ridiculed him, rejected him many times, and he keeps returning. In the old Soviet Union he was buried, not for a couple of days, but for sixty years! Seminaries were closed. Churches were turned into museums. Nobody but little old ladies attended worship. And now, as we know from our recent missionaries-in-residence, Marina and Natalia, Christ is back, giving credence to the rumor of resurrection.

What we must all do, of course, in the end, is test the rumor for ourselves. For myself, I cannot claim that I have ever met Christ the way you meet someone on the street, or the way Paul encountered him on the Damascus Road. Maybe you have, but I haven't. What I do experience, sometimes, when I am lost and don't know which way to turn, is an Inner Voice that says, "Try this way," or "Open that door." I know that when the candle is burning low and I am wondering how I will ever manage to do the things that are waiting for me, there is Someone greater than I who helps me. In ways I cannot predict and sometimes do not even recognize, help comes. I know that Someone has taught me — hard-headed as I am — what the really valuable things in life are, and how different they are from the things that money can buy. I also know that, sometimes, when I am less sure about the rumor, but try to live "as if" it were all true, that it becomes truer somehow. I've learned, in other words, that I'm most likely to realize that Christ really is risen, not when I am taking my spiritual pulse, but when I try to do the things he said and answer his call of service to others. Maybe I am deluded. Maybe the rumor isn't true after all. I'll take the risk. I would far rather join the long line of followers from Peter, Paul, and Mary down to Bonhoeffer, Blake, and Buechner, than to be part of those who reject the greatest story ever told.

*   *   *

Good Friday is verifiable. It's as John Vannorsall says: "We continue to kill one another. The reasons are as myriad as we are in number. The ways are as diverse as we are different from one another; smooth stones in a slingshot, smooth words on the tongue; barbed arrow, barbed tongue; with all the intentionality of a swung sword, the unintentionality of lead paint on a nursery window sill, with all the indifference of starvation. We kill in the name of God, in the name of the clan, the country. . . . We kill from the ground, the air, at sea. We kill one by one, by gangs, by armies, by general mayhem and holocaust."[7] We have every reason to know that Good Friday is for real.

And Easter? It's still a rumor, but a hardy one. It's lasted a long time. While I believe it is true, I can't prove that it is. What I can do is urge you to keep your eyes open for the risen Christ. Sometime when you are mired in grief, he will come to you. When you need the grace of forgiveness, or the strength to forgive, he will come to you. When all around is darkness and the road ahead is uncertain, he will come to you. In sadness and in joy, he will come. In the company of believers, he will come. In the sacrament of baptism, in the breaking of bread, in the word read and spoken, in the splendor of an anthem, in the quietness of prayer, he will make himself known to you. In one way or another, he will knock at the door of your life, and if you let him, he will come in. Then you will know that the rumor is true: Christ is risen! Alleluia!

1. Barbara Brown Taylor, *Journal for Preachers,* Volume XVIII, Number 3, p. 11.
2. Joan Evheart Cinelli, unpublished poem.
3. Samuel Terrien, *The Elusive Presence* (San Francisco: Harper & Row, 1978).
4. Theodore Parker Ferris, *What Jesus Did* (Oxford University Press, Forward Movement Edition, 1963), p. 100.
5. Douglas John Hall, *Professing the Faith* (Minneapolis: Fortress Press, 1993), p. 391.
6. Cited in Hall, Ibid.; p. 389.
7. John Vannersall, *Lectionary Homiletics,* April 1995, p. 28.

~

The Voice That Wakes the Dead

Readings: Ezekiel 37:1-14   **March 16, 1997**
           John 11:1-44

When he had said this, he cried with a loud voice, "Lazarus, come out!"

— John 11:43

The raising of Lazarus is the seventh, last, and by far the most important, of what John calls "signs," and most of us would call "miracles." Other "signs" in the Fourth Gospel include the changing of water into wine, the healing of the child of a Roman official, the feeding of the five thousand, the restoration of a blind man's sight, and so on. John speaks of these events as "signs" because he believes they point beyond themselves. They reveal something about who Jesus is and what he does. He concludes his Gospel by saying: "Now Jesus did many other signs . . . which are not written in this book." These were not the only ones. "But these are written so that you may come to believe that Jesus is the Messiah, the Son of God, and that through believing you may have life in his name."

John would be astonished to learn that, rather than confirming in our hearts and minds who Jesus is, his reports of these extraordinary happenings, for many, get in the way. I know that these so-called miracles are serious problems for some of you, and understandably so. We are not at home in the atmosphere of the miraculous. When we come upon stories like that of the raising of Lazarus, our immediate reaction is probably not to exclaim, "How wonderful!" but to ask, "Is this true?" "Did this really happen?"

Let me say two things which you may find helpful. First, these miracle stories have something behind them. Now, it is highly likely that details were added or exaggerated as these stories were told and re-told. But it is very unlikely that they were made up out of whole cloth. If we have any confidence in the integrity of the authors of the Gospels, we cannot conclude that they manufactured these events. John Meier, who has written a careful and massive three volume work on the historical Jesus, concludes that "the tradition of Jesus' miracles is more firmly supported by the criteria of historicity than are a number of other well-known and often readily accepted traditions about his life and ministry."[1] Specifically, as regards the Lazarus story, the ever-so-cautious scholar Raymond Brown says, "there is no conclusive reason for assuming that the skeleton of the story does not stem from the early tradition about Jesus."[2] The claim that this extraordinary man called Jesus did extraordinary things rests on a solid foundation.

Nonetheless, and this is the second thing I wish to say: the author of the Fourth Gospel has not the slightest interest in satisfying what another calls "the curiosity of our eighteenth century minds."[3] John would tell us that our question, "Is it true?" is absolutely the wrong question. What we ought to be asking is the question of meaning. What is the point of these "signs"? Toward what end does John relate these events? What is the meaning? Regarding the raising of Lazarus, that is the question to which we now turn. To find the answer we have to look more closely at the story itself.

* * *

It begins in an odd way. Mary and Martha, the sisters of Lazarus, send word to Jesus that their brother is ill. Jesus treats this news in what appears a most cavalier fashion. Despite his affection for Mary, Martha and Lazarus, Jesus delays going to their aid. He stays two days longer where he is. This is strange. I know what I would have done. I have done it hundreds of times. I might be writing a sermon, or in a meeting, or weeding my garden. The phone rings. So and so has been rushed to the emergency room. And I immediately rush to the hospital. Any caring and competent pastor would do the same. But it's *not* what Jesus does. He procrastinates.

When, at last, he makes up his mind to go to Bethany, there is a curious exchange with his disciples. They remind him that, not long ago, his enemies seemed ready to do him bodily harm. What makes him think that the danger has passed? Jesus, however, brushes aside their worries.

"Our friend Lazarus has fallen asleep," he says, "but I am going there to waken him." Like others whom we have met in the Fourth Gospel — Nicodemus and the Samaritan woman, for instance — the disciples are clueless as to Jesus' meaning. Finally he puts it in a way they cannot misconstrue. "Lazarus is dead," he says. Whereupon honest, plain-speaking Thomas, from whom we will hear more on Easter morning, says, "Let us also go, that we may die with him."

When Jesus arrives in Bethany, sure enough, Lazarus is dead. He has been four days in a tomb. Hearing that Jesus has come, at long last, Martha goes to meet him. "Lord," she says, "if you had been here, my brother would not have died." How do you hear what she says? "Lord, if you had been here . . ." Is it a rebuke? An expression of regret? A word of confidence in Jesus' power to heal? Or maybe some of each? "Lord, if you had been here . . ."

This is a good place for a pastoral observation. Grief typically provokes a multitude of emotions, among which are likely to be anger, bitterness, resentment, or other negative reactions. Sometimes people are reluctant to express such feelings, especially to God. They worry that God can't take it. Learn from Martha. You can be honest with Christ, with God. There's no better place to take your despair, your disappointment, your anger — whatever it is you are feeling.

Returning to our story, Jesus tells Martha, "Your brother will rise again." She is not consoled, in part because she, too, misunderstands. She thinks Jesus is offering pious talk about heaven. "I know," she says, "I know all about that." "I know that he will rise again in the resurrection on the last day." But Jesus is not talking about some vague promise of another life sometime, somewhere. Here I give you Eugene Peterson's translation. Jesus says: "I am, right now, Resurrection and Life. The one who believes in me, even though he or she dies, will live. And everyone who lives believing in me does not ultimately die at all. Do you believe this?" To which Martha responds with the most explicit and extravagant confession of faith of anyone to this point in John's Gospel. "Yes, Lord," she says, "I believe that you are the Messiah, the Son of God. . . ."[4]

With that, Jesus heads for the cemetery, and Martha goes to get Mary. Martha's words to Mary are the ones carved in stone over the front entrance of this church. Have you noticed them there, in the charming language of the King James Version? "The master is come and calleth for thee." This story is the source of those words. "The master is come and calleth for thee." And so, Martha, Mary, and their grieving friends all go out to meet Jesus. Seeing Mary weeping, Jesus is himself moved to tears. And here we come to a crucial point in the story. How are we to understand these tears of Jesus?

There are two or three possibilities. Perhaps they are evidence of Jesus' empathy. We would welcome that. It would be good to know that Jesus feels our sadness. One can imagine the families of those young girls in New York City, killed when a tree fell on the car in which they were riding: those families would like it if they could be sure that Jesus is weeping along with them. A little later in our story, Jesus inquires as to where Lazarus is buried, and the mourners say, "Come and see." All of us who have buried our loved ones hope that, in some way beyond our knowing, Jesus will "come and see" where we have laid them. Maybe the tears of Jesus are tears of empathy.

According to John, "the Jews" who are there with Mary and Martha draw the obvious inference. "See how he loved him," they say; loved Lazarus, they mean. And there is surely something to that. Jesus did love Lazarus, and so perhaps he weeps just as we do when somebody close to us dies. We feel the loss, and we weep. And so does Jesus.

If, however, you have been with us throughout this series, you may remember what I said in an earlier sermon about this phrase, "the Jews." John uses this term to refer to those who really don't understand who Jesus is, or what he is about. So, when we read, "The Jews said, 'See how he loved him!'" it is a signal that we have to dig deeper. Jesus' tears likely represent something more than his affection for a dead friend.

The clue is way back at the beginning of the story. You remember that, when Jesus learns of Lazarus' illness, he says: "This illness does not lead to death; rather it is for God's glory, so that the Son of God may be glorified through it." Here's something else you have got to understand if you are ever going to get what John is saying. Whenever in the Fourth Gospel Jesus speaks of being glorified, it is a reference to his death, to his coming crucifixion. So, next Sunday, when we read John's version of the entry into Jerusalem, we will hear Jesus say, "The hour has come for the Son of Man to be glorified." The reference is not to the little parade, with the "Hosannas!" and palm branches. The reference is to his approaching death. Prior to this John has said of Jesus, "His hour had not yet come." But now, here in Bethany, his hour is coming and Jesus knows it. What we have here is the Fourth Gospel's version of the Garden of Gethsemane.

Standing in the cemetery preparing to call Lazarus out of the tomb, Jesus knows that he will soon be in a tomb of his own. John intends us to see in this scene a kind of preview, a foretaste, of Good Friday and Easter. As we watch Jesus come to the tomb of Lazarus and as we hear the women weeping and wailing, we are to think of another tomb soon to be occupied and of other women gathered before a cross. As we hear Jesus order the stone rolled away, we are to be reminded of another stone and of another tomb. As we observe Jesus weeping there in the graveyard at Bethany, we are to realize how much it costs Jesus to free, not just Lazarus, but all his sisters and brothers — that is to say, all of us — from the burden of our sins and the sting of our death.

Jesus goes to the tomb of Lazarus, knowing that he and Lazarus are about to exchange places. He cries with a loud voice — he shouts! — "Lazarus, come out!" And, when the dead man comes forth, still wrapped up in his burial clothes, Jesus says, "Unbind him, and let him go."

There is so much to wonder about, isn't there? So much John does not tell us that we would like to know. What did it mean for Lazarus to have this second chance at life? Did he live any differently from before? Did he stop more often to smell the roses? Did he speak his love or express his gratitude more frequently? Having died once, was he better prepared to die again? These and other of our curiosities go unsatisfied.

The reason is that John has told us what he wants us to know — all really that we need to know: to encounter Jesus is to live; to hear the voice of Jesus is to come alive. As true for you as for Lazarus. For, John's Jesus says: ". . . I tell you, *anyone* who hears my word and believes him who sent me has eternal life, and does not come under judgment, but has passed from death to life." Without God, the whole world is a graveyard. But you are not without God — at least you do not have to be without God. God comes to you in Jesus, revealing divine love, releasing divine power. God comes to you in Jesus so that you "may have life, and have it abundantly."

*   *   *

The voice that wakes the dead. Are you listening? Do you hear it? It's not Lazarus to whom Jesus is calling, this morning. It's you. It's me. "Come out!" he is saying. Come out from among the dead. Come out from whatever has you entombed. Come to me and live. You haven't been so long dead that you cannot hear, have you? Have you?

1. John P. Meier, *A Marginal Jew*, Volume II (New York: Doubleday, 1994), p. 630.

2. Raymond E. Brown, *The Anchor Bible, The Gospel According to John* (Garden City, NY: Doubleday & Co., 1966), p. 429.

3. Peter Gomes, *More Sundays at Harvard* (Cambridge, MA: The Memorial Church, Harvard University, 1996), p. 136.

4. Eugene H. Peterson, *The Message* (Colorado Spring, CO: Nav Press, 1993), p. 212.

~

The Loving Father

Readings: Psalm 32   **March 18, 2001**
               II Corinthians 5:16-21
               Luke 15:11-32

Then Jesus said, "There was a man who had two sons."
— Luke 15:11

Some months ago, when I was trying to decide which of the many stories of Jesus to include in this sermon series, I thought at first of omitting the parable of the prodigal son, as it is called. It is so familiar, and has been the subject of so many sermons, that I wondered if its "shock value" has not been lost.[1] But then it occurred to me that, if it were not a part of the series, some of you might never speak to me again. So, included it is.

But, before plunging into the parable itself, permit me three preliminary comments. First, the name by which this story has long been known — "the prodigal son" — is misleading. The important person, the central figure of the story, is the father. As the opening words make clear, it's about the father: "There was a man who had two sons." The story needs a new name, something like, "The Loving Father."

Second comment: While "Father" appears to have been a favorite metaphor of Jesus in speaking of God, it was not his only one. In the parable immediately preceding this one there is a feminine image: that of a woman who has lost a coin and sweeps her house until she finds it. Moreover, according to one New Testament scholar, the word "Father," as used by Jesus, "encompasses . . . something of what the word 'Mother' signifies among us."[2] It's something you will want to keep in mind as we go along.

Comment number three: I realize that, for some, the parental figure in the story is simply unrecognizable. There are those who have longed for, but have never known such a father. There are some whose father was never there, either not there physically, or not there emotionally. There are others whose father was there and they wish he hadn't been because he was so abusive. One can only hope that these persons can hear and believe the gospel message despite their experience.

*   *   *

Now to the story itself. I begin where the parable does: with the younger son. It is, I believe, a mistake to think of him as the class cut-up, mischievous but lovable, a charming rogue: an ancient version, say, of a certain recent President. The portrait Jesus paints is not that of a young man who is only exercising his freedom, sowing a few wild oats, living for a while in the fast lane, before settling down and becoming a responsible citizen. Let me be blunt: the younger son is a self-centered jerk. He demands that he be given his inheritance, that which would fall to him upon his father's death. What he asks is an insult: "Too bad you have hung around so long, old man, give me what is mine." In effect, he wishes his father dead!

The father's response is astonishing. Then and there, "he divided his property between (the two sons)." According to the custom of the time, one-third to the younger, two-thirds to the elder. Presumably the younger son gets cash, the older one gets the farm. Off goes the younger son "to a distant country" where he squanders his property "in dissolute living." You are free to imagine whatever forms of "dissolute living" appeal to you: booze, drugs, women, gambling casinos, the racetrack. You might even imagine a greedy day-trader who invests in dot com stocks, gets over extended, borrows heavily, and, when the NASDAQ plunges, loses everything. Whatever the form of "dissolute living," the younger son ends up destitute, disgraced, and desperate. That's what all the business about the "pigs" is meant to say.

Then, one day, or more likely, during one restless night, he has a thought. Why not go home? Now right here, it is easy to get off the track, and many preachers have done so. They have taken the phrase, "he came to himself," as an indication that the younger son has experienced pangs of remorse; he realizes what a jerk he has been; and he is ready to repent. Don't believe it. The speech the younger son rehearses sounds pious —

"I have sinned against heaven and before you" — but what prompts the piety is immediately obvious — the old man's hired hands are far better off than he is. David Buttrick thinks of it as a "soup kitchen conversion."[3] The boy is hungry. The church has a feeding program. And if, to get a meal, you have to listen to some preacher's boring sermon and sing a few gospel hymns, well, it's a small price to have to pay to get a full belly.

*   *   *

So, the younger son heads for home, speech all memorized. Anybody who either is, or ever was, an adolescent knows what that's like. We have all been there and done that. We have all done something we realized afterward our parents were not going to be happy about. And we have carefully considered what it is we could say that might make mom and dad ease up on the punishment. Such a speech as the younger son prepared and rehearsed we can all understand.

What is difficult to understand, astonishing really, is the behavior of the father in Jesus' story. Maybe he is weeding the garden, or mowing the lawn, or just sitting on the front porch. He looks up, sees a figure in the distance, recognizes his son, "is filled with compassion," runs to meet the returning scoundrel, hugs him, kisses him — all before the son has uttered the first word of his carefully crafted speech.

One commentator says the father's behavior has "the quality of burlesque."[4] He is, after all, a patriarchal figure. One expects a certain dignity. A typical father of that time and place — perhaps of any time and place — might have welcomed the prodigal home, but not without an apology, not without some appropriate groveling. This father, on the other hand, disregards dignity, hikes up his long robe, runs down the lane, embraces and kisses the boy. He acts like a mother, if you ask me.

There is one detail I don't want you to overlook. The father's embrace precedes any admission of wrongdoing on the part of the son. "The father . . . ran and put his arms around him and kissed him. *Then* the son said to him, 'Father, I have sinned against heaven and before you. . . .' " The son's confession does not trigger the father's love; it is the other way around. It is the father's warm embrace that elicits the son's confession. And that, dear people, is why in our worship, the corporate prayer of confession is always preceded by a pastoral word that, in one form or another, says, "A gracious God awaits you; you, therefore, can be honest; you don't need to pretend; let us confess our sins." As another puts it: "We are not forgiven . . . because we have made ourselves forgivable or even because we have had faith; we are forgiven solely because there is a Forgiver." He continues: "We may be unable, as the prodigal was, to believe it until we finally see it; but the God who does it, (who forgives) like the father who forgave the prodigal, never once had anything else in mind."[5]

*   *   *

The younger son is back. His father has not only permitted his return. He has not put him to work as one of the hired hands. He has embraced him as his son. His long lost boy has come home. There is, says the father, only one thing to do: Let's have a party. "Get the fatted calf and kill it," he tells the servants, "and let us eat and celebrate for this son of mine was dead and is alive again, he was lost and is found."

The "fatted calf" is an important symbol. Says one commentator: "A calf is slaughtered for the marriage of the eldest son, or the visit of a governor of the province, or some such occasion. The calf means . . . a joy so great that it must be celebrated with the grandest banquet imaginable"[6] — or, in this case, a Texas-sized barbecue.

Enter the older son — the villain of the piece. Yes? No? Some of you, I know, view him sympathetically. My guess is, many of you do. I am not surprised, because many of you are older brother types, or older sister types, even if you really are not the eldest. That's why you are where you are. It's why I am where I am. Most of us good Bryn Mawr Presbyterians are not like the younger son — irresponsible, selfish, uncaring. We do not treat our living parents as if they were dead. We are faithful, decent, diligent, hard-working people. We expect a lot of ourselves, we give a lot of ourselves, and we don't much like it when we are taken for granted.

I'm not making fun of you. I, too, have a lot of sympathy for the older sibling. I grew up in the home of two older siblings. Both my father and my mother were the eldest in their families. I well remember how, when my grandparents became frail or sickly, how it was my parents who took them in and cared for them, nursed them until they died. Both of my parents had younger siblings. They were all nice people, I liked them all. So far as I know, they did not engage in "dissolute living." But they didn't come around all that much either. And I don't remember them doing much in the way of emptying bedpans, helping with baths, changing sheets, and dispensing pills. I am not sure they even told my parents that they were grateful they did those things. Older siblings can and often do get taken for granted. They shouldn't, but they do.

But not always. Years ago, there was a baseball player named Tommy Henrich. He played for the New York Yankees along side Joe DiMaggio. He was DiMaggio's teammate longer than any other player. Henrich's career batting average was a highly respectable .282. Every year he drove in a lot of runs. He played well in the field. He was a fine player. DiMaggio was the star, the idol of the fans, the favorite of the press. But you know what nickname his teammates gave Henrich? "Old Reliable." Every day he showed up, put on his uniform, did his job. "Old Reliable." It's how I think of the older brother. It's how I remember my parents. And that's how many of us are, too: "Reliable," whether or not we are "old."

The trouble is, sometimes we are so reliable that we become a bit self-righteous. Like the older son: "For all these years I have been working like a slave for you, and I have never disobeyed your commands. . . ." And self-righteousness can so easily lead to self-pity: "Yet you have never given me even a young goat so that I might celebrate with my friends. But when this son of yours came back, who devoured your property with prostitutes, you killed the fatted calf for him."

One wonders just how it was the older brother knew the particular kind of "dissolute living" his younger brother had been guilty of. Up to this point there has been no mention of "prostitutes." One wonders if he was not betraying his own sexual fantasies. But we better not go there.

What does need to be said is this: The sins of the older son are not the sins of the younger. The sins of the younger son are open, obvious, even flamboyant. The sins of the older son are more discreet, private, even clandestine, hidden — hidden, so much so that he may not even recognize them as sins — anger, resentment, bitterness, self-righteousness, a tendency to divide the world up into winners and losers, good people and bad people, the sheep and the goats, the saved and the lost. Of the two sons, Peter Gomes says: "The prodigal is willful, foolish, profligate, self-centered, . . . and indulgent. He comes home only when there is no where else to go. The elder brother is petty, spiteful, jealous, self-righteous. . . . I think," says Gomes, "we should pity the poor father, who has to live with this conspicuous vice and the even more conspicuous virtue: perhaps *he* should have run away and left the place to the two of them to fight it out."[7]

*   *   *

But, as you know, that is not what happens. And now with the older son, perhaps even more than with the younger, the father earns his title.

He is "the loving father." Having learned of the anger of his eldest, the "father came out and began to plead with him." And after allowing the older son to spill his resentment and bitterness, the father declares his affection for him, too. I have given you everything, he says. He has, you remember, already handed over to the older son two-thirds of his estate: "All that I have is yours." It's like the psalm says: "The earth is the Lord's" — and it has all been handed over to us. That's what the father says: I love you, too, he tells the older son, and not because of your obedience, your hard work, or even your reliability. I love you because you also are my son, my child. And here, too, it strikes me that the father is behaving more like a mother.

*   *   *

Now, two important questions. First, where in this story is God, and what is God doing? You know the answer. God is the father who gives away all that he has. God is the father who acts like a mother — disregarding dignity and running to one son with forgiveness, pleading with the other to join the party. God is the father who does not so much have mercy as he is mercy. God is the father who does not seem to care about appearances. He will do almost anything, it seems, to reconcile his two children to himself and to each other. The extravagance of his love is almost as absurd as a lovely figure hanging on a cross so as to reconcile you and me and the whole world to God.

Question number two: Where are we in this story? Where are you? Maybe you are the younger one to whom the father says, "Welcome home." Or maybe you are the older one to whom the father says, "Won't you please come in?" Or maybe — could this be? — maybe you and I are a blend of the two sons. Maybe some days we are like the younger, and some days we are like the older. The one who stays the same is the father who acts like a mother. And, which ever one of the children you are, what I want to say to you this morning is this: do not let this Lenten season go by without seeing how greatly you are loved. Do not let another Lent pass without recognizing how far the God we know in Jesus Christ goes to reconcile you to himself. Then you will know what the hymn writer means:

> "Love so amazing, so divine,
> Demands my soul, my life, my all."

1. As suggested by Thomas G. Long in *Christian Century*, March 14, 2001.
2. Joachim Jeremias, *The Prayers of Jesus* (Philadelphia: Fortress Press, 1967), p. 11.
3. David Buttrick, *Preaching Parables* (Louisville, KY: Westminster John Knox, 2000), p. 202.
4. Bernard Brandon Scott, *Hear Then the Parable* (Minneapolis: Fortress Press, 1989), p. 117.
5. Robert Capon, *The Parables of Grace* (Grand Rapids, MI: Wm. B. Eerdmans Publishing Co., 1988), p. 140.
6. Kenneth Bailey in Buttrick, Ibid., p. 203.
7. Peter S. Gomes, *Yet More Sundays at Harvard* (Cambridge, MA: The Memorial Church, Harvard University, 1997), p. 117.

~

The Rich Man and Lazarus

Readings: Isaiah 58:5-12   March 25, 2001
            I Corinthians 12:14-26
            Luke 16:19-31

There was a rich man who was dressed in purple and fine linen and who feasted sumptuously every day. And at his gate lay a poor man named Lazarus . . .
— Luke 16:19-20

When was the last time you heard a joke having to do with "St. Peter and the pearly gates"? Yesterday? Last week? There is a whole genre of these stories. They have been around for a long while. At the time of Christ there was one making the rounds that scholars believe originated in Egypt. It seems that Jesus borrowed it and made it into a parable.

As we approach it, there is something important to keep in mind: just as our "pearly gates" jokes and stories typically have more to do with this world than the next one, so with the parable of the rich man and Lazarus. Its purpose is *not* to document heaven and hell. The focus of the parable is the here and now, not the hereafter. And it is yet one more confirmation of the point I made four Sundays ago in introducing this Lenten sermon series. I warned then that the stories of Jesus "have a prophetic purpose. They have an edge to them," I said, "often a sharp edge." That's certainly true of this one. Only its edge may not be exactly where you think, or even where you fear. Now to the story itself.

*   *   *

It begins by introducing two individuals who live in physical proximity to one another, but who, in other ways, are miles apart.

67

One is "a rich man" who wears the finest clothes and eats the best food that money can buy. He is "dressed in purple," Jesus says, which is probably meant to signify a person of power and prestige, as well as wealth. We are to imagine him residing in a mansion surrounded by a wall, within which there is a gate. Keep your eye on the gate!

Lying on the opposite side of the gate is "a poor man," not only poor, but helpless. He is "covered with sores." The wild dogs roaming about the streets harass him. He hopes to satisfy his hunger with the scraps from the rich man's table. His condition is desperate. But there is one thing about him that we should not overlook: he has a name — Lazarus. Which is to say, he is more than a problem, or a statistic, he is a person with a name. It is worth noting that this is the only person in all of Jesus' parables who is given a name. Maybe Jesus means to remind us that all whom we tend to speak of as "problems" or "statistics," have names — the children in Iraq unable to access the medicines they need, the emaciated victims of the AIDS virus, the lonely inhabitants of our nursing homes, the people locked up in our prisons. Perhaps Jesus wants us to remember that all such have names, even though to us they may appear nameless, faceless.

It would seem, at first, that the rich man and Lazarus have nothing in common. But, as it turns out, there is one thing. They are both mortal; they both die. Whereupon, the scene shifts from this world to the next. Once again, the conditions in which the two men find themselves are very different. Only a great reversal has occurred. The name "Lazarus" means "one whom God helps," and in the story it is so. The poor man, having died, is carried to the bosom of Abraham, the great patriarch of Israel, and there he is comforted. The rich man, on the other hand, is in Hades and in torment.

Such a reversal of fortune would have come as quite a surprise, not only to the rich man and Lazarus, but to many of those who heard Jesus tell this story. According to Luke, among those listening were "the Pharisees who were lovers of money." Their assumption was that material prosperity should be taken as a sign of divine favor. The opposite was also believed to be true: poverty is somehow what the poor deserve. These attitudes, as you must know, far from having disappeared, are still around. If you don't believe it, listen more carefully to the conversation at your next cocktail party. But in our story, it is not so. Lazarus is with Abraham, and the rich man is in a place "where," as one commentator puts it, "the accommodations are well below his accustomed standards."[1] The Four Seasons Hotel it is not!

You remember what happens next: the rich man looks up to see Abraham and Lazarus "at his side." Obviously, he has to have seen Lazarus before, and even known who he was. For now he is able to identify him, and call his name, and he asks Abraham to "send Lazarus" to relieve him of his "agony." The rich man is still operating on the assumption, apparently, that if Lazarus is good for anything, it is as someone who can serve the rich man's needs. Abraham answers that it is impossible to honor such a request. "A great chasm has been fixed," he says, so that there can be no traffic between the two realms. It was possible, once upon a time for a relationship to exist between the rich man and Lazarus. Only a gate kept the two apart, a gate that could have easily been opened. But that time has passed. Now, "a great chasm has been fixed," Abraham says, "so that those who might want to pass from here to you cannot do so, and no one can pass from there to us."

Perhaps you have noticed that, up to this point, the sole concern of the rich man has been himself, numero uno. In life he lived by himself, and he protected himself from the realm of human suffering by means of a wall. In death, and in Hades, he seeks relief for himself and from his agony. It is only at this point in the story, when his self-concern has come to naught, that the rich man begins to think of others. Having been told that his own rescue is out of the question, the rich man remembers his brothers. He pleads with Abraham to send Lazarus to warn them, lest they, too, end up where he is. Abraham answers: they don't need Lazarus; "they have Moses and the prophets; they should listen to them." Here, one guesses, the rich man may have realized that he, also, at one time had Moses and the prophets, but failed to listen to them. And so he says: "No, Father Abraham; but if someone goes to them from the dead, they will repent." But to this Abraham responds with the punch line of the parable: "If they do not listen to Moses and the prophets, neither will they be convinced even if someone rises from the dead."

*   *   *

Last Thursday afternoon I made a pastoral visit to one of our members, someone who is physically afflicted but very much with it mentally. During our conversation he asked about today's sermon. This is somebody who is well acquainted with the Bible, especially the Gospels. When I told him that I would be preaching on the parable of the rich man and Lazarus, his response was, "That's a tough one." I knew instinctively what he was thinking. He knows the community in which we live, the congregation of which you are a part and which I serve. While not all of us are wealthy by any means, in the total scheme of things, compared to most of the rest of the world, all of us here are well off — even if we are less well off today than we were a few months ago! Your fellow parishioner knows all this. He is familiar with this parable, and knows that the rich man does not come off well in it, and he was worried, I think, that this parable might occasion a sermonic tirade about the evils of wealth. I am sure that something of the sort concerned him because when we parted, he said, "I will pray for you this Sunday."

I am glad for his prayers. But his fears, and perhaps yours, are somewhat misplaced. For, while both wealth and poverty are featured in the parable, what Jesus is getting at is something else. Which is not to say that Jesus did not warn about the dangers of riches. He did. "It is easier," Jesus said, "for a camel to go through the eye of a needle, than for a rich person to enter the kingdom of God." The problem is less the wealth itself, than the attitude it can foster: the illusion of self-sufficiency, the feeling that one does not need anybody else — including God. All of which is illustrated by the rich man in the parable.

It is, however, my contention that the main concern of Jesus is revealed in the last part of his story, which, by the way, is where we come in. Those of you who have been here throughout this sermon series will recall that, with regard to each of the stories of Jesus, we have been keeping two questions in mind. One has to do with God: Where in the story is God? The other question concerns ourselves: Where are we in the story? This morning, I want to take the second question first.

Where in the story are we? Not with the rich man, and not with Lazarus. We are still on this side of the great divide, so we cannot be with Lazarus, and, thankfully, we can not be in Hades with the rich man, either. Not yet, anyway! Where, then, are we? We are in the only place left: with the five brothers — which is to say, we still have time to listen to Moses and the prophets, and that is exactly what Jesus hopes we will do. In telling this story, Jesus is inviting, even pleading for us to listen and learn while we still have time to do so.

What do Moses and the prophets say? There is time to give you only a small sample, but it will be enough for you to get the point. Here, for example, in Chapter 15 of Deuteronomy, is Moses: If there is among you anyone in need, . . . do not be hard-hearted or tight-fisted toward your needy neighbor. You should rather open your hand. . . ." As for the prophets, you heard earlier what Isaiah had to say on behalf of God. Originally he was rebuking Israel for its self-serving religious practices. The prophet asks: "Is not this the fast that I choose . . . : to share your bread with the hungry, and bring the homeless poor into your house; when you see the naked, to cover them, and not to hide yourself from your own kin?"

Do you get it? The rich man's sin was not his wealth, but his indifference. It was his habit of isolating himself, protecting, insulating himself from suffering with his wall, hiding himself, in Isaiah's words, from his own "kin" in the person of Lazarus. He ignored his moral duty. He failed to understand that he was a member of a community and not an isolated, self-sufficient individual. He never understood that those to whom much has been given, of them much is required. All of which he would have known if only he would have listened to Moses and the prophets. And his brothers would know it, and so, too, would we — if we were to listen to what, not only Moses and the prophets, but the Bible as a whole is trying to tell us. It does not take somebody coming to us from the dead. We already have the means to know what God wants and expects. Where are we in this story? Right there with the five brothers. The opportunity is ours to listen and to learn. The consequence of doing so is life — whether we are rich or poor. The failure to do so means death — for it is to be cut off, not only from our neighbor, but from God.

*   *   *

This story of Jesus has many implications and applications. You might, and I hope you will, apply it personally. Many of you already do, and for that I commend you. We might think of the parables' implications for this congregation. It might be good to ponder it when we get together to decide on our budget, for instance. In any number of ways we are trying to take seriously our neighborly responsibilities: through the ministries of the Outreach and Mission Councils, the Hunger and Homeless Task Forces, the tutoring programs, and others. Surely the Urban/Suburban Partnership is one way in which we are trying to open the gate between ourselves and others.

Beyond the personal and the congregational, I want to suggest one other application. It has to do with that greater society of which we are all a part. One of the things I do to sniff out the mood of our society is to read letters to the editor that appear in various publications. In doing so, I sense a rising tide of individualism among us. A recent rather sarcastic one about tax cuts began this way: "Let me get this straight; Congress is willing to return my money to me if there is a surplus. The last time I checked," the writer went on, "the only way there could not be a surplus is if spending exceeds the amount of money collected. . . . So," he continued, "if the Beltway elite cannot come up with a way to spend my money, they will graciously return it to me. How kind of them."[2] Nowhere in the letter was there any thought that this individual might bear some obligation for the welfare of the community of which he is a part. There was no indication he knew anything about, or cared anything about, the Lazaruses who are part of our society. There was no sense that some of his money might be needed to help others.

In the lesson read earlier from First Corinthians, there is a quite different point of view. Admittedly, Paul was speaking with reference to the church, but what he says applies equally to the larger community I believe, to our society as a whole, and indeed, to the world beyond our shores. We are one body, Paul says, with many members. We cannot say to one another, "I have no need of you." We are instead so connected to one another that "if one member suffers, all suffer together . . .; if one member is honored, all rejoice together."

That's the message of our parable, too. It stands as a sharp rebuke to the world of greed and self-indulgence. At our gate, says the parable, there is a neighbor — indeed many neighbors. They are kinfolk, and we ignore them at our peril. We are part of a body, a commonwealth, if you please, and we share a moral responsibility to assist our most vulnerable sisters and brothers. The question of how may be open for discussion and debate, but Moses and the prophets have long since told us about the what: "If there is among you anyone in need, . . . open your hand." This, then, is a parable about mutuality and community. It reminds us that we are responsible for one another. We are to bear one another's burdens. It has nothing to do with liberalism or conservatism or any other "ism." This, quite simply, is the gospel of Jesus Christ.

*   *   *

So, we know where we are in this story. We are with the five brothers. We still have the opportunity to listen to and learn from Moses and the prophets. But what of our other question: where is God? You may think God is represented by Abraham, and I suppose in a way that is so. But I suggest you look elsewhere. I believe we are to see God in the person of Lazarus. If we want to meet God, it is to Lazarus that we are meant to go. It's what Jesus said once. Not in this story, but in another one. "I was hungry and you gave me food, I was thirsty and you gave me something to drink, I was a stranger and you welcomed me, I was naked and you gave me clothing, I was sick and you took care of me, I was in prison and you visited me. . . .Truly I tell you, just as you did it to one of the least of these who are members of my family [my kinfolk!], you did it to me." If you want to meet God, especially in the person of Christ, look just beyond the gate. You will find him waiting for you there, in the disguise of Lazarus.

1. Robert Farrar Capon, *Parables of Grace* (Grand Rapids, MI: Wm. B. Eerdmans Publishing Co., 1988), p. 156.
2. *The Philadelphia Inquirer*, March 16, 2001.

~

The Crucified God¹

Readings: Isaiah 50:4-9a   **April 8, 2001**
                Philippians 2:5-11
                Luke 23:1-56

As he came near and saw the city, he wept over it. . . .
                     — Luke 19:41

Those of us who share responsibility for shaping and leading our services of worship try to do so in a way that produces a semblance of unity. Our hope is that the music, lessons, prayers, and sermon will all fit together, resulting in harmony, not dissonance. Maybe you are thinking that today we have failed miserably. For, we seem to have encouraged two quite different moods.

It was all upbeat in the beginning. "Blessed is the one who comes in the name of the Lord," I said, and you responded, "We bless him from the house of the Lord." Luke's account of the "triumphal entry" was read. And that was followed by a jubilant hymn and the procession of children waving palms, and soon thereafter the lovely anthem by the children, urging us to open wide the gates of our hearts so as to welcome the wonderful King, "strong" and "mighty to save." There were happy, smiling faces all around.

Suddenly it was as if we took a sharp left turn. The song, "All Glory, Laud and Honor" gave way to shouts of "crucify, crucify him." The laments of the women overtook our laughter. The triumphal atmosphere was replaced by a sense of tragedy as we heard how the one of whom it was said, "Blessed is the king who comes . . . ," was nailed to a cross, and over his head there was a mocking inscription, "This — this! — is the king of the Jews."

Why do this? Why bring together the palms and the passion? One reason, as you have heard me say before, is to try to make up for the absence of so many of you from the Maundy Thursday and Good Friday services. So many of you go directly from the Hosannas of Palm Sunday to the alleluias of Easter without bothering to stand at the foot of the cross. We read the passion narrative today to help you remember that the living Lord of Easter is none other than the Jesus who "suffered under Pontius Pilate, was crucified, dead, and buried."

But that's only part of it. The main reason for bringing these seemingly contradictory themes together is that they really do belong together. I mean Palm Sunday no less than Good Friday is a day of tragedy. The tragic part of it is that so few, at the time, had any clue as to what was going on, just as many today still fail to comprehend. Not that it was, or is, easy. He is a strange sovereign, this Jesus, riding on in lowly majesty, not to a throne, but to his death.

*   *   *

On the five preceding Sundays of this Lenten season, our attention was drawn to a few of the parables of Jesus. In each instance we asked, where in the parable is God, and what, according to the parable, is God said to be doing? It's an appropriate question to be asking today, as well. For, the story of Palm Sunday is also a parable of sorts — not of words, but of action.

It may have been something Jesus learned how to do from the prophets. Acting out a message was something the prophets had done on occasion when their words seemed to be falling on deaf ears. So, for example, when Jeremiah predicted that his country was going to come under foreign rule, and nobody believed him, and ridiculed him, the prophet put a yoke around his neck and went parading with it up and down the streets. Just so, he said, the nation of Judah would soon be under the yoke of King Nebuchadnezzar of Babylon. And when, in anger, somebody got hold of the wooden yoke and broke it, Jeremiah had one made of iron and went about with it.

Well, Jesus had been trying to tell the people, especially his disciples, that they had the wrong idea about the messiah they were wanting and expecting. He had tried to undermine, subvert, their fantasies of a triumphant God of domineering force who would come some day and fix everything. Jesus had spoken of God in terms not of power and glory, but in terms of self-giving love, gentle mercy, and lowly vulnerability. But they did not get it, mostly I think because they did not want to get it.

And so, down from the Mount of Olives he came on that first Palm Sunday with none of the customary trappings of power, astride a donkey. To call it a "triumphal entry" is somewhat ludicrous, don't you think? Where are the symbols of power? There is no brass band, no soldiers marching with their weapons, saluting as they pass the reviewing stand. Just a man on a donkey. But they did not get it, did not see the lowliness, the modesty, the pathetic powerlessness of it. Which, one surmises, is why when he reached the brow of the hill and saw the city "he wept over it." According to Luke, that's when he said, "If you, even you, had recognized on this day the things that make for peace! But now they are hidden from your eyes."

*　　*　　*

But let's not leave it back there in the distant past, because I am not at all sure that we are much different from those observers of the first Palm Sunday parade. I am, as a matter of fact, fairly certain that we have as much difficulty seeing the meaning of this day as they did. And if we do see it, I think we have about as much difficulty accepting it as they did. And I wonder if Jesus is not weeping still — because despite, not only his acted-out Palm Sunday parable, but despite even more what got acted out on that Friday afternoon when, because the church saw him as a religious heretic, and the state feared he was a political danger, they combined to execute him; I say, despite even that, we still, much of the time, do not seem to get it.

The problem is, just as in some of Jesus' stories, the parable he acted out on Palm Sunday gives us a God different from the one we imagine and believe we need. And his death on the cross just plain collides with our preferred notions of God. The apostle Paul calls Jesus' death on the cross a scandal. He says "the message about the cross" seems like "foolishness." And it's every bit as true today as when he first said it.

We are Americans, after all, and as another puts it, we "are into self-fulfillment, success, the necessity of self-esteem, and the uses of power."[2] Just the other day, I came upon a bumper sticker I had not seen before. It had what looked to me like the insignia of the Marines on it, and what it said was, "When it absolutely has to be destroyed overnight." We believe in power: military power, economic power, political power — even, God help us, ecclesiastical power. It's all about power, we think, and so we project onto God absolute power.

Those who were there that day and who witnessed the crucifixion believed in a God of power, too, a triumphant God. "He saved others," they mocked; "let him save himself — if! — he is the Messiah of God, his chosen one!" "Are you not the Messiah?" asked one of those hanging next to him. When are you going to start acting like one, instead of hanging there like any other pitiful victim? "Save yourself and us!" When will you do the God-like thing? Our form of the question is: "Why do bad things happen to good people?" Where is a little divine omnipotence when we need it?

Well, here is a different kind of question: What if God is like Christ Jesus, the lowly, ludicrous man on the donkey, the lonely, impotent figure on the cross? What if the death of Jesus was not necessary in order to change God, to persuade God to love us and forgive us? What if the death of Christ on the cross was necessary in order to change us, instead, and especially to change our false notions of God? Suppose, in other words, "the sovereignty that sways the universe is not a domineering force but self-giving love calling us all to a similar way of being with one another?"³

Precisely that, if I understand him correctly, is what Paul is saying in his letter to the Philippians. "Though (Christ) was in the form of God," Paul writes, "he emptied himself. . . ." Another writes: "The word *form* as Paul is using it does not mean outward shape, but rather inner essence."⁴ It is, Paul seems to be saying, this death on the cross that illuminates the essence of the divine.

It is, of course, only Easter that makes it possible to say so. For, without Easter, we would have nothing more than a dead — and deluded! — Jesus. What Easter give us — and by far the most important thing to celebrate next Sunday — what Easter gives us is a risen Lord who was crucified. And so, at last, we may begin to glimpse the true nature of God's glory and the real essence of God's power — nothing other than modest, lowly, cross-shaped love.

∗   ∗   ∗

Well, so what? Does it matter? Will it make any practical difference in the way you live your life? Will it have any influence on how the church thinks of itself, how it behaves? I think I will just remind you of Paul's answer to those questions. The way it works, he says, is that we have this astonishing example to look to and to learn from. "Do nothing from selfish ambition or conceit," Paul writes, "but in humility regard others as better than yourselves. Let each of you look not only to your own interests, but to the interests of others. Let the same mind be in you that was in Christ Jesus, who, although he was in the form of God, did not regard equality with God as something to be exploited, but emptied himself. . . ." If, in other words, that is the picture of who God is and a sample of what God does, it should not be too hard to figure out the kind of people we are meant to be, the kind of things we are called to do. The church that understands, the people who finally "get it," will not have ambitions of grandeur. Such a people, such a church, will seek not to be served, but to serve. Such a church will be ready, even, to give its life on behalf of others.

*   *   *

So, dear friends, here we are at the beginning of another Holy Week. On Thursday we will watch in astonishment as Jesus washes our feet, and then sit at table to receive from his hands the Bread of Life and the Cup of Salvation. On Friday we will stand beneath the cross of Jesus, lost in wonder, love, and praise. And next Sunday, it will be the most glorious day of the Christian year. We will begin our worship, as is our custom, with the Hallelujah Chorus. Only try to remember, as you listen to it, that the "one who is said to reign forever and ever" is that very one in whose death, as Paul puts it, "God has made foolish the wisdom of the world."

1. The title of a book by Jürgen Moltmann.
2. David Buttrick, *The Mystery and the Passion* (Minneapolis: Fortress Press, 1992), p. 126.
3. Penelope Duckworth, *I Am* (Nashville: Abingdon Press, 1998), p. 77.
4. Ibid., p. 40.

~

Easter in the Church of Saint Mark

Readings: Acts 10:34-43   **April 20, 2003**
I Corinthians 15:1-11
Mark 16:1-8

> **As they entered the tomb, they saw a young man, dressed in a white robe, sitting on the right side; and they were alarmed. But he said to them, "Do not be alarmed; you are looking for Jesus of Nazareth, who was crucified. He has been raised; he is not here. Look, there is the place they laid him. But go, tell his disciples and Peter that he is going ahead of you to Galilee; there you will see him, just as he told you." So they went out and fled from the tomb, for terror and amazement had seized them; and they said nothing to anyone, for they were afraid.**
> **— Mark 16:5-8**

Everything about the way our worship began this morning signaled both the significance and the splendor of the day. We entered a sanctuary gorgeously appointed with lilies and ferns, carnations and roses. The music of the prelude was unmistakably jubilant. Then came the choir's singing of the Hallelujah Chorus with its rousing affirmation that "he shall reign forever and ever." Soon thereafter we were all singing the glad and grateful "Jesus Christ is Risen Today." Who could doubt that we are celebrating Easter, the crown of the Christian year, the church's most holy festival?

A little later on the lessons from Scripture were read. From the Book of Acts, a sample of an early Christian sermon in which Peter declares of the crucified Jesus: " . . . But God raised him on the third day." From

Paul's letter to the Corinthians, the unequivocal assertion "that Christ died for our sins . . . , that he was buried, . . . that he was raised on the third day . . . , and that he appeared" not just to one or two of the disciples, but "to more than five hundred brothers and sisters," and even, miracle of miracles, to Paul himself. Finally, we listened to the story of the first Easter morning as it appears in the Gospel according to Mark.

I wonder if Mark's account of the resurrection seemed anti-climactic to you, or even disappointing. His is a curious narrative in which there are "no joyfully amazed women rushing with news of the empty tomb, no awe struck exclamations to the disciples that 'he is risen!' and no reassuring appearances by the risen Christ himself."[1] All we have is a mysterious "young man," sitting in an otherwise empty tomb, "who announces the Resurrection and then issues two commands to the frightened women: don't be afraid and go tell Jesus' disciples that they will see him in Galilee."[2] But the story ends with the women disobeying both commands. Mark says: "They said nothing to anyone, for they were afraid." Not a very auspicious beginning to Easter!

*   *   *

Nonetheless, according to the oldest manuscripts, that is how Mark's Gospel ends: "They said nothing to anyone, for they were afraid." Perhaps, as the reading concluded, you thought to yourself, "There must be more." In our Bibles there are a few additional verses. But these additional verses, virtually all New Testament scholars agree, were added later, probably in the second century. Some editor, that is to say some scribe, also thought Mark's version of the story incomplete and added summaries of stories from the other Gospels. But the most ancient manuscripts end with the women saying nothing because they are afraid.

We are left, then, with what seems like an unfinished Gospel. What are we to make of it? Some suggest that Mark must have intended for there to be more. Maybe he was interrupted in his writing and was never able to return to his desk. Or maybe, originally, there was more. Maybe the manuscript was torn in being handed around, and the last part of it lost. There is, of course, another possibility: that what we have is the ending Mark intended, that Mark deliberately left the ending as we have it. That is what I believe. Let me tell you why.

We know that each of the four Gospels was written for a particular Christian community. Mark's Gospel was the first, written around 65 or

70 A.D. By that time there were already in existence a number of churches in various places: in Corinth, Philippi, Ephesus, Rome, and elsewhere. In the congregation for which Mark was writing, what I am calling the Church of Saint Mark, people were not hearing the Easter story for the first time. In other words, they were like you. I doubt that there is anyone here today who didn't know about Easter before coming to this service. You knew, before you entered the door, without having to look in the bulletin, what the preacher was going to talk about today. You knew the subject of the sermon would be the Resurrection of Jesus. You can assume the same thing was true of the people in Mark's church. They were familiar with the basic story. They were already Christians. Mark tells the story the way he does in the hope that they — and we — might hear it afresh. He concludes the way he does because he wants to draw us into the story. There is no proper ending on purpose. If there is to be one, you have to write it.

*   *   *

So, here you are on this fine Easter morning. You come, with Mark's help, to the tomb. You are greeted by a young man who says: "You are looking for Jesus of Nazareth, who was crucified. He has been raised; he is not here. . . . He is going ahead of you to Galilee; there you will see him." Now what? You have been reminded of the belief that created the Christian church in the first place and has sustained it ever since. You have heard the good, glad news of Easter. Jesus has been raised from the dead. Now, what will you do? You know what the women did. They were afraid and told no one. What will you do?

You are in the tomb, courtesy of Mark. Jesus "is not here," we are told. "He is going ahead of you to Galilee; there you will see him. . . . What does that mean? Are you supposed to charter a plane and go to the Holy Land, retrace the footsteps of Jesus, visit Cana and Capernaum and Nazareth, sit on the hillside where it is believed Jesus spoke the Beatitudes? I know people who have done that and who have been terribly disappointed. No wonder! Jesus is not there.

In Mark's Easter narrative, "Galilee" is not about geography. "Galilee" is a metaphor; Galilee is where ministry occurs. "Galilee is the place where Jesus turned the world on its head."[3] Galilee is where Jesus found Peter and Andrew, James and John, and said: "Follow me." Galilee is where Jesus ate with sinners, healed the sick, fed the hungry crowds, preached a gospel of grace, and taught with authority about the coming kingdom of God. Galilee symbolizes the ministry of Jesus. And when, in Mark's Easter narrative the young man tells us to go to Galilee, he is inviting us to celebrate Easter by participating in the on-going ministry of Jesus — right here, right now. "Are you looking for Jesus? He has been raised; he is not here. . . . He is going ahead of you to Galilee; there you will see him."

My friend Joanna Adams tells about a young man she knew who volunteered regularly at a foot clinic that was part of a homeless shelter in Atlanta. He was "an advertising executive on the rise in his profession," Joanna says, and he "came every Tuesday night and sat on a low stool at the feet of the homeless men. Gently he would place their feet in a basin of warm water. Then he would dry [the feet] and apply ointment to their sores. The ritual always ended with the gift of a clean pair of white socks for each sheltered guest." Joanna says: "It was not unusual . . . for the guests to shed a tear of two. For many, it had been a long time since anyone had offered them any tenderness." One night Joanna asked the young man why he participated in this compassionate ministry. He said: "I just figure I have a better chance of running into Jesus here than almost anywhere else."[4]

I wonder if, sometime, that young man had not celebrated Easter in the Church of Saint Mark. Somewhere he had heard if you are looking for the risen Christ, you have to go to Galilee.

Where, exactly, is Galilee? No one place. That's the marvelous thing. Galilee might be a foot clinic in a homeless shelter. Or a church basement in West Philadelphia where children come for tutoring. Or a place like Graterford Prison. Or a Habitat for Humanity house. Maybe Galilee is a nursing home where lonely people are waiting for someone to come for a visit. Or a food cupboard where people with little or no money go to get something to have for dinner. Galilee might even be a church schoolroom full of bright, rambunctious youngsters. Or a church pew with a stranger sitting in it on Easter morning right next to you. Galilee might be a group of Christian people meeting regularly and wrestling with issues of war and peace, or even the Boardroom of a community agency or church committee where scarce resources are allocated to meet the needs of people who are down on their luck. Someone has suggested that Galilee could even be where you live or where you work,[5] where maybe there is a terminally ill

spouse or parent to care for, or a rebellious adolescent to love, or a difficult colleague to be kind to. I cannot tell you where your Galilee might be.
All I know is what the young man in the empty tomb says: If you want to
see Jesus, Galilee is where you have to go.

*   *   *

What it means is that Albert Schweitzer had it right after all. Do you
know about Schweitzer? That many talented man who spent most of his
life in Africa as a medical missionary? He was also a Biblical scholar and,
long before there was a Jesus Seminar, Schweitzer went looking for the
historical Jesus. He concluded it is an impossible quest. He said, you can't
find Jesus in history. He is not there. Where is he? This is what Schweitzer
said, and even if you have heard his words before, they are worth hearing
again in the light of Mark's version of Easter. Schweitzer said of Jesus:
"He comes to us as One unknown, without a name, as of old, by the lake-
side, He came to those men who knew him not. He speaks to us the same
word: 'Follow thou me!' and sets us to the tasks which He has to fulfill
for our time. He commands, and to those who obey Him, whether they be
wise or simple, He will reveal himself in the toils, the conflicts, the sufferings which they will pass through in His fellowship, and, as an ineffa-
ble mystery, they shall learn in their own experience who He is."[6]

It is what Mark knew all along. You won't find Jesus by going to a
tomb, or anywhere else where people have tried to confine him. He is
not there. ". . . He is going ahead of you to Galilee; there you will see
him. . . ." Those who have ears to hear, let them hear.

1. Tomas G. Long, "Preaching Easter From the Gospel of Mark," *Journal for Preachers*, Easter, 2003, p. 10.
2. Ibid.
3. O. Wesley Allen, Jr., *Preaching Resurrection* (St. Louis, MO: Chalice Press, 2000), p. 27.
4. Joanna Adams, *"The Edge of the Story,"* Trinity Presbyterian Church, Atlanta, Georgia, March 28, 1999.
5. David Bartlett in *Lectionary Homiletics*, April 23, 2000.
6. Albert Schweitzer, *The Quest for the Historical Jesus* (New York: The MacMillan Co., 1964), p. 403.

~

The Lost and Found Department

Readings: Psalm 32   March 7, 2004
          II Corinthians 5:16-6:2
          Luke 19:1-10

For the Son of Man came to seek out and to save the lost.
                              — Luke 19:10

Tradition has it that Luke, the author of the Gospel bearing his name, was a physician. "The beloved physician," Paul calls him. As such we can assume he had a firsthand familiarity with human frailty and fallibility. No only our susceptibility to physical illnesses and ailments, but our vulnerability to spiritual and moral trials and temptations. It's my guess that Luke's experience as a physician helps to explain his compassion for sinners and outcasts, his empathy with the least, the left out, and the lost.

Each of the Gospels has its own particular slant on the life and ministry of Jesus. Matthew's Jesus is a teacher. Mark's Jesus is a man of action. John portrays Jesus as "the word made flesh," the personification of truth. Luke's Jesus is the "friend of sinners."

Luke alone tells about the unnamed woman who, having received Jesus' forgiveness, barges in on a dinner party to "bathe his feet with her tears and to dry them with her hair." Only Luke reports Jesus' parables of the shepherd who goes after the lost sheep, of the woman who searches for the lost coin, and of the father who welcomes home the lost son. Only Luke gives us the parable of the Pharisee who thanks God that he is not like other people and the Tax Collector who prays: "God, be merciful to me, a sinner." And, only in Luke, do we come across the story from which we get today's text: "For the Son of Man came to seek out and to save the lost."

*   *   *

If my records are to be believed I have never before preached on this text or the story from which it comes. Strange, since the story has to be among the best known and most popular of Biblical tales. Once upon a time, children learned of it by way of a Sunday School song:

> Zacchaeus was a wee little man,
> A wee little man was he;
> He climbed up into a sycamore tree,
> The better his Lord to see.

The song suggests that Zacchaeus is the subject of the story and, in many respects, he is. Zacchaeus, we are told, "is a chief tax collector." As such, he is considered to be a "sinner" to be shunned, an outcast, someone who is unwelcome in respectable circles. Tax collectors were Jewish agents of the Roman Empire, despised for being collaborators with the enemy. The fact that theirs was a kind of "cost plus" operation added to the ill-feeling. The system permitted them to collect, not only what was due to Rome, but an extra amount for themselves. It was "a license to steal."

While not an esteemed occupation, it was a lucrative one. So, it is no surprise to learn that Zacchaeus, a chief tax collector, is "rich." Which does not mean, necessarily, that he is happy or that his is a carefree life. Many people do make such an assumption, assume, for example, that anybody who can afford to live on the Main Line must "have it made." But, as we who do live here know, it is not necessarily so. Wealth is no guarantee of health or happiness, provides no assurance that marriages will last or that children will grow up free of heartache.

We are left to guess at Zacchaeus' state of contentment and his motivation. Luke tells us only that he wishes to see Jesus, about whom presumably he has heard, and who is coming through Jericho on his way to Jerusalem. Frustrated by his shortness of stature and the crowd that blocks his view, Zacchaeus runs ahead and climbs a sycamore tree from which vantage point he will have an undisturbed view as Jesus passes by.

*   *   *

This is the point in the story when the scene shifts dramatically. Another actor enters and claims center stage. It is quickly evident that, not Zacchaeus, but Jesus is the subject of the story.

If you were with us last Sunday you may remember my saying that Lent is a time in which we are to pay particular attention to Jesus. We are to listen closely to what he says and watch closely what he does because his words, together with his deeds, provide important clues as to what he wishes to do and can do, in and for us. In today's lesson we get both word and deed, the one showing and the other saying what the ministry of Jesus is all about — why and to whom he has come.

The deed comes first. Observing Zacchaeus up in the tree, Jesus calls his name and says: "Hurry and come down for I must stay at your house today." Jesus invites himself to the house of Zacchaeus, asks hospitality from one who is a notorious sinner — as all the witnesses are quick to point out. Luke leaves to our imagination what transpires inside the house of Zacchaeus. But he leaves us in no doubt as to the consequences of the time Jesus and Zacchaeus spend together. Zacchaeus repents of his ways, makes a huge financial commitment to benefit the poor, and offers restitution to those from whom he has extracted exorbitant funds. All of which prompts Jesus to say: "Today salvation has come to this house because he too is a son of Abraham." Then, lest we miss the meaning of what has just happened, Jesus explains: "For the Son of Man came to seek out and to save the lost."

*   *   *

The time and place in which this encounter occurs are not insignificant. Jesus is on his way to Jerusalem. It will not be long, in Luke's account, before the Palm Sunday parade and, not long after that, until Jesus' arrest, trial, and execution. All of which, Luke tells us, Jesus is anticipating. Here in Jericho, in the person of Zacchaeus, Jesus has one last opportunity for show and tell; one final and dramatic moment to declare and to demonstrate the purpose for which he has come: "To seek out and to save the lost."

In our story it is Jesus who takes the initiative. It is true that Zacchaeus demonstrates some initiative as well. He climbs the tree in order to see who Jesus is. But there is no indication of any other move on his part. It may well be that, once in the tree, Zacchaeus wishes to see but not to be seen. But Jesus does see him, calls to him, bids him come down from his hiding place and goes home with Zacchaeus to dine.

Notice that nothing is asked of Zacchaeus except his hospitality. He is not called upon to confess his sin and repent and thus to become a worthy host. He is not required to change his ways or clean up his act so a condition of being accepted by Jesus. Jesus sees Zacchaeus as he is, calls to him as he is, takes him as he is, and, as he is accepts his hospitality. Recall the hymn we sang moments ago: "Just as I am thou wilt receive, wilt welcome, pardon, cleanse, relieve. . . ." Just as I am.

As we noted, repentance does occur in our story. Zacchaeus changes his ways and does so in a big way. Not, however, as a condition of Jesus' visit, but as a consequence. It is in response to Jesus' embrace, not as a requirement of Jesus' embrace, that the change occurs.

What we are not to miss, is how this story is a symbolic representation of the entire life and ministry of Jesus — and of his death, as well. The good news of the gospel, what makes the gospel good news, is that God, in Jesus Christ, seeks out and saves the lost. The initiative, the first move, is God's. As the Apostle Paul puts it in our Epistle Lesson: "God was in Christ reconciling the world to himself, not counting their trespasses against him. . . ." Or, as he puts it in the famous passage from Romans: "God proves his love for us in that while we were yet sinners Christ died for us. . . ."

The story before us today is one of divine initiative and human transformation. It is a commentary, if you will, on that verse from the First Letter of John: "We love because God first loved us." The divine initiative is both testified to — "the Son of Man came to seek and to save the lost" — and demonstrated: "Zacchaeus, hurry and come down; for I must stay at your house today." The result, the consequence, is one of transformation. In the person of Zacchaeus we are to see what happens when the divine initiative is recognized and responded to. The name for it is "salvation." In this story we learn that "salvation" concerns, not as much what happens to us after we die, but what happens to us when we begin to live. "Salvation" is the manifestation of a spiritual revolution that begins when we surrender to the grace of our Lord Jesus Christ, and permit his transforming love to go to work in and through us.

This past week I received in the mail from a former colleague and cherished friend a copy of a book entitled *Credo*. It is a collection of the wit and wisdom of one of my heroes, William Sloane Coffin. Yesterday morning I opened the book in order to savor a few paragraphs. My eyes fell upon these words: "Of God's love we can say two things: it is poured out universally for everyone from the Pope to the loneliest wino on the planet; and secondly, God's love doesn't seek value, it creates value. It is not because we have value that we are loved, but because we are loved that we have value. Our value is a gift, not an achievement." Coffin adds: "Because our value is a gift, we don't have to prove ourselves, only to express ourselves. . . ."[1]

The story of Zacchaeus in a nutshell. A "sinner" in the eyes of all save one who sees a potential "Son of Abraham" and who, loving him as such, makes it possible. Loved into a person of value, Zacchaeus no longer needs to prove himself, but is free to express himself — which he does gratefully and generously.

*   *   *

The critical question in this, as in all the gospel stories, is where we find ourselves. Where are we in the narrative?

I know where we are meant to be, where our Lord Jesus Christ hopes to find us. Not among those who grumble about Jesus being "the guest of one who is a sinner." Not with those who protest the grace that seeks out and saves the lost. We are rather to see ourselves, like Zacchaeus, as those to whom Christ comes knowing everything there is to know about us, calling us by name, and inviting himself into our hearts, into our lives. When, in other words, we hear Jesus say, "the Son of Man came to seek and to save the lost," we are to understand that he means us.

We are in this story, along with Zacchaeus. We are to trust that what happened to him can happen to us as well whenever we hear Christ calling our name to come down from our hiding places and offer him hospitality — take him home with you know, us.

It could happen right here, this morning. You have come to the lost and found department of the kingdom of God. The spirit of Jesus Christ is here today, in this very place, offering the transforming power of his love. Do you hear his voice? "Hurry and come down, for I must stay at your house today." Is it your name he is calling? Is it with you, and in your house, that Jesus wishes to dine today? May you, like Zacchaeus, be happy to welcome him.

1. William Sloane Coffin, *Credo* (Louisville and London: Westminster John Knox Press, 2004), p. 6

~

The Sufferings of This Present Time

Readings: Jeremiah 17:5-13   March 14, 2004
              Romans 8:18-28
              Luke 13:1-9

He asked them, "Do you think that because these Galileans suffered in this way they were worse sinners than all other Galileans? No, I tell you; but unless you repent, you will all perish as they did."

— Luke 13:2-3

I consider that the sufferings of this present time are not worth comparing with the glory about to be revealed to us.

— Romans 8:18

They asked him: "Have you heard the news? Do you know what happened up in Galilee?" Perhaps Jesus had not heard, did not know. There was no KYW to provide "all the news, all the time," no CNN to whisk the curious, by way of satellite, to the scene of the latest disaster. News traveled by word of mouth as in this instance: "At that very time there were some present who told him about the Galileans whose blood Pilate had mingled with their sacrifices."

Worshipers massacred in Galilee. It's the kind of newspaper headline with which we have become all too familiar. Gunmen murder Pakistani Christians inside their church. Synagogue bombed in Istanbul. Shiite worshipers in Baghdad blown to bits while saying their prayers. And, while the 199 Spaniards who were killed just this past week, and the 1400 others who were wounded, were not in worship, it was, to be sure, a massacre.

89

They told Jesus about "the Galileans whose blood Pilate had mingled with their sacrifices. He asked them, 'Do you think that because these Galileans suffered in this way they were worse sinners than all other Galileans? . . . Or those eighteen who were killed when the tower of Siloam fell on them — do you think they were worse offenders than all the others living in Jerusalem?'" The second calamity to which Jesus made reference was different from the first: an accident, not an atrocity. We are familiar with those kinds of headlines, too. Hundreds die in Iranian earthquake. Tornado rips through Oklahoma. Tidal wave strikes Japan. Such natural disasters occur all too frequently.

Some of those who were there with Jesus had a ready explanation for both the accidents and the atrocities. Calamities were divine punishment. There were parts of their Bible that lent support to the idea, texts suggesting that the righteous are rewarded, while the wicked are punished. That sometimes there is a connection between sin and suffering is undeniable. A spouse who has engaged in adultery may well suffer estrangement from family members or friends once the unfaithfulness is known. The trouble is, the family members and friends may suffer, too, and the sin was not theirs. A drunk driver runs a red light and crashes headlong into a car full of children, killing them all. Had the driver been more responsible the accident would not have happened. Yet he or she may escape injury while the children — presumably innocent — all die. So, who is being punished?

Actually, very little of suffering as we see it appears to be distributed according to a person's righteousness or the lack thereof. Some of the worst sinners suffer the least, and some of the greatest saints suffer the most.

". . . Worse sinners than all other Galileans?" No, said Jesus. ". . . Worse offenders than all the others living in Jerusalem?" No, Jesus said. Trouble is, that is not all he said. He went on to say: ". . . But unless you repent, you will all perish just as they did."

What's that all about? We witness calamities such as those mentioned earlier, and the proper response is repentance? Why would Jesus think that and say it aloud? I'm going to ask you to put that question on hold for a while. We'll come back to it.

*　　*　　*

Moments ago, I reminded you — as if you needed reminding — of tragedies in our time similar to those that occurred back there in Galilee and Jerusalem. Such calamities inevitably bring to the surface questions about suffering, especially the question of why "bad things happen to good people." I do not have the answer, and I don't know anybody who does. So, I am not going there this morning.

My concern is a different one, and I must say that what prompted it was not so much the catastrophes of our time but pastoral realities right here within our own congregation, within the BMPC family. There has just been a lot of personal suffering of many different kinds. Young people and old people. Physical and mental. Emotional and spiritual. Long and drawn out and mercifully brief. All of it painful to bear, painful to watch, painful to share. Just a lot of suffering.

As your pastors, we have witnessed it, sought to share as much of it as we can, offered our support, our care, our prayers. It has prompted us, prompted me, anyway, to think anew about the human experience of suffering and to look again at what our Christian faith has to say about it. One place to which I have turned and found something of worth is the eighth chapter of Paul's Letter to the Romans. I have thought you might find it of value, as well.

*   *   *

One thing to keep in mind is that the Letter to the Romans is not a theological treatise. It is a letter, a pastoral letter. Paul is writing to people for whom pain and poverty, trouble and turmoil, disease and death are daily realities. One of the things I appreciate about what Paul has to say to them is his honesty.

One of the things I always try to be with you is honest. I don't like preachers who are not honest. I don't like preachers who get up in the pulpit and say: "If you just believe in God, you can't imagine how good your life will be, how peaceful, serene, trouble-free." I don't like preachers who don't tell the truth.

Paul is an honest preacher. He doesn't offer the Christian faith as an insurance policy against suffering. He knows that everybody suffers in some way, every life bears some pain. Paul says it isn't just a few people here and there, not just some people now and then. It's "the whole creation." "The whole creation has been groaning in labor pains," he writes. And "not only the creation but we ourselves, who have the first fruits of the Spirit" — in other words we believers, we Christians — "groan inwardly while we wait . . . for the redemption of our bodies."

Some people respond to suffering by asking "why me? I have been a Christian all my life. I have tried to be a good person, a faithful Christian. Why is this happening to me?"

Paul is honest. Everybody is vulnerable to suffering. As a matter of fact, being a Christian makes you more vulnerable. Why? Because, as a Christian, your capacity for love expands, and the more you love, the more you learn to care about others, the more suffering there is to share.

The Christian faith offers no protection against suffering. What it offers is hope in the midst of suffering — the hope that in all things, including our suffering, God is present, working for good.

"We know that all things work together for good for those who love God," is the way Paul puts it. It's a verse that requires careful interpretation. Paul is not promising that for those who love God, everything will turn out for the best. Remember, Paul is an honest preacher. He knows better than to say something so naive as that. He knows better than to say that, for those who love God, everything will be just fine. Things do not always work together for good. Things can and often do work together for evil. Paul knows as much.

What Paul means, I believe, is that God is present in all things, including the bad things, the hurtful things, the inexplicable things, and that those who love God should expect God to be with them. There is, in other words, no set of circumstances, no experience, no suffering, where the love of God is unable to go. Paul's conviction is that in everything God is at work, working as he says a little later, not against us but with us and for us.

That's what Paul says. Even though "the whole creation is groaning," we can have hope because, no matter what, God is with us, God is at work in all things. The question is, can we believe it? Can we trust it to be so? On what basis? Is there something more here than wishful thinking?

Paul, honest preacher that he is, knows that is our question. So, he takes us — where else? — to the foot of the cross. "If God is for us," Paul asks, "who can be against us?" Well, yes, but how do we know God is for us? Because of him "who did not withhold his own Son, but gave him up for us all. . . ."

Not today, but three weeks from today, I plan to devote an entire sermon to the meaning of the cross. What I will say this morning is this: What matters most about the cross of Christ is not the amount of suffering, as Mel Gibson seems to think. What matters is not the cross alone for, as another puts it, "If salvation could ever be in a cross alone, there have been enough crosses to save the world a million times over."[1] There have been lots of crosses. What matters most is the identity of the one who is on the cross. "It is Christ Jesus," Paul says, "who died, yes, who was raised, who is at the right hand of God. . . ." If that is so then, in his suffering, we may be able to catch a glimpse of the God who shares our suffering. The God who loves us so much that, in the person of his Son, he identifies completely with us, walks with us in and through the valley of the shadow of death.

It's what enables Paul to promise that there is nothing in life or in death, nothing in the present or future, nothing in all creation that has the power to separate us from the love of God in Christ Jesus our Lord. It's what enabled me to have anything of worth to say to that member of this congregation whom I have visited for the last four years as he suffered from the dreaded disease ALS — Lou Gehrig's disease. As it was, *his* faith in the Christ Jesus who died, and was raised was such that while the ALS slowly but surely ravaged his body, and on Monday claimed his life, it never touched his spirit. He epitomized the truth of St. Augustine's words: what distinguishes Christian is not the ills they suffer, but the way they suffer their ills.

I confess, there was a time, years ago, when I thought that the Apostle Paul was overdoing it when he told the Corinthians: "I decided to know nothing among you except Jesus Christ, and him crucified." But, no longer. I have lived long enough, and I have seen and shared enough, to know why Paul insisted on the centrality of the cross — because only one who has been there can help us, only a God who suffers with us can save us. He is our hope: all we have and all we need. The old gospel hymn we will sing a little later has it right:

> My hope is built on nothing less
> Than Jesus' blood and righteousness;
> I dare not trust the sweetest frame,
> But wholly lean on Jesus' name.
> On Christ the solid rock, I stand;
> All other ground is sinking sand. . . .

*   *   *

"Do you think that because these Galileans suffered in this way they were worse sinners than all other Galileans? No, I tell you: But unless you repent, you will all perish as they did."

Let's return to the question we set aside earlier: Why, having denied the connection between suffering and sin, does Jesus nonetheless urge repentance? Why, in the face of calamity, does he call upon us to repent?

I am guessing, but I think it is because such calamities can and do serve to remind us all of our frailty and fragility. They can and often do serve to remind us of just how perilous and precarious life is. When we are safe, or we think we are, when we are in control, or we think we are, when all is well, or we think it is, we can easily imagine we can do without the resources of our faith. Calamities, as we all remember from 9/11, remind us how vulnerable we are, how defenseless in the face of suffering and death we are with only ourselves to rely on, and how much we need the presence and power of God. So, you know what? The call to repentance is good news: an invitation to move from self-reliance to God-reliance, an invitation to discover and depend upon that solid Rock which is the only hope we have, and the source of our strength and salvation — in this world and in the world to come.

1. Carlyle Marney, *The Crucible of Redemption* (Nashville and New York: Abingdon Press, 1968), p. 30.

~

The Death of Jesus

Readings: I Corinthians 2:1-10   **April 4, 2004**
              Luke 23:1-57

When they came to the place that is called The Skull, they crucified Jesus there with the criminals, one on his right and one on his left.

— Luke 23:33

For I decided to know nothing among you except Jesus Christ, and him crucified.

— I Corinthians 2:2

Everybody is talking about it. That is certainly one of the consequences of Mel Gibson's movie. The *Passion of the Christ* has become a frequent topic of conversation. Not only in church circles, where you might expect it, but in newspapers and magazines, around dinner tables and at cocktail parties, among professional colleagues and even casual acquaintances. If nothing else, Gibson's movie has provoked an unusual public discussion about the death of Jesus, his death on the cross.

The cross, of course, has long been the central symbol of our faith. Wherever it appears — whether on the top of a great cathedral, or in the window of a ghetto storefront — it "signals the presence of Christians."[1] Among the most beloved of the church's hymns are those that do not simply remind us of the manner of Jesus' death, but prompt us to exult in it. "In the Cross of Christ I Glory," for example; or "Lift High the Cross," or "When I Survey the Wondrous Cross." Within the pages of the New Testament the cross has a prominent place. About one-third of each of the

Gospels is devoted to the words and deeds that lead to the cross. And earlier this morning, you heard what the Apostle Paul told the congregation at Corinth: ". . . I decided to know nothing among you except Jesus Christ, and him crucified."

Paul was not the only one. He was the most eloquent. But all who first went out to tell the story of Jesus did the same thing. They talked first and foremost about the death of Jesus. They did not report his teachings, repeat his parables. They did not describe how he healed the sick and forgave sins. Not at first. It was all about his death on the cross. "We preach Christ crucified," they said.

They did not go into many of the details of the drama, in the beginning, did not dwell on the gore, as Gibson does. Most remarkably when they spoke about the cross of Christ they were neither mournful nor apologetic. Quite the opposite. You might even say that Paul and the others boasted about the death of Jesus. They gloried in the cross.

It is an odd thing when you stop to think about it. Crucifixion was such a terrible way to die: shameful, excruciatingly painful, degrading, humiliating. Rome's way both of punishing trouble-makers and warning everybody else that they had better toe the line. Paul himself recognized that, on the face of it, "the message about the cross is foolishness." So why did he and the others make it the centerpiece of their message? That is the question around which the rest of this sermon will revolve. Why did Paul say, "I can't preach anything else"?

I have to be honest and say, I don't know for sure why Paul said that. All I can do is tell you what I think, what I believe it is about the cross of Jesus that has made it the most prominent and pervasive symbol of the Christian faith.

*   *   *

First, there is what the cross tells us about ourselves.

Part of it is not complimentary. In the death of Jesus we can see the evil we human beings are capable of. We read the story, as we did earlier, watch and listen as Jesus is arrested, tried, and condemned, and we see religious leaders acting out of self-interest. We see Pontius Pilate acting on the basis of political expediency; going along to get along as Sam Rayburn used to say. We see Herod playing the part of a buffoon and soldiers doing their duty, obeying their orders. We see ordinary people becoming a lynch mob, and many others who are indifferent. "It is," as another has put it, "like looking in a mirror. We see ourselves, and our own sins! We see the crimes and follies of our own day."[2] Need I mention Fallujah? It is not a pretty picture, but we need to see it, realize that the attitudes and actions that led to Jesus' death are still very much in evidence in ourselves as well as in others.

There is, however, something else the cross tells us about ourselves. This second thing is even more important than the first, because it is so easy to lose sight of, or to have doubts about, especially given the current condition of the world.

In a recent book of his, the Canadian theologian, Douglas John Hall puts it this way: ". . . What (the cross) says . . . is not that God thinks humankind so wretched that it deserves death and hell, but that God thinks humankind and the whole creation so good, so beautiful, so precious in its . . . potentiality, that . . . its redemption is worth dying for."[3]

An old Scottish preacher by the name of James Denny saw it in much the same way. Near the end of his life, he stood before the General Assembly of the Church of Scotland, and Presbyterian though he was, he held up a crucifix — a Roman crucifix! — and in his inimitable brogue said: "If I had my time to do it again, I would go through the length and breadth of Scotland, and I would stand in every Presbyterian pulpit, and I would hold up this cross and say, 'God loves you like that!' "

I believe that is one of the reasons why Paul had to preach the cross. He wants us to recognize how much we are valued in the eyes of God, despite all our failures and follies. "God proves his love for us," he says, "that while we were yet sinners Christ died for us." Sometimes, when you stand beneath the cross of Jesus, you can see it.

*   *   *

I think one reason Paul made the cross the centerpiece of his message is because the death of Jesus shows us what we need to know about ourselves. Another reason, I believe, and by far the more important one, is what the death of Jesus on the cross tells us about God. There are actually a number of things. I am going to mention just two.

First of all, we can see in the death of Jesus how God takes the initiative in dealing with sin and evil.

It seems clear that Jesus did not have to die; he chose to die. He did not have to go to Jerusalem; he went there on purpose. We cannot be sure how or when Jesus made the decision, but at some point he seems to have come to the conclusion that the relationship between human beings and God was broken, and that if it was going to be mended, there was only one way to do it. So he told his disciples: "No one takes my life from me; I lay it down of my own accord." Somehow he seemed to know that, in his death, God would do what needed to be done to save the world from itself and save it for God. It is what the Christian faith has ever since proclaimed: in his death Jesus took upon himself the sins of the world. As Paul was to put it: "God was in Christ reconciling the world to himself.

Over the years a number of theories have been developed in an attempt to explain it. As the Presbyterian Church's Confession of 1967 says: "God's reconciling act in Jesus Christ is a mystery which the Scriptures describe in various ways. It is called the sacrifice of the lamb, a shepherd's life given for his sheep, atonement by a priest; again it is ransom of a slave, payment of a debt, vicarious satisfaction of a legal penalty, and victory over the powers of evil." The Confession of 1967 goes on to say: "These are expressions of a truth which remains beyond the reach of all theory in the depths of God's love."[4]

I myself am content to leave it there. Not to try to explain it, but to see in Jesus' decision to go to the cross the initiative of a God who values us so much, cares for us so deeply, that for our sake and for our salvation he puts on human flesh, empties himself, takes the form of a servant, and is obedient onto death, even death on a cross, so that sin might be forgiven and evil overcome. Sometimes, when you stand beneath the cross of Jesus, you can see it.

What you can see, as well, is a God who identifies with human suffering. Dorothee Soelle is right, I believe, in saying that we should not think of Jesus' suffering as being greater than others.[5] This is where Mel Gibson's film misses the mark. It is not the severity of Jesus' suffering that makes it unique. It is rather the identity of the one who suffers, and who, by his suffering, shares our suffering, and by sharing it, hallows it. As Rowan Williams, the Archbishop of Canterbury puts it: "There is a place for God now in all suffering, at the heart of suffering and even of death, because we have seen the glory of God abiding in the squalor and humiliation of Jesus' execution."[6]

Perhaps you recall how in the weeks following 9/11, when workers were clearing away the debris at Ground Zero, one of them pulled from the site of what had been the World Trade Center a piece of the destroyed steel structure that was "shaped like a perfectly symmetrical cross." It was immediately "raised over the wreckage." The New York Times said of it: "The cross has become an inspiration to many workers and others at the site."[7] Nobody had to explain why. Everybody knew. That steel cross was a symbol of God's identification with human tragedy, human suffering, human pain, human death.

Sometimes, when you stand beneath the cross of Jesus, you can see it. I believe that's why Paul says he has to preach "Jesus Christ, and him crucified." He wants everybody to know about the God who shares in and thereby sanctifies human suffering.

Paul wants everybody to know. The loved ones of the men who were so brutally murdered in Fallujah and dragged through the streets. Paul wants them to know. The African children in the AIDS hospice. The North Korean children on the verge of starvation. Paul wants them to know. The parents of the little girl just diagnosed with leukemia, and the girl herself. Paul wants them to know. Those who are waiting, and have been waiting for so long, for a transplant. Those of you — so many of you recently — who have lost a spouse, a parent, a friend to death. I believe Paul makes the cross the centerpiece of his message because he wants all of us to know that none of these hard and hurtful things can separate us from the love of God in Christ Jesus our Lord.

*   *   *

Paul says, I have to preach the death of Jesus. " I decided to know nothing among you except Jesus Christ, and him crucified." It is a hard thing to understand at first. Jesus was such a good man, "the man for others," as Bonhoeffer called him. And the cross on which he died was such a cruel instrument of state-sponsored brutality. It seems odd, at first, that Paul would want to make the cross the center of his message, and that the church would want to make the cross the central symbol of its faith. It is all because of Easter, of course. It is only because of Easter! When, in the light of Easter, you stand beneath the cross of Jesus you can begin to understand why that symbol of death is at the center of it all. What else is there that can show us so much of what we need to know about ourselves? What else is there that tells us what we need to know about God? I don't know of anything. Do you?

1. Wm. Placher, *Jesus the Savior* (Louisville: Westminster John Knox, 2001), p. 111.
2. Theodore Parker Ferris, *When I Became A Man* (New York: Oxford University Press, 1957), p. 64.
3. Douglas John Hall, *The Cross In Our Context* (Minneapolis: Fortress Press, 2003), p. 24.
4. In *The Book of Confessions,* published by the Office of the General Assembly.
5. Dorothee Soelee, *Suffering* (Philadelphia: Fortress Press, 1975), p. 81.
6. Rowan Williams, *A Ray of Darkness* (Cambridge, Boston: Cowley Publications, 1995), p. 59.
7. Reported in Fleming Rutledge, *The Undoing of Death* (Grand Rapids, MI: Wm. B. Eerdman Publishing Co., 2002), p. 226.

~

Our Resurrection, Too

Readings: Revelation 21:1-7   April 11, 2004
           II Corinthians 5:11-21
           John 20:1-18

**And the one who was seated on the throne said, "See, I am
making all things new."**
                                              — Revelation 21:5

**So if anyone is in Christ, there is a new creation: everything
old has passed away; see, everything has become new!**
                                              — II Corinthians 5:17

**Mary Magdalene went and announced to the disciples,
"I have seen the Lord": and she told them that he had said
these things to her.**
                                              — John 20:18

Today marks the eighteenth and final time that I will have the privilege of preaching the Easter sermon in this congregation, and I take as my
text the seventeenth verse of the fifth chapter of Second Corinthians: "So
if anyone is in Christ, there is a new creation; everything old has passed
away; see, everything has become new." Paul is telling the Corinthians,
and telling us: on Easter we celebrate not only the resurrection of Jesus,
but our resurrection, too. Not only is Jesus raised to new life but so, too,
can we be. Earlier, in the reading from Revelation you heard the risen
Christ say so himself: "See, I am making all things new." That includes
you. That means you — and it means here and now. Easter morning greets
us with an offer of new life — and we do not have to wait until we die to
experience it.

*   *   *

According to the Gospel of John, Mary Magdalene was the first to do so. ". . . It was still dark," John says, "when she came to the tomb." With that comment I think John means to tell us more than what time of day it was. The darkness was not just around; it was within.

There had been darkness in Mary's life before. Tradition has it that she had been a prostitute, though there is absolutely nothing in the Bible to support such a claim. What the Bible does say is that Mary had been possessed by "seven demons." She had, in other words, been troubled emotionally — severely, pathologically troubled. And Jesus had healed her, had sent the demons packing, had filled the darkness of her life with light. Ever since, she had been one of his most loyal followers. She had supported his ministry financially. John says she followed Jesus to the cross and stayed to the end, watching as the flickering flame was snuffed out on the candle she had come to believe was the light of the world. On the first Easter morning Mary assumed that light was gone; had not only disappeared; had been destroyed. When she came to the tomb, "it was still dark."

Yet, not so dark that Mary could not see that the stone "had been removed from the tomb." Her reaction? Not a joyful outburst of praise. Mary did not infer a resurrection. She assumed treachery, foul play. The corpse had been stolen, the grave robbed. That's what she ran to tell Peter and "the other disciple": "They have taken the Lord out of the tomb, and we do not know where they have laid him." The two disciples ran to the tomb and saw for themselves that it was empty. But if they thought Jesus had walked out on his own two legs, and not been carried out by grave robbers — if that's what they thought, they had a strange way of showing it. They did not jump for joy. They did not launch into the Hallelujah Chorus. John says "they returned to their homes," leaving Mary to weep by an empty tomb.

The two disciples seem not to have been consoled by an empty tomb. Certainly Mary was not. Nor should we be. An empty tomb is no assurance of resurrection, brings no cheer, gives no hope. If that's all there is to the Easter story we are left weeping along with Mary.

Praise be to God, that is not all. There is more to the story. As Mary stands outside the tomb, the light that once before had come into her life comes again. A voice she at first mistakes as that of a gardener calls her by name. That is when her darkness, along with that of the morning, turns to dawn. I wonder: did she at that very instant remember what Jesus had told his followers not long before? The Good Shepherd "calls his own sheep by name," Jesus had said, and the sheep follow him because they know his voice." Now, in this tenderest, most precious of moments, the risen Christ says, "Mary!" She knows that voice. "Rabbouni!", she says — teacher!

The light is back in Mary's life. What did it was not an empty tomb but a living Lord. When Mary goes to the disciples, she doesn't say, "I have seen the empty tomb." She doesn't say, "I have seen angels." She doesn't say, "I have this feeling that the spirit of Jesus lives on." She says: "I have seen the Lord!"

Gradually, in the days that follow, the darkness lifts for the rest of them as well. For Peter. For Thomas. For the two on the Emmaus Road. Little by little, it begins to dawn on the entire community, all who had loved Jesus and been loved by him — it begins to dawn on them: the light that had shone in the life of Jesus is shining again. As one of them was later to put it: "The light shines in the darkness, and the darkness did not overcome it." Only because of a living Lord could anybody say so then. Only because of a living Lord can we say it today.

Mary was the first to know. She was followed by many others. As different as they all were, there was one thing they all had in common: once they had been in the dark and now they were in the light — the light in the life of Christ which not even a brutal, horrific crucifixion had been able to extinguish.

*   *   *

In an earlier letter to the Corinthians, in a passage which is actually the earliest written testimony to the resurrection, Paul had listed a number of the people who, by virtue of Easter and the days following, had been lifted out of darkness and back into the light, people to whom the risen Lord had appeared. Peter, James, the other disciples, and, says Paul, "more than five hundred brothers and sisters at one time." Male chauvinist that he is, Paul does not include Mary in the list. Surprisingly, one person he does include is . . . himself! "Last of all," Paul says, "as to one untimely born, he" — that is, the Risen Christ — "appeared also to me."

When, then, we hear the words of our text, we can assume Paul is being autobiographical. ". . . If anyone is in Christ, there is a new creation:

everything old has passed away; see, everything has become new!" Paul might have gone on to say: All you have to do is look at me. I am a new man, a new being, "a new creation."

I will not try to say all the ways in which Paul was made new. I am going to trust that you know the basic facts of his story. How the persecutor of Christians became the foremost apostle of the Christian faith. How the legalist who wanted everybody to follow the rules became a proponent of freedom. How, as he tells us in Philippians, compared with knowing Christ, he came to think of all that had once been of utmost importance to him as so much rubbish. In all these ways and more Paul had become "a new creation."

How had it happened? Not because of any effort on Paul's part. He did nothing to make it happen. Paul would be the first to say so. He did not make himself "a new creation." Just as Mary did nothing to bring back the lost light. In both instances it was something that happened to them — a consequence, in Paul's own words, of knowing "Christ and the power of his resurrection."

Which is where you and I come into the picture. What has been the case now for two thousand years is the case today: we may know Christ and the power of his resurrection. Easter is not just about the resurrection of Jesus; it's about our resurrection, too. We are not here today to try to prove Easter — something that cannot be done in any case. We are here, not to prove but to participate; not to explain Easter, but to experience it.

What does that mean? What might it mean for you? I hesitate to say because it could mean different things to different people. For somebody who is stuck in a well paying, but life-draining job, it might mean a decision to quit and do something else, something that doesn't pay nearly so well, but is far more life-giving. For the person who has only a few months to live, it might mean making the most of everyday that is left, using the days to connect with old friends, or to spend time with grandchildren, telling them about the part of the family's history nobody else knows. For the high school or college student it might mean not asking, "What can I do to make the most money?", but "What can I do to make the most difference? What can I do with my life to make it count for something?" For the person who has long been estranged from a sister or a brother, maybe it means sitting down and writing a letter aimed at reconciliation. And maybe for somebody who has grown weary of reading about yet more 18- and 19-year-olds coming home from Iraq in a box, maybe for such a person it means getting involved, perhaps even running for office.

"Easter," someone once said, "is to be taken internally,"[1] Just what that might mean for you I dare not say. But you know. And, if you want to, you can do something about it. If you want to, you can claim the promise of resurrection for yourself. Because "if anyone is in Christ, there is a new creation."

*   *   *

Because this is my last Easter as your pastor, I want to say a word about the responsibility of this congregation to represent the power of the risen Christ to make all things new. Often we refer to the church as "the body of Christ." What that means, as I understand it, is that the church is the community in which people are to come into contact with Christ. It may not be the only place, but it is, or should be, one of the primary places. I believe this congregation has been such a place, and I hope it always will be. So I want to ask you to do what you can to make it so: the kind of place, as Bill Coffin puts it, that doesn't sympathize with the crucified Christ, but pledges its loyalty to the risen one.[2] The kind of place that remembers him saying: "Blessed are the peacemakers," and "In as much as you did it to one of the least of these you did it to me." The kind of place where, when strangers come, they will be able to hear Christ calling them by name, where our own children and youth will be able to hear Christ call their names. A place where there is a climate of acceptance, so that each unique person who comes here can be him or herself. A community, not of legalism, but of love. The kind of community where those who walk through the valley of the shadow do not have to walk alone. A church that thinks boldly, cares deeply, loves passionately.

Clarence Jordan, the founder of the Koinonia Community in Americus, Georgia, out of which the great Habitat for Humanity movement emerged, once wrote: "The proof that God raised Jesus from the dead is not the empty tomb, it is not a rolled-away stone; it is a carried away church."[3] I hope you will remember that: If there is to be any proof of Easter, you are it. That is what it means to be the body of Christ: being the sort of place in which there is on-going evidence that, "if anyone is in Christ, there is a new creation; everything old has passed away; see, everything has become new!" To be the church of the Risen Lord is to be the kind of place where that happens — not once — but again, and again, and again, and again.

1. Raymond Lindquist, in a book that has long since disappeared from my library.
2. Wm. Sloan Coffin, *Living the Truth in a World of Illusions* (San Francisco: Harper & Row, Publishers, 1985), p. 70-17.
3. Joanna Adams in *"Locked Doors,"* a sermon preached in Fourth Presbyterian Church, Chicago, April 7, 2002.

PART THREE

*Sermons for
the Seasons of
Ordinary Times*

~

The Monday Connection

Readings: I Peter 2:4-10   November 1, 1992
           Matthew 4:18-22; 5:13-16

**But you are a chosen race, a royal priesthood, a holy nation,
God's own people, in order that you may proclaim the mighty
acts of him who called you out of darkness into his marvelous
light.**

                                            — I Peter 2:9

The man who entered his pastor's office was prominent in the community: president of the city's third largest bank and clerk of Session in
his Presbyterian church. Bill got quickly to the reason for his visit:
"I would like you to talk with one of my associates at work," he said.
He explained how a fellow bank officer had spoken to him about some
ethical problems related to his work. As Bill recounted their conversation,
the pastor could see the wisdom and sensitivity with which his parishioner
had responded to the man, not offering advice, but listening and assisting
his colleague to clarify his options.

Bill said: "When we finished talking the fellow asked me to pray for
him, right then and there. I didn't feel adequate to do it, but I was caught
— so I did. It was . . . special," he said. "My colleague asked if he could
see me again. Of course," he went on, "*you* are the one he needs to see.
I want to ask him to call you for an appointment."

The pastor responded: "Bill, you have used well your gifts — listening, caring, clarifying, praying not as some expert but as a fellow strug-
gler. I could not do as well what you are doing. You can identify with your
colleague's business-related ethical dilemmas. And you have with him an

already built bridge of friendship and trust that I do not have." "Maybe so," Bill said, "but this is serious stuff. And you're the minister. I'm just a layman. I'm not the one to do this."[1]

*   *   *

Behind Bill's remark — "You're the minister. I'm just a layman." — is an often unspoken, but widely held, assumption that there are two categories of Christians. There is a "first string" of ordained ministers who are called into the profession and trained to do what Bill would call "serious ministry," and there is a "second string" of lay people whose responsibility it is to help the professionals run the church and carry out its programs.

Such a distinction has little basis in the New Testament. To begin with, Jesus was not a religious professional. He was neither a priest nor a Pharisee. His profession was that of a carpenter. And the movement he began was made up of what we would call "lay persons" — the fisherman, Peter and Andrew, James and John; the tax collector, Matthew; and women such as Joanna, Mary Magdalene, and Suzanna. Christianity began as a "grass-roots" movement.

In the early church, while offices such as deacon, elder, and bishop, were eventually created, there was never any second level category of laity. The Greek word, "laos," from which "laity" comes, simply means "people" and was used to refer to all Christians, to all who had been baptized. Those who were set apart — "ordained" — to teach or preach or serve in some other capacity, were still part of the "laos." There may have been a difference of function, but there was no difference in terms of status.

In the years that followed, this all changed, of course, so that by the time Martin Luther came along, in the sixteenth century, there *were* two classes of Christians. One, made up of the priests, was active, while the other, consisting of the laity, was passive. The priests dispensed God's grace, and the laity received it. The priests ran the church, and the laity went along for the ride. Most important of all, the priests alone were viewed as being Christ's representatives in the world. Anyone could be a Christian, of course, by confessing his or her faith in Christ and being baptized. But, if you were really serious about following Christ in day to day living, you joined the ranks of the "clergy."

One result of the Protestant Reformation was the rediscovery of the

New Testament idea of ministry. Luther, for example, came across passages such as the one read earlier from I Peter: "You are a chosen race, a royal priesthood, a holy nation, God's own people, in order that you may proclaim the mighty acts of him who called you out of darkness into his marvelous light." Luther realized that, originally, such words had not been addressed to "clergy," but to ordinary Christians. He came to the conclusion that all Christians, not just a few, are to be Christ's representatives in the world, to bear witness to the Christian way of life, to be "priests."

"The priesthood of *all believers*" is what it came to be called. The Reformers never meant, by the way, that we can all be our own priests, that we don't need anybody else to support, encourage, and pray for us as we try to live the Christian life. They meant, rather, that we are all to be priests to each other. The Reformers rediscovered the New Testament notion that the responsibility for ministry, and the privilege of ministry, belong to every follower of Christ. Whatever our occupation or profession, or even if we have none, we share one vocation, one calling — which is why that phrase appears on the front of our worship bulletin week after week: "Ministers — *all* the members of the church."

*   *   *

My purpose today is to encourage you in your ministry. My sense is that like Bill, the bank president, you sometimes underestimate the significance of your ministry. You may not even realize that you are engaged in ministry when you are.

I do not, by the way, mean to suggest that the special calling of people like myself is unimportant. The church will always need the best pastoral leadership it can find, and a church like this one, with 3,600 members and a seven day a week program, requires more rather than less professional leadership, if our corporate ministry is to remain vigorous and vital. It is on behalf of that corporate ministry — of everything from worship to education, to pastoral care, to outreach and mission, and all the rest — that we are making our pledges of financial support today.

But, there is another form of ministry that is almost entirely in your hands. It takes place, not here, where you spend, at most, a few hours a week, but out in the everyday world where you spend most of your lives. It's what William Diehl, a Lutheran layman, calls "The Monday Connection." "In today's world," he writes, "'Sunday Christians' are irrelevant. The hymns, sermons, prayers and creeds of Sunday morning have no impact upon the outside world unless they shape the lives of Christians during the rest of the week. The false idols and pernicious values of society remain unchallenged unless 'Monday Christians' act and witness to their faith in everyday life and in a relevant manner. Yet," says Diehl, "most Christians are unable to bring into . . . everyday life the basic elements of the faith they express on a Sunday morning. When asked how the experiences of . . . Monday connect with what they experienced . . . on Sunday, in church, most Christians are at a total loss for words."[2]

The main reason this is so, Diehl contends, is because people like you don't get enough help from people like me. I take his criticism seriously and personally. Today, therefore, I want to suggest some ways in which you can make the Monday connection; I want to call to your attention some of the places where, if you don't do it, there will be no ministry.

To begin with, *you can make the Monday connection in and through your work.* I'm not speaking, now, only to those who have a "job." Some of us are paid to work and some of us are not, but almost all of us work. A parent who stays home to raise children works. So does a student in school or college. So does the unpaid volunteer. And, in and through our work, there are opportunities for ministry.

Diehl suggests that just doing your work competently can be an expression of ministry. As an illustration, he reminds us of how David Cronin, an airplane pilot, used all his knowledge and experience, back in 1989, to safely land a jumbo jet after its cargo door had been blown open, tearing a huge hole in the side of the plane. "A few days after the harrowing experience, an interviewer asked Captain Cronin about his first thought following the loss of the cargo door." Cronin answered: "I said a prayer for my passengers momentarily and then got back to business." Diehl writes: "The passengers who survived that night of terror can say a prayer for Captain Cronin. They can thank God that he was a man of such high competence."[3]

But it's not just in such rare and dangerous moments that competency counts in making the Monday connection. The CEO who takes charge of a troubled company, and makes the tough decisions that save it, is doing something which affects the well-being of a host of people. He is making the Monday connection. So is a nurse who does her work with skill and compassion. So is the builder who doesn't take short cuts or substitute inferior materials. So is the reporter who works hard to dig out the truth.

So is the scientist who, with unflagging persistence, dedicates her life to AIDS research. So is the secretary who handles a myriad of details effectively and efficiently for her organization. So is the volunteer who tutors a child, or helps in the waiting room of a hospital. And so is the parent who, with skill and compassion nurtures a child. Simply by their competence, such Christians are making the Monday Connection.

Viewing your work as ministry doesn't mean what many think. It doesn't mean becoming the office evangelist, and badgering colleagues about their faith. It doesn't necessarily mean that you gather with other employees for Bible study at lunchtime. It *could* mean that. But, of more importance is the honesty and integrity with which you do your work, the nature of the opinions you express at work, the manner in which you treat colleagues with whom you work, and the policies you help put into place in the workplace. In these and all kinds of other ways, the Monday connection can be made in and through your work.

A second way to make the Monday connection is in and through your relationships: as spouse, parent, colleague, neighbor, friend, as one member of the congregation to another. I wonder if you ever think of yourself as a "priest" in these relationships as one who mediates God's love? It's what you do: whenever you stop and stoop to listen to a child, or go by to check on a neighborhood shut-in, or write a note to someone whose spouse has died. You are a priest: whenever you forgive a wrong, or greet a stranger, or confront a friend about her excessive drinking. You might even be a priest to the checkout person in the supermarket, to the one who delivers your mail, to the person who cuts your hair. It's what Diehl calls a "ministry of presence," just "being there" for another.

A third way to make the Monday connection is in and through all the institutions that you are part of: Rotary, the garden club, United Way or Women's Way, all those boards you "sit" on, the professional associations you belong to, and yes, the political parties on whose behalf you work!

I once heard another pastor bragging how he had persuaded one of his members to resign from the School Board in order to go on the Session of the church. Now, I would be the last to minimize the importance of having good Session members. But I don't want somebody to resign from a School Board in order to do church work. I want Christians in such places to help humanize them and lead them and make them what they ought to be. It's a point Diehl makes this way: "There can be no large-scale changes in our nation until we have many small-scale changes. We must make changes in our families, our schools, our health systems, our industries, our governmental agencies, and our basic sense of values. It is Christians," says Diehl, "who constitute the largest religious group in our nation, who must largely bear the responsibility for the deterioration of our institutions; it is Christians who must lead the way in turning things around."[4] Helping to do that is an important way to make the Monday connection.

In truth, there are all kinds of ways to make the Monday connection. What is required is the imagination to see a situation where Christian influence, or Christian compassion, is needed, and to respond: to see a lonely person and respond with a gesture of friendship; to see some poisoned area of life and respond with some reconciling act; to see someone who is disheartened and to respond with encouragement. What is required is an awareness that in law office and laboratory, in media and medicine, in corporate office and union hall, in private clubs and public forums, you are there as a representative of Jesus Christ. Whatever you say and whatever you do, will reflect on him. To use the bank president's words, that's "serious stuff," it's all ministry.

*   *   *

I happen to believe that what we do here on Sunday is of supreme importance. I work hard and worry a lot to make it as alive and vital as I can. But Diehl is right: " 'Sunday Christians' are irrelevant."[5] If Christian ideals are to be realized, if Christian values are to survive, if the cause of Christ is to go forward, if the Christian church is to make any difference, it will be because wherever you are, you find a way to "make the Monday connection." As a Christian, that is your calling; that is your vocation. There is none higher.

1. Robert S. Smith, "A Theology by the Laity" in *Journal for Preachers* (volume and number unknown).
2. William Diehl, *The Monday Connection* (San Francisco: Harper, 1991), p. 1.
3. Ibid., p. 26.
4. Ibid., Chapter 4.
5. Ibid., pp. 34-35.

~

A Sacrament for Failure

Readings: Jeremiah 20:7-13   October 15, 1995
          II Corinthians 4:7-15
          Mark 6:1-13

If any place will not welcome you and they refuse to hear you, as you leave, shake off the dust that is on your feet as a testimony against them.

— Mark 6:11

There are times when what we *expect* and what we *experience* are very different things. Not long ago, the novelist Kurt Vonnegut called attention to such a disparity within our society. The American library, he wrote, "is full of stories of supposed triumphs, which makes me suspicious of it. It's misleading for people to read about great successes, since even for middle-class and upper-class white people, in my experience, failure is the norm." Vonnegut went on to say: "It is unfair to youngsters particularly to leave them wholly unprepared for . . . monster screw ups and starring roles in Keystone Kop comedies and much, much worse."[1]

Perhaps Vonnegut exaggerates when he says that "failure is the norm." But we all experience times when things do not go well. In the world of sports, no team or individual performs perfectly. Even Penn State loses one occasionally. Superstar or not, Ken Griffey, Jr. fails to get a base hit roughly seven out of every ten times at bat. And did not Jack Nicklaus shank a tee shot during the Masters Golf Tournament last spring?

As a preacher, I have had my share of sermons that went nowhere, and failed, so far as I could tell, to enlighten or energize anyone. I was comforted to learn that George Buttrick felt the same on occasion. Buttrick

114

was such a fine preacher that other preachers would go to hear him — a rarity. But after one Sunday morning service, as he stood at the door greeting people, there were no compliments. Finally, a woman, the last person out the door, said: "Thank you, Dr. Buttrick, for your sermon." He responded: "I appreciate the compliment. But it was too long." "Oh no," the woman replied: "it just seemed long."[2]

Failures occur. Business plans don't always work out. Not every marriage is made in heaven. Not every surgery is successful. Not every investment decision is wise. Not every new product is a winner. Not every one who walks into the Bryn Mawr Presbyterian Church on a Sunday morning is coming off a terrific week. Most college students do not make the Dean's list or graduate with honors. Interpersonal relationships are filled with blunders and betrayals. Spouses fail each other. So do parents and children, teachers and students, pastors and parishioners, friends and colleagues. We should not be surprised when these things happen, but often we are. Vonnegut is probably right about the reason. We are taught to expect success, but are left unprepared to experience failure.

One of the books I remember having read to me as a child was entitled, *The Little Engine That Could*. As I recall it, the story concerns a long train filled with toys and other goodies for children which are being transported to a farm on the other side of a high mountain. A locomotive is needed to pull the train. For one reason or another, two or three likely candidates decline, one of which is pessimistic and keeps saying, "I can not, I can not." Despite its inadequate appearance, the little engine is optimistic. It says, "I think I can," and it does! Moral of the story: Believe in yourself and you will achieve great things.

I was curious to know if that book is still being read to children, so the other day a call was made to one of the local bookstores. Question: "Do you have *The Little Engine That Could*?" Answer: "Which version do you want?" "Which version"? "There is the board version, a pop-up version, a hard cover edition, a paperback, and an anniversary edition." Why am I not surprised? The reason the book was read to me, and the reason it is still being read, is that it reflects the optimistic, "can do" spirit of America. It's one of the "stories of supposed triumphs" that Vonnegut was referring to. It creates in children an expectation of success. Perhaps an unrealistic one. For, eventually, we all experience situations where we can say, "I think I can," all we want, but the reality is we cannot either — the train is too heavy, or the mountain is too steep, and our little engine simply isn't adequate. Vonnegut's point is: It is unfair to teach our children always to expect success when, inevitably, they will experience failure. One can only wonder, by the way, if the high suicide rate among the adolescents doesn't have something to do with the notion that failure is unacceptable.

The contemporary theologian, Douglas John Hall, takes up this theme and expands upon it. He contends that our society's "doctrinaire optimism" — the belief that we can do whatever we put our collective mind to — has left us all but defenseless against our recent experiences of failure. We expected to win in Vietnam, but we didn't. As a consequence of "The Great Society" programs, we expected to win a war on poverty, but we didn't. More recently, a war on drugs was declared, with similar disappointing results. We expected to outgrow racism, but we have not. Nor have we overcome crime, or homelessness, or hunger, or violence, or war. Hall calls upon two figures of Greek mythology to describe our plight. One is Prometheus, who stole fire from the gods, and the other is Sisyphus, whose efforts to push the stone up the hill always came to naught. American mythology, says Hall tells us that we are like Prometheus, but, these days, many are feeling more like Sisyphus. The expectation is one thing, our experience is quite different.[3]

*   *   *

There is much neglected saying of Jesus that addresses this experience with frustration and failure. According to Mark, Jesus himself had just experienced rejection. He had returned to his hometown with a reputation of having performed "deeds of power" — such as stilling a storm, healing the sick, and even raising the dead. The reception he received in Nazareth was a disappointing one. His former neighbors dismissed Jesus as something of a fraud, leading him to say, "Prophets are not without honor, except in their hometown. . . ." Mark says that since Jesus "could do no deed of power there . . . ," he went on to other villages. It was during that time that he sent his disciples out on their first mission. Among the instructions he gave them was this one: "If anyplace will not welcome you and they refuse to hear you, leave, shake off the dust that is on your feet as a testimony against them."

John Oman called this act "the sacrament of failure."[4] It corresponded to a gesture used by pious Jews at the time when they returned to Israel from a Gentile land. Dust was stamped from their feet to symbolize separation from any clinging remnant of ritual defilement. Bothered by its seemingly judgmental tone, some commentators wonder if Jesus could have actually given such an instruction to his disciples. Ernest Campbell asks: "But what if Jesus instituted this symbolic act for his disciples' sake, to prevent them from falling victim to undue anxiety about the need for immediate success? Perhaps, says Campbell, "Jesus graciously anticipated . . . that there would be times when we would be less than invincible. Every home will not receive you. Every city will not listen to you. What then? When this happens do not get uptight. Take your leave graciously. Shake the dust off your feet and move on. Someone may come after you who will succeed where you have failed. You may do battle in the next place."[5]

*   *   *

In what ways does this ancient "sacrament" speak to us? It is not necessarily the only thing that might be said about our subject. But does it not provide a corrective to that "doctrinaire optimism" mentioned earlier? Does it not only teach us to anticipate failure, but also to carry on in spite of it?

To be more specific, there is in our text a *graceful affirmation of the Biblical notion of human fallibility.* We human beings are not without limits. There are problems for which there may not be solutions. Few, if any, politicians have the courage to say so, but it is true. Some things that are broken cannot be fixed. Try as we will, some of our relationships with others aren't going to take off. Parents may do the right things, and a child may still go astray. A marriage may fail, despite the good attempts of both husband and wife to make it work.

As our Prayer of Confession, this morning, I deliberately chose one of the ancient classics. I chose it because it counters the notion that we are, or can be, like Prometheus. We are not. We are creatures, fallible human beings, who "have erred and strayed . . . like lost sheep," who "have followed too much the devices and desires of our own hearts," and who will continue doing so. To admit as much is to be saved from a perfectionism that is destructive to ourselves and others. Instead of endlessly berating yourself for your human frailty, acknowledge it, admit your failures, trust the promise of forgiveness, and move on.

I also hear in our text *a warning against unrealistic expectations.* Jesus seems to be saying, "You will win some and you will lose some."

When things do not go well, it is not necessarily your fault. You are in charge of the effort, but you are not in control of the outcome. Some days, no matter how hard you work, no matter how skillful you are, you are not going to succeed.

The psychiatrist Carl Jung believed that some objects have a will of their own. One should spend some amount of time hunting down a lost object, he said, but after a while it behooves the searcher to accept the fact that some things want to stay lost. Sometimes our Clerk of Session refers to inactive church members as lost sheep. Inspired by one of Jesus' parables, we do our best to locate them and bring them back into the fold. But some sheep don't want to come back. If we have done something to drive them away, that's one thing. In that case, we ought to try to make amends. But it's another thing if they simply prefer to stay lost. It happens. Our text invites us to be more realistic in our expectations, and not always take it personally when things do not go well.

Finally, our text suggests that *what matters most in God's sight is not success, but faithfulness.* In this respect, as in others, God's judgments are quite different from those of the world. Vince Lombardi, the late coach of the Green Bay Packers used to say, "Winning isn't everything; it's the only thing." Call it the idolatry of success. Let's be clear about what comes from worshipping at this shrine. If succeeding is what counts, than anything goes. If you are a student, you cheat on exams if you have to. If you are a politician, you distort your opponent's views if that's what it takes to win. If you are in business, you try to destroy your competition. If you are an athlete, you look for anything that will give you an edge. If success is the god you worship, then you do whatever it takes.

It is the witness of the gospel that, not success, but faithfulness is the issue. Jesus himself is our model in this, as in all else. From beginning to end, from the temptations in the wilderness to the trial before Pilate, and everywhere in between, he refused to trade faithfulness for victory, he rejected success if it meant surrendering his integrity or his identity. Jesus trusted that in God's own way and in God's good time, his life would not be for naught or his work in vain. He calls his followers to do the same: To worry less about our success or failure, and more about our faithfulness — doing what we can to the best of our ability, leaving the results in God's hands.

*   *   *

As for *The Little Engine That Could*, no doubt I will read it to my grandchildren — if I can figure out which of the five versions to buy. I will encourage them to believe that sometimes they will succeed in difficult tasks if they think they can. But I will also tell them to expect failures, too — to expect them, and not to be dismayed or defeated when they come. And, I will tell them that, far more than success or failure, integrity and faithfulness are what count. It's a message I hope all Christian parents and grandparents will want to convey to the next generation

1. Kurt Vonnegut, *Hocus Pocus* (New York: Berkley Books, 1990), p. 33.
2. A story I heard Buttrick relate at a conference years ago.
3. Douglas John Hall, *Professing the Faith* (Minneapolis: Fortress Press, 1993), p. 283.
4. Quoted in *The Interpreter's Bible, Volume VII* (New York and Nashville: Abingdon Press, 1951), p. 367.
5. In *To God Be the Glory*, Theodore A. Gill, editor (New York and Nashville: Abingdon Press, 1973), pp. 146-147.

~

On Dying and Caring

Readings: Psalm 16   January 28, 1996
        II Corinthians 4:7-5:1
        John 12:27-36; 19:25-27

The sermon I am about to give is not the one I had planned for today. The change was prompted by a combination of recent pastoral experience and the reading of a book.

The experience involved helping two people prepare to die: one a much loved member of this congregation, the other a total stranger up until the time I was asked to visit her in the hospital. I have done this many times before, of course. Yet whenever I do it again, I find it to be profoundly moving. These most recent experiences not only touched me personally, but caused me to think that it might be helpful if I were to talk with you about dying and caring – and to do so, not from a psychological point of view, which you can get elsewhere, but utilizing the insights and resources of our Christian faith.

Which is where the book comes in. It's by Henri Nouwen, who has written so perceptively and personally on a number of topics related to Christian faith. This particular book is entitled, *Our Greatest Gift*, a meditation on dying and caring.[1]

Let me acknowledge at the outset that our topic is not an easy one. You may find it depressing. It may bring to the surface painful memories. It may be a topic you would just as soon avoid. Yet, sooner or later, we are all obliged to die, and we all have opportunities to care for others who are dying. So, from time to time, we ought to think and talk about dying and caring. There is, of course, only so much that can be said in one sermon, but perhaps enough can be said to begin to affect both your attitude and your actions.

*   *   *

Nouwen's book is divided into two parts: the first he entitles, "Dying Well," and the second, "Caring Well." But do not think of these as unrelated. They are two sides of the same coin. As Nouwen says, when we "befriend" our own death, we can care for others who are dying.

Befriending death. This is not how we usually think of it, is it? Avoiding death seems to be the common goal, and denying death the prevalent attitude in our culture. Nouwen is not suggesting that we should be enthusiastic about dying. That's beyond most of us. By and large, we are not looking forward to leaving this world. Some are, to be sure: those for whom living has become too burdensome, too painful, without purpose. But, for the most part, we enjoy living too much to be enthusiastic about dying.

It's not enthusiasm, but readiness that is called for. Nouwen says that being ready to die involves two sets of relationships: those with family and friends, and that with God. With regard to family and friends, Nouwen suggests that we ask: "How can we prepare ourselves for our death in such a way that our dying will be a new way for us to send our and God's spirit to those whom we have loved and who have loved us?" With regard to God, Nouwen writes that dying involves the on-going "struggle to surrender our lives completely," to be ready, at the last, to say as Jesus did, "Father, into your hands I commend my Spirit."

Befriending death, Nouwen acknowledges is not easy. It "is a life-long spiritual task." Yet every step we take in that direction enables us to live our own lives more fully, more gratefully, more profoundly, and brings us closer to one another, helps care for each other. "Befriending our own death and helping others to befriend theirs are inseparable." Together they comprise "our greatest gift."

*   *   *

There are, says Nouwen three dimensions, three components, to dying well and to caring well. These are not things that happen automatically, effortlessly, or by chance. Rather, they are attitudes that must be claimed, chosen. A word about each.

First is the conviction that *we are children of God*. For the dying this means acknowledging dependence upon God, remembering that, whatever else might be said about us, what matters most is that we are divinely loved. What is most important in caring for the dying is to help them make that claim. "To care for the dying is to keep saying, 'You are the beloved daughter of God, you are the beloved son of God.' . . . The ways (of doing so) are countless: through words, prayers, and blessings; through gentle touch and the holding of hands; through cleaning and feeding; through listening and just being there." Sometimes we refer to it as a "ministry of presence." It's what the three Marys and the beloved disciple were doing at the cross: by their presence reminding Jesus of his belovedness.

Among the dying, Nouwen says, the "greatest suffering comes from losing touch with . . . our belovedness and thinking of ourselves only as a useless, unwanted presence. . . . Dying and death always call forth, with renewed power, the fear that we are unloved and will, finally, be reduced to useless ashes." As I mentioned at her memorial service, a dying Gail Bentley said to me, with reference to her nurses and physicians: "They are concerned about my pain. But it's not just my physical suffering that I am concerned about. I care about my whole person. I want my whole person to be addressed." I took it as a desire for her to hear and as an invitation for me to say: "You are God's child. You are loved."

Not only does dying threaten us with a sense of uselessness, it also threatens to separate us from others. Therefore, says Nouwen, the second thing we need to claim in order to die or to care well, is our oneness with each other. We need to understand that *we are brothers and sisters of each other.*

The one who is dying may think, "I am sick; everybody else is healthy. I am dying; they will go on living." But, the fact is, we are all dying, and that's something which should bind us together. Some of us are just closer to it than others, that's all. Moreover, whatever differences there may be among us – of wealth, education, status, race – whatever the differences are, they disappear when we die. "We all die powerless." In that sense, we are all poor. We are all dependent upon God's grace and mercy. "Our greatest challenge," says Nouwen, "is to discover this truth as a source of immense joy that will set us free to embrace our mortality with the awareness that we will make our passage to new life in solidarity with all the people of the earth." "We are all mortal beings called to surrender our lives into the hands of a loving God."

It occurs to me that our own Chapel Garden bears a profound, if silent witness, to our ultimate destiny of oneness. All whose ashes are interred there are treated alike. There are no tombstones, no monuments to individual egos. Just plaques with the names of the deceased and their dates of birth and death, an affirmation that we are brothers and sisters of one another.

The third component of dying well and caring well involves the matter of our legacy, or what Nouwen calls "fruitfulness," the recognition that *"we are parents of generations to come."* For most of us, this requires seeing ourselves, and valuing ourselves, in a new way — not because of what we accomplish, but because of who we are. Nouwen writes: "Our death may be the end of our success, our productivity, our fame, or our importance among people, but it is not the end of our fruitfulness. In fact," he goes on, "the opposite is true: the fruitfulness of our lives shows itself in its fullness only after we have died. We ourselves seldom see or experience our fruitfulness. Often we remain preoccupied with our accomplishments and have no eye for the fruitfulness of what we live. But the beauty of life is that it bears fruit long after life itself has come to an end." It this not what Jesus meant when he said, "In all truth I tell you, unless a grain of wheat falls into the earth and dies, it remains only a single grain, but if it dies it yields a rich harvest"?

Dying well, says Nouwen, means that we shift "our attention from doing to being. Our doing brings success, but our being bears fruit. The great paradox of our lives is that we are often concerned about what we do or still can do, but we are most likely to be remembered for who we were."

Caring well means reminding each other that it is not what we do so much, and not at all what we have, that endures. Our greatest legacy will be who we are. Nouwen encourages us "to remind each other that we will bear fruit far beyond the few years we have to live."

*   *   *

Neither Nouwen nor I wishes to underestimate the difficulty involved in either dying well or caring well.

As for **caring**, I wish to affirm what a privilege it is, and also to assure you that you can do it. You can learn to care for the dying. You don't have to be a minister, a nurse, a hospice worker, a physician, a funeral director. "Caring is the privilege of every person and is at the heart of being human." The temptation is to think we have little or nothing to offer, that we can't change anything. We may be frightened by another's suffering or disheartened by physical or mental deterioration. That's why befriending our own mortality is critical. Then you will have a sense of what the other is experiencing, you will see that there is much that you can do to become a source of healing and hope. As Nouwen puts it, "When we have the courage to let go of our need to cure, our care can . . . heal in ways far beyond our expectations."

As for **dying**, we need not pretend that faith makes it easy or takes away all our fears. After all, we are part of a culture that assumes death is the end: there is nothing more. That culture is part of us, is in us. And the truth is, we don't know much about what lies beyond. The apostle Paul acknowledged as much when he said, "Now we see in a mirror dimly. . . ." What we do have, in the life, death, and resurrection of Jesus Christ, is the assurance that God is faithful, in the words of our denomination's Brief Statement of Faith, the assurance that "in life and in death we belong to God." Ultimately, what enables us to die well and to care well is the trust that God will not let us fall.

In that regard, I conclude with a story from Nouwen's book. He tells of having gone to the circus and witnessed The Flying Rodleighs, famous trapeze artists. Then he writes: "One day, I was sitting with Rodleigh, the leader of the troupe, . . . talking about flying. He said, 'As a flyer, I must have complete trust in my catcher. The public might think that I am the great star of the trapeze, but the real star is Joe, my catcher. He has to be there for me with split-second precision and grab me out of the air as I come to him in the long jump.' 'How does it work?' I asked. 'The secret,' Rodleigh said, 'is that the flyer does nothing and the catcher does everything. When I fly to Joe, I have simply to stretch out my arms and hands and wait for him to catch me and pull me safely over the apron behind the catch bar.'

'You do nothing!' I said, surprised. 'Nothing,' Rodleigh repeated. 'The worst thing the flyer can do is to try to catch the catcher. I am not supposed to catch Joe. It's Joe's task to catch me. If I grabbed Joe's wrists, I might break them, or he might break mine, and that would be the end for both of us. A flyer must fly, and a catcher must catch, and the flyer must trust, with outstretched arms, that his catcher will be there for him.'"

Nouwen concludes: "When Rodleigh said this with so much conviction, the words of Jesus flashed through my mind: 'Father into your hands I commend my spirit.' **Dying** is trusting in the catcher. To **care** for the dying is to say, 'Don't be afraid. Remember that you are the beloved child of God. He will be there when you make your long jump. Don't try to grab him; he will grab you. Just stretch out your arms and hands and trust, trust, trust.' "

1. Henri J. M. Nouwen, *Our Greatest Gift, A Meditation on Dying and Caring* (San Francisco: Harper, 1994). All the quotations in this sermon are taken from this book.

~

The Power of a Blessing

Readings: Genesis 27:1-4,18-27a, 30-36   October 13, 1996
Romans 12:14-21

Then he said, "Have you not reserved a blessing for me?"
— Genesis 27:36

Bless those who persecute you; bless and do not curse them.
— Romans 12:14

The Biblical tale concerning Isaac and Rebecca and their twin sons, Jacob and Esau, contains an abundance of fascinating material, the kind of material that could keep a preacher occupied for a long time, or a psychiatrist, for that matter! There is the brothers' sibling rivalry which, it is said, began at their birth, and which produced animosity, alienation, and ultimately physical separation. There is Rebecca's undisguised favoritism towards Jacob, her youngest, through whom she seeks to live her life. There is her willful deceit of her husband, and Jacob's collusion in that episode. There is the contrast between the two sons: one who lives for the moment, the other who plots and schemes in order to secure his future. So dysfunctional is this family that one wonders why its story has not been made into a television soap opera! Most peculiar of all, of course, is the Biblical contention of how it is through this all too human family that God's purpose is carried forward.

The aspect of the story to which I invite your attention, this morning, concerns the matter of "blessing." Isaac's wish, prompted by a growing awareness of his mortality, to give a blessing. The trouble Rebecca and Jacob go through to secure it. Esau's great disappointment — and anger! — when he discovers that he has arrived at his father's bedside too late to be blessed — not because the old patriarch has died, but because the blessing which was rightfully Esau's as the eldest son, has been given to Jacob and cannot be withdrawn. Is there a more plaintive plea in all of Scripture than Esau's question to Isaac: "Have you not reserved a blessing for me?"

*   *   *

There is what may seem like a superstitious or magical quality to the Biblical notion of blessing. The word itself connotes a favor, or a benefit, which is conferred upon another. There was thought to be what one Old Testament scholar calls an "inscrutable power" associated with a blessing,[1] so that to receive a blessing meant that one was, in fact, blessed. Divine favors, mercies, gifts, are sometimes referred to as "blessings." It's what people often have in mind when they talk about "counting" their blessings. In the Bible such favors may be material in nature: "The blessing of the Lord was on all that he had, in home and field" — or, they may be spiritual: "Blessed be . . . God . . . who has blessed us in Christ with every spiritual blessing. . . ." Our story, of course, has to do with how human beings can bless one another, and even be channels or agents of God's blessing. It's what Paul, echoing an admonition of Jesus, urges upon us even when we have been on the receiving end of some hurtful behavior by others: "Bless those who persecute you; bless and do not curse them."

We cannot understand the Biblical notion of a blessing apart from its opposite, a curse. It was believed that both could transform a situation or a person, the one for good, the other for ill. So, in another Biblical story, one individual says to another: ". . . I know that whomever you bless is blessed, and whomever you curse *is* cursed." Or, as Isaac says with reference to Jacob: ". . . I have blessed him? — yes, and blessed he shall be!"

Well, perhaps you are wondering, How does any of this connect with us? We seem to bless and curse quite casually. Someone sneezes and we say, "Bless you!" Does it mean anything? The driver of a car who, quite unintentionally, perhaps, inconveniences another driver, may be greeted with a barrage of curses. The practical effect seems to be of no earth-shaking consequence. "God bless America," nearly every President says at the end of nearly every Presidential address. Does he really expect anything to happen? Compared with the time of Isaac and Rebecca, Jacob and Esau, the power of a blessing, or of a curse, seems greatly diminished.

But is it, really? I want to suggest that, while we do not understand very much about why or how it happens, our relatedness to one another gives us an enormous power to bless or to curse. Another puts it this way: ". . . There are deep connections between all human beings. . . . We are not made to stand alone, . . . we were made for life with one another, just as we were made to live in relationship with God." To be sure, "there is an empty space at the center of our souls that can be filled only by God," but "there is (also) something about our soul stuff that needs positive relationships with all kinds of people. . . . When we bless one another, we are sending energy across the lines of these invisible connections, using them in the way they were meant to be used, with a result that we feel healed and whole. But when we curse one another, we are sending a destructive energy across them which actually hurts us, both the one who curses and the one who is cursed."[2]

The scary thing is how we unconsciously send out the positive and the negative signals, the healing messages and the hurtful ones, the blessings and the curses. In his book, *A Whole New Life: An Illness and a Healing*, Reynolds Price describes his decade-long battle with spinal cancer, during which he endured several long stays in Duke University Hospital. He contrasts what was communicated to him during his hospital stay by a highly-skilled but aloof oncologist — an unconscious, but nonetheless real "curse" of a sort — he contrasts that with the blessings which were communicated to him by his night nurses. "My presiding oncologist saw me as seldom as he could manage," says Price. "He seemed to know literally no word or look of mild encouragement or comradeship in the face of what, as I later learned, he thought was hurried death. . . . What I wanted and needed badly from that man," but never received, "was the frank exchange of decent concern."[3] The night nurses, on the other hand, were able "to blend their professional code with the oldest natural code of all — mere human connection, the simple looks and words that award a suffering creature his or her dignity."[4] Additional forms of blessing came from Price's friends. "Keith and Brenda Brodie gave me a small crystal ball "to contemplate (your) happy future," and ". . . David Sabiston promised to be at my ninetieth birthday party. I learned," says Price, "that such homely offerings . . . can have a weight that even the giver may not foresee. They can quickly swell into amulets for health and hope. . . ."[5]

You and I can learn something important from the experience of Reynolds Price. When it comes to our power to bless, we are not necessarily talking about huge or heroic undertakings. The power of a blessing often comes by way of a small gesture. an expression of gratitude, a note letting a bereaved friend know that he or she is in your thoughts, a phone call or a visit to a shut-in, paying attention to a child who wants to tell you what happened in school, reading psalms to a sick friend. All that's needed, sometimes, is a simple gesture that tells another he or she matters.

*   *   *

I don't believe the human need to be blessed has diminished at all. And, I believe that our power to bless or to curse remains as strong as ever. And the family, I suppose, is still the place where we feel most profoundly the impact of the one or the other.

As for cursing — we know what happens to children who live continually in the presence of criticism, how hard it is for them to accept themselves or learn to take risks. We know that abused children experience an assault on their self-worth that scars them for life. Children who are physically abused often pass on the heritage of abuse to the next generation. We know that children of alcoholics typically grow up believing that it is always their fault when things do not go well. We know that children who have been told by their parents that their worth depends upon their accomplishments typically become driven adults who are never satisfied, never able to live and rejoice in life.

Such is the reality of our human connectedness that our ability to wreck havoc on one another is powerful indeed. But so is our power to bless. And that's what I hope you will take away with you, this morning: an awareness of your power to bless — especially the younger generation.

Next Sunday we will join the national observance of Children's Sabbath and we will read again the story of how Jesus blessed children who were brought to him one day. There is no evidence that they were sick or in any way afflicted. Their parents simply wanted them to experience the love of God in Jesus Christ. We will read how "He took them up into his arms, laid his hands on them, and blessed them." One wonders what it came to mean to those children as they remembered, in their later years, that they had been embraced by that loving and gracious figure.

It is, of course, the purpose of our ministries with children — Church School, Weekday School, choirs, mini-music, Young-In-Arts — and the purpose of all our ministries with youth — to enable what happened long ago to keep on happening: to introduce these precious children and adolescents to Jesus Christ, and to help them experience his love, his acceptance, his "blessing." You ought to be, and I assume you are, grateful for those who give their time and energy to these ministries. It's hard for me to imagine a greater blessing than that of a Christian faith, rooted in on-going tradition, and experienced in a lively community — which is what we are trying to give these children and young people.

But, in addition to the "blessing" our children and young people receive here, I dare to suggest that there is a specific blessing that they can receive best from those of us who are their parents and grandparents. Perhaps you read the op-ed piece in the *New York Times* the other day, by Robert Coles, the child psychiatrist. What prompted him to write were the charges of "sexual harassment" that were made recently against two six-year-old boys. In the article, Coles was arguing against "psychological . . . interpretations" of inappropriate behavior on the part of children, and commending, instead, "the day-to-day moral lessons that shape a child's conscience." Said Coles: "Boys and girls need to know 'no,' and need to have absorbed any number of 'no's' within their thinking and feeling minds." But, he asked, "when more and more adults seem to lack a firm sense of what is right and wrong, how do our children then acquire a firm conscience?"[6]

In a Chicago Tribune essay entitled, *"Moral Poverty,"* John DiJulio wrote in a similar vein: "Moral poverty," he said, "is the poverty of being without loving, capable responsible adults who teach you right from wrong. It is the poverty of being without parents and other authorities who habituate you to feel joy at other's joy, pain at other's pain, happiness when you do right, remorse when you do wrong. It is the poverty of growing up in the virtual absence of people who teach morality by their own everyday example and who insist that you follow suit."[7] Is there a greater curse we can pronounce upon our children than to leave them morally impoverished?

I want to say to you that one of the most powerful of all blessings you can give to your children and grandchildren is the loving gift of "character." Perhaps I am thinking of this in no small part, this morning, because it was exactly six months ago today that my own mother died, and because I have no doubt that her greatest legacy to my brother and me was her loving gift of character, her example of kindness, compassion, integrity, and goodness. In a culture that, as Coles puts it, "flaunts and exploits sex and aggression — in movies, television, the Internet, rap music and, not least, the version of theater called politics,"[8] what greater blessing can we give our children?

* * *

Let me return, for a moment to that plaintive plea of Esau to his father: "Have you not reserved a blessing for me?" Says the Biblical scholar, Walter Brueggemann, "Nobody wants to live a life that is unblessed."[9] Which is why, when all is said and done, we come here on a Sunday morning. Because above and beyond all else we need the blessing of God. We bring our sins and need an assurance of pardon. We bring our confusion and uncertainty and need to hear some clear word of truth. We bring our loneliness and need for community. We bring all the scars of all the curses we have endured over the years and need to experience the grace of our Lord Jesus Christ, the love of God, and the communion of the Holy Spirit.

Having thus been blessed, we are empowered to bless others with the blessing of God — in our homes, among our colleagues and friends, in the meetings we will attend or in the thousand and one casual conversations in which we will engage in the coming week. This is something everyone of us can do. No great wealth is required. No Ph.D. No special gifts. Just an awareness of our interrelatedness as human beings, a realization of our power to bless one another. I would like you to know that when you exercise that power, it is a continuation of the ministry of him who, once upon a time, took children in his arms and blessed them.

1. Walter Brueggemann, *Interpretation, Genesis* (Atlanta: John Knox Press, 1982), p. 227.
2. Morgan Roberts, *Are There Horses In Heaven?* (Pittsburgh, PA: Lighthouse Point Press, 1996), p. 61.
3. Reynolds Price, *A Whole New Life* (New York: Plume/Penguin, 1995), p. 56.
4. Ibid., p. 132.
5. Ibid., pp. 32-33.
6. *New York Times*, October 10, 1996.
7. Quoted in *Context*, October 1, 1996.
8. *New York Times*, October 10, 1996.
9. Brueggemann, Ibid.; p. 229.

~

Fate, Luck, and God

Readings: **Ecclesiastes 8** *(selected verses)*   **October 13, 1996**
                   Colossians 1:3-14
                   Luke 13:1-5

He asked them, "Do you think that because these Galileans suffered in this way they were worse sinners than all other Galileans?"

                                                                        — Luke 13:2

Back in July, a few days after the plane crash that killed John F. Kennedy, Jr. and the Bessette sisters, there appeared in *The New York Times* an essay by William Safire. As this deadly accident was the latest in a series of family tragedies, there was, you may recall, a good deal of talk about a "Kennedy curse" — speculation that this family had been singled out, somehow, to suffer misfortune. Safire argued against any such notion. "I don't believe in curses or any other form of predestination," he wrote. "Allowing for genetic breaks," he went on, "we are free to make much of our own fate." The Kennedy accident, Safire argued, was "brought on by a lack of judgment," by the taking of an unnecessary risk. He concluded his essay by saying: "The icon-busting Book of Job teaches that God does not micromanage the universe, and that free-willed human beings are responsible for actions and injustices."

The emphasis on human choice and personal responsibility was, I thought at the time, and still do, a helpful corrective to much of what was being said and written about that sad event. I would suggest, however, that Mr. Safire re-read the Book of Job. It doesn't teach precisely what he says. What that story actually does is refute the notion that suffering and tragedy are always deserved, that they are the consequence of sin, wrong-

132

doing. There is recognition, in other words, that bad things do happen to good people. As for the role God does or does not play, Job does not get an answer one way or the other. What he gets and submits to is a sense of God's awesome majesty and mystery. But, leaving aside the question of whether or not he has the backing of the Book of Job, what caught my attention at the time, and perhaps now has caught yours, is Safire's belief that "God does not micromanage the universe."

*   *   *

It is a quite different point of view from that which assumes God is intimately involved with the details of everyday earthly events. Like the television producer, for instance, who, after the death of Princess Diana, called a certain theologian and said: "Can you appear on our show? We want you to explain how God could possibly allow such a terrible accident." Or like the young woman who wrote a well-known evangelist. "Four years ago," she said, "I was dating a man and became pregnant. I was devastated! I asked God, 'Why have you allowed this to happen to me?' "[1]

*   *   *

I suppose all of us wonder from time to time why certain things happen that we have not planned or prepared for, especially if it is a tragedy of some kind. We wonder who or what, if anybody or anything, is behind it. The same can be said about the good things that come along, which we did not expect and did nothing to deserve. Last Sunday I told you about my car's collision with a deer. The question, "Why me?," could be asked from both directions. On the one hand, how to account for the fact that the deer and my car arrived at the same place at the same time? I can't speak for the deer, but I certainly had not planned on such a meeting! On the other hand, why was it that I emerged unscathed when, as has been the case with others, I might have been injured or even killed?

Earlier we heard about the time when Jesus was teaching, and somebody in the crowd said, "Say, Jesus, did you hear about the people Pilate, the Roman Procurator, massacred while they were worshipping?" It was as if one of you were to interrupt me now to ask, "Hey, preacher, did you hear about the crazy character down in Fort Worth who walked into the Baptist church with his gun and started mowing down the kids who were there for a prayer service?" Jesus had heard. He said: Do you think it was because they were bad people? That wasn't it. Nor, he added, were those eighteen who were killed when the big tower over at Siloam collapsed worse people than you. We can imagine him saying the same thing about those who lost their lives, a few weeks ago, in that Indian train wreck, or about those who died in the earthquake over in Turkey, or about the two girls in Delaware who were swept away by flood waters just this past week. There were some among the ones to whom Jesus was speaking who assumed, and there are still some today who assume that the explanation for any kind of suffering is sin. We get what we deserve. That's what the Book of Job protests, and Jesus says that isn't it.

Sometimes it is, of course. Our behavior does have consequences. If we abuse our bodies, the chances are pretty good that we will pay for it eventually. As for the earthquake over in Turkey, it seems that tragedy was made worse, and some people died who didn't need to, because the construction of the places people were living in was poorly done, corners were cut so that the builders could make more profit. Some of the suffering there was caused by sin. Yet it soon becomes obvious, once we look around, that neither the bad things, nor the good things, are distributed according to what people deserve. "There *is*," Reinhold Niebuhr said once, "reward for goodness in life, and there *is* punishment for evil, but not absolutely."[2]

*   *   *

So how are we to account for these mysterious happenings, these unexpected events? One response in every age has been Fate. It's the notion that nothing happens by chance or by choice. It is all predetermined. Safire called this "predestination" which it really is not — but that's another sermon for another day. Believers in Fate contend that a script has been prepared and each of us has been assigned a part, and all we do is play out our role as it has been written for us. Belief in Fate takes many forms. There is the stoicism, for example, that is prepared to take whatever comes. There is so-called scientific determinism which holds that everything happens according to an impersonal process which is beyond human control. Then, of course, there is astrology, the belief that it is all written in the stars.

Actually, there is probably nobody who believes in any kind of absolute fatalism. I mean someone who thinks he or she has no choice at all, and just sits around waiting to see what is going to happen. Somebody, for instance, who after breaking a leg, does nothing but watch to see what Fate has in mind.

Much more common is the belief that chance or luck plays a role in human affairs. The other night I was watching the Walker Cup on television. One of the players hit a ball that looked like a good shot until it bounced in a way that the ball ended up in a sand trap, a bunker. "Bad luck," the announcer said. One of you said to me at the door last Sunday, with reference to my deer accident, "You were lucky!" Even though this person had just emerged from a service of worship, I noticed he did not say, "God must have been looking out for you."

Now, I am not being critical. I happen to agree with him. I was lucky. And I don't see how we can deny that there is an element of luck in human affairs. Safire was right to stress human choice, personal responsibility, yet that's not the whole story, is it? There is the success that comes from hard work. But there are also those who benefit just because they happen to be in the right place at the right time. There is the accident-free record that comes from careful driving. But there is also the traffic jam that causes a person to miss the plane that crashes on takeoff, killing all on board. Leave it to the writer of Ecclesiastes to tell it like it is: ". . . I saw that under the sun the race is not to the swift, nor the battle to the strong, nor bread to the wise, nor riches to the intelligent, nor favor to the skillful" — not always anyway! "But time and chance happen to them all."

Perhaps you are thinking, what about God? What *about* God? What *are* we to believe about God's role in the things that happen to us? More specifically, what about "the will of God"?

It is something about which Scripture speaks frequently. Jesus, too. He taught us to seek God's will and to pray "thy will be done." He himself sought to understand and obey what he called "the will of my Father." On the last night of his life, he prayed, "not my will, but thine be done." Paul was constantly praying, he told the Colossians, that they might "be filled with the knowledge of God's will," so that they might "lead lives worthy of the Lord, fully pleasing to him. . . ."

An essential ingredient in Christian faith is the confidence that there is a will of God for us and for the human race, and no small part of our Christian duty is to try to ascertain what that will is and live in accordance with it. Yet we must be careful in talking about God's will, for a lot of damage can be inflicted when people casually or carelessly attribute things to "the will of God" — especially personal tragedies, and natural catastrophes — earthquakes, hurricanes, tornadoes.

Jesus seems to have had a different idea of the will of God: not as something evil, not as something capricious, but as God's good intention toward us and toward the world. Once, speaking of the children in whom he delighted, Jesus said, "It is not the will of your Father in heaven that one of these little ones should be lost." Jesus did not, it seems, believe that everything that happens is according to the will of God. Otherwise, why would he ask us to pray, "thy will be done, on earth as it is in heaven"?

One of the things many of us need to do, I believe, is re-think notions of God's omnipotence and God's sovereignty. It's what Safire is doing when he says that "God does not micromanage the universe." To put it positively, maybe what we have to say is that while God cares, God does not control, and *chooses* not to control everyday earthly events. The question of God's ultimate sovereignty is another matter — but that, too, is another sermon for another day. As for here and now, we find ourselves in a world which by design, it seems, has its own ways of working with which, for many good reasons, there is neither divine interference or manipulation. It is something we have to come to terms with.

Recently I was reading about a chaplain whose ministry is with the terminally ill, mostly with those afflicted with cancer. He said that most cancer victims who have any faith at all will try to see their suffering as part of the larger plan of God. He spends considerable energy trying to move them from what he sees as a theologically untenable position. He tries to tell them they are ill because they are *part of the planet*, not because they are *part of a plan!*" The one who reported this wisely comments: "There is more here than a clever play on words. Much that befalls us, whether of good or ill, is the result of laws and processes that are at work in the earth irrespective of our faith. Botulism is botulism and one gets it from eating spoiled food. Period. To say that God wills it, under the rubric of some 'hands-on' providence, is to turn the grace of God into a travesty. Cancer happens. Earthquakes happen. Plagues and pestilences happen. They work their deadly harm on the evil and the good, upon the just and the unjust. Faith has nothing to do with it." This individual concluded: "To suggest that stronger faith would produce for us a more favorable providence is to suggest that God plays favorites. Where others sit, we sit. What others feel, we feel. The faith difference shows through not in what happens to us, but in how we respond to what happens to us."[3]

That brings me back to that puzzling response of Jesus to those who told him about Pilate's massacre. "Do you think that because these

Galileans suffered in this way they were worse sinners than all other Galileans?" Jesus asked. "No, I tell you; but unless you repent, you will all perish as they did." In the wake of what just happened in Fort Worth, and what has been happening all over, with a kind of nauseous regularity, there is a particular pointedness about Jesus' warning, isn't there? Wake up America! But there is a deeper meaning to this saying of Jesus. It is that the things about which we have been thinking this morning — these unforeseen, unpredictable events of life, especially those with a tragic dimension — when we see these things occurring, we should think not of our superiority, but of our own vulnerability. They should prompt us to notice what fragile creatures we all are, and should underline for each of us our need for God.

There is a mystery to life, and an even more profound mystery to God. There is so much we cannot know. At the end of the day, we fall back on the promise of Christ that God loves us and longs to hold us close. But it will not do to understand this promise in any shallow, sentimental, or superficial way, as if, as believers, we are not subject to the hazards of history, and the trials of tribulations of life as are all others. In baptizing these children, this morning, we are not giving them some mantel of protection. We are putting on them a sign that, come what may, they belong to God and are precious in his sight.

Do you remember the time when Jesus was talking about the sparrows, seemingly of such little worth that you could buy two for a penny? He did not say, God never lets anything happen to the sparrows. He said, "Not one of them will fall to the ground apart from your Father." Sparrows do fall, and we fall, tragically sometimes and inexplicably sometimes, but never from God's everlasting arms. That being so, what Paul wished for those Colossians can be so for us: Made strong by the strength that comes from God, we are "prepared to endure everything with patience, while joyfully giving thanks to the Father, who has enabled (us) to share in the inheritance of the saints. . . ."

1. Philip Yancy, as quoted by Martin Marty in *Context*, February 1, 1998.
2. Reinhold Niebuhr, *Justice and Mercy* (New York, Evanston, San Francisco, London: Harper & Rowe Publishers, 1974), p. 18.
3. Ernest T. Campbell, in *Campbell's Notebook* (the month and year of the publication unknown).

~

God's Promise and Our Perseverance

Readings: Deuteronomy 31:7-8, 14-15, 23   January 16, 2000
II Corinthians 5:16-21
Luke 4:16-30

It is the Lord who goes before you. He will be with you; he will not fail you or forsake you. Do not fear or be dismayed.
— Deuteronomy 3:18

I may have missed it. That's entirely possible, since I refused to be captured by the Y2K hype and hoopla. It was my own little protest against media manipulation. I wasn't paying close attention, so I may have missed it. But in what I did read or hear in the way of predictions as to the issues or problems which we will need to address in this new century, there was nothing about the one dilemma that has bedeviled this nation since its beginning: the matter of race. All the attention seemed to be focused on global markets and global politics, on cyberspace and telecommunications, on genetic research and bio-technology. It was as if nobody noticed the elephant that has lain so long in American's living room. Or, perhaps it is that we have grown tired of the subject. The failure of President Clinton's effort to promote a national conversation about race would seem to indicate such a weariness. But the elephant is still there. And if few others are concerned about it, we in the religious community, we who, more than any others, have the obligation of moral leadership, ought to be attentive. And so, as the nation prepares to celebrate the birthday of Martin Luther King, Jr., I invite you to join me in thinking about the state of race relations in America as we enter the twenty-first century.

* * *

138

The text that I believe can help us focus our reflections, and serve as well to instruct and inspire us, is from the Book of Deuteronomy where Joshua, the successor to Moses, is told: "It is the Lord who goes before you. He will be with you; he will not fail you or forsake you. Do not fear or be dismayed."

You may know something of the occasion for these words. Moses had served as the divine instrument in leading the Hebrew people out of Egypt, where they had long been enslaved. For the forty years in which his people had been wandering in the wilderness, waiting to enter the Promised Land, Moses had borne the burden of leadership. And a burden it had been. For the people were impatient and subject to fits of whining and whimpering. They did not take kindly to the hardships which were their lot. They were painfully slow to learn the ways of the Lord which Moses sought to teach them. But, at long last, the time had come for them to enter the Promised Land. Only, Moses was not to go with them. According to the story, he was permitted to climb a mountain — Mt. Nebo — from where he could see the land which his people were soon to enter, but, Moses was told, "You shall not cross over there." Joshua was the one who would take the people the rest of the way. The story read earlier describes the passing of the torch of leadership from Moses to his successor.

Now, one reason for recalling this story today is because it was the one much in the mind of Martin Luther King, Jr. on the last night of his life. In what was to be his final sermon, he seemed to have a premonition that, like Moses, he would not be able to accompany those whom he had been leading to the completion of their journey. "Like anybody," King said, "I would like to live a long life. . . . But I'm not concerned about that now. I just want to do God's will. He's allowed me to go to the mountain," King said. "And I've looked over. And I've seen the Promised Land. I may not get there with you," King told the congregation. "But I want you to know . . . that we, as a people will get to the Promised Land."[1]

This biblical image of a people poised to leave the wilderness and cross over into a new and better place, was one that sustained and strengthened this latter-day Moses. But I bring this story to your attention for another reason. For, I believe it serves to symbolize the state of things, today, with regard to black and white in America. Here's why.

The end of the Civil War brought an end to slavery. It constituted our exodus from Egypt, and like that of the Hebrews, it was bloody. Then came, not a mere forty years, but a hundred years, of wandering in the wilderness of legal segregation and blatant discrimination. We have emerged from that. No question about it. The world I grew up in south of the Mason-Dixon Line, the world in which I began my ministry nearly forty years ago, is long gone. Some of you are too young to remember how bad it was and how much it cost to change the way it was. Things are different today — thank God!

When, however, the question is asked, How far have we come, and how far do we have yet to go?, black Americans and white Americans tend to answer differently. So, at least, one researcher recently discovered. The whites he surveyed overwhelmingly expressed the belief that while discrimination has not disappeared, it is getting much better, and that blacks have pretty much the same opportunities as whites to participate in "the American dream." The blacks, on the other hand, spoke about the persistence of racism. Some even expressed the belief that discrimination is worsening, and said that equal access to "the American dream" is still a long way off.[2] White Americans of good spirit are apt to consider that, for the most part, the struggle is over and victory is secure. Few black Americans believe this.

One of their number, Gayraud Wilmore, a Presbyterian minister who grew up in Philadelphia, who is now retired and living in Atlanta, compares our situation to something he witnessed in Tuscany during the Second World War. Whenever there was a lull in the fighting, Wilmore observed, the residents would come out to shore up and even to rebuild the terraces where they grew their olives and grapes. "My Italian was pretty good in those day," says Wilmore, "so (one day) I asked one of them why they risked their lives rebuilding terraces with a war going on all around them." He was told: "Every winter the ground freezes, thaws — rains come, and winds — maybe there's even an earthquake, or a war — the soil constantly erodes, the terraces crumble and slide down the mountain-side. So every year we have to build them up all over again. For hundreds of years we have done this. It is our life." Says Wilmore: ". . . I believe the struggle against racism is like that. . . . It is perennial. Every year we have to do all over again what we did to combat it last year and many years before. That should not so much discourage us as it should clarify for us what our moral obligation is in the best and worst of times. We need to know . . . that it falls to every generation . . . to rebuild the terraces . . . ; to tidy up the world of interracial . . . relations in obedience to Christ."[3]

Throughout the years of my ministry, in parish after parish, and in many and various ways, I have been part of efforts to seek racial justice and to diminish racial isolation. And, I am glad to say, and grateful for the fact, that in all those congregations, including this one, especially, I have been joined by Christian men and women whose contributions have been far greater than my own. Some of you have devoted years to tutoring inner city children. All of you have joined in funding outreach ministries which, for many years now, have made a difference in places such as North and South and West Philadelphia, and Chester. Some of you have taken initiatives to increase employment opportunities, to open up membership in private clubs, to welcome minority families into your neighborhoods, and to recruit, not only African Americans, but Asian and Hispanic Americans, to serve on corporate and community boards. More recently, you have embraced, encouraged, and many of you are engaged in the Urban/Suburban Partnership. I commend you for all of that.

At the same time, I must tell you: we are not yet where God intends for us to be. We have emerged from the wilderness. But we have not yet entered the Promised Land. There is a long way still to go. When you learn, as we have just this past week, of threatening letters, filled with racist and anti-Semitic diatribes, being sent to thirty colleges of mostly African American students, and when you realize that you have seen similar remarks on the internet, or heard them in the locker room, then you know that Gay Wilmore is right: the struggle against racism is perennial. Perhaps even of more consequence than these ignorant and bigoted attitudes is the point of view of some who having "made it themselves," do not care about those who have not. There is a kind of selfish complacency abroad not unlike that in the story — maybe apocryphal, maybe not — about President Calvin Coolidge. "It seems that some friends decided to call upon the Coolidges in their retirement in Plymouth, Vermont, and arrived at the homestead close to the supper hour. They knocked on the door, and Mr. Coolidge answered and said, 'Had your supper? We've had ours.'"[4]

*   *   *

We are not yet where God beckons us to go. And so, this morning, I urge us not merely to remember Martin Luther King, Jr., or to honor him as a martyr, but to recapture his vision and renew our own commitment to it.

Were he with us today, I believe King would not be wanting us to put him up on a pedestal. He would, I believe, confess his own weakness, and call our attention to how God worked in and through him despite his all too human frailty. He would encourage us to trust God to work in and through us. We may not be the stuff of which heroes are made, but we are a people God can use to make a difference somewhere, somehow. I believe King would challenge us to give ourselves to that agenda which is, after all, a biblical agenda, to "let justice roll down like waters, and right-eousness like an everflowing stream." It is, as we heard earlier, the agen-da Jesus made his own: to proclaim release to the captives, to let the oppressed go free. . . . It is, according to the apostle Paul, the calling of every follower of Christ: to be part of his ministry of reconciliation.

No less an American icon than Billy Graham has called Christians to devote themselves to the agenda of overcoming racial injustice and racial isolation, and in doing so, he alludes to this very passage from Second Corinthians. "Tragically," says Graham, "too often in the past evangelical Christians have turned a blind eye to racism or have been willing to stand aside while others take the lead in racial reconciliation, saying it was not our responsibility." ("I admit," says Graham, "I share in that blame.") But now, he says to himself and to us, "Our consciences should be stirred to repentance by how far we have fallen short of what God asks us to be as agents of reconciliation. . . . Of all people, Christians should be the most active in reaching out to those of other races, instead of accepting the sta-tus quo of division and animosity."[5]

Here we are, then, like Joshua, bearing the responsibility of moral leadership. With him, we recognize it will not be easy to go the rest of the way. Like the Promised Land to which his people were summoned, that place to which we are beckoned is filled not only with opportunity, but also with obstacles and opposition of all kinds. We need, then, along with Joshua, to listen to the assurance of Moses: "It is the Lord who goes before you. He will be with you; he will not fail you or forsake you. Do not fear or be dismayed." Even more, we need to trust God's own promise: "Be strong and bold. . . . I will be with you."

In its first year, our Urban/Suburban Partnership has made remarkable progress. We have made a good beginning. But that is all it is: a begin-ning. Last Tuesday, in reporting to the Session, Patrice Nelson warned that the real test of our commitment is yet to come. Building relationships takes time, she reminded us. There are differences in the styles of ministry, in the way things get done, between us and our partners. We should expect that there will be bumps and potholes on the road we are traveling — maybe even detours. We will have to learn to practice what white Americans have for so long urged upon their black brothers and sisters — namely patience and perseverance. If our relationship is indeed to be one of partnership and not paternalism, we will need to learn to listen and to respond to other people's agendas, to others' perceptions of what is needed. What we are seeking to accomplish will not be achieved quickly or easily. Our partners have long known this, and we must learn it.

We live in a quick fix culture, but neither the achievement of racial justice, nor the overcoming of racial isolation, lends itself to a quick fix. Endurance, staying power, what was once called "the perseverance of the saints" — that's what it is all about. We are required to remember: "It is the Lord who goes before you. He will be with you; he will not fail or forsake you. Do not fear or be dismayed."

1. *A Testament of Hope*, the Essential Writings and Speeches of Martin Luther King, Jr., James Melvin Washington, editor (San Francisco: Harper, 1986), p. 286.
2. Alan Wolfe, *One Nation After All* (New York, NY: Viking Press, 1998), pp. 210-212.
3. *Journal for Preachers*, Volume XXIII, Number 2, Lent 2000, p. 34.
4. Peter S. Gomes, *Sermons*, Biblical Wisdom for Daily Living (New York: Wm. Morrow & Co., Inc., 1998), p. 156.
5. Quoted by Peter J. Gomes in *The Good Book* (New York: Wm. Morrow & Co., Inc, 1996), p. 100.

~

The Time Jesus Lost An Argument

Readings: Ephesians 2:11-14   September 10, 2000
          Mark 7:24-30

Then he said to her, "For saying that, you may go — the demon has left your daughter."

                                          — Mark 7:29

If the story read earlier, about the encounter between Jesus and the Syrophoenician woman, left you perplexed, or even troubled, I am not surprised. Most of us imagine Jesus to be warm and welcoming — the sort of person whose office door is always open, so that anyone can walk in at any time for any reason, be graciously received and treated with kindness and compassion. Yet, when this Syrophoenician woman approaches Jesus, she gets the cold shoulder. The story is told in Matthew's Gospel, too, and in a little more detail. According to Matthew, the woman "started shouting, 'Have mercy on me, Lord. . . .' But (Jesus) did not answer her at all." She, however, continued to press her case, plead for help. And that's when Jesus called her a "dog" — not only the woman, but all her people. "Let the children be fed first," Jesus says, "for it is not fair to take the children's food and throw it to the dogs." It is a saying one might wish were not in the Bible, and certainly not on the lips of Jesus. But there it is. How are we to understand it? What are we to make of it?

                        *   *   *

It is possible, I suppose, that Jesus was just having a bad day. As a matter of fact, when you examine the context, read what Matthew and Mark say was going on prior to this incident, you might draw that con-

144

clusion. For one thing, Jesus has experienced frustration with his followers, with the disciples. They just don't seem to be getting the message, or
getting with the program. They seem to be the original "slow learners,"
and it's discouraging. Even more disconcerting has been the growing
resistance of the religious leaders. Like modern day heresy hunters, or
moralistic police officers, they seem intent on catching Jesus saying or
doing something they can criticize. According to both Matthew and Mark,
Jesus has just had a run-in with them over purity regulations. Exasperated
by their nit-picking, Jesus calls them "hypocrites." You honor God with
your lips, he tells them, but not with your hearts.

Put all this together with the everyday stresses and strains of his ministry, and it's easy to see why Jesus wants to get away. He goes "to the
region of Tyre." He leaves Israel, in other words, and ventures into Gentile
territory. That, in itself, was highly unusual. It meant crossing a boundary
that normally wasn't crossed. It would be like an Israeli today going into
a Palestinian village, or like a Roman Catholic taking a walk in the
Protestant neighborhood of Belfast, or . . . maybe like someone from Bryn
Mawr venturing into North Philadelphia after dark. It was a bold move on
the part of Jesus, and an indication, not only of how much he needed to
get away, but of his determination to do so.

Having made his way to Tyre, Mark says, "He entered a house, and
did not want anyone to know he was there." You can understand that. I can,
certainly. As much as I like my work and love all of you, when summer
comes I am ready to get out of here. And when I arrive at our little cottage
in the Adirondacks, I don't even want the next door neighbors coming
around. Just let me be a hermit for a day or two! After a little while, I'm
willing to socialize, and, in time, I'm ready to return. But only after some
time for rest and relaxation, for reading and reflection, and for preparing
myself for the challenges and opportunities that lie ahead.

And I am thinking that's what Jesus was wanting, too. And, before he
has a chance even to begin to relax, along comes this woman wanting his
time, his attention, and a favor. She is an uninvited disrespectful intruder
— a nuisance. One can easily imagine Jesus saying to himself, If I help
her, she will go and blab it all around, and soon the whole neighborhood
will be at the door. But there is more to it than that. The woman is a
Gentile, a pagan. Try to put yourself back in that time and place. Jesus was
a Jew. Some Christians forget that. We have to remember: Jesus was a

Jew, and the custom of the day dictated that Jews did not socialize with Gentiles. And there is something else: it was a patriarchal society in which women knew their place. According to one scholar, the woman's solicitation would have been considered "an affront." "No woman," he writes, "and especially a Gentile, unknown and unrelated to this Jew, would have dared invade his privacy at home to seek a favor."[1] This woman has some nerve!

But there she is. In Matthew's version of the story, the disciples, in an effort to be rid of her, urge Jesus to do what she asks. That's when Jesus states what is only implied in the Mark's version: "I was sent only to the lost sheep of the house of Israel." It seems harsh. But try to stand in Jesus' shoes for a moment. The focus of his ministry, as he has understood it, is Israel. As this Gentile woman stands before him she represents a kind of temptation. She is enticing Jesus to dilute his ministry. It's not that the woman's need is not worthy. But Jesus cannot be expected to do everything, to be all things to all people. Heretofore he has understood his particular calling to be "the lost sheep of the house of Israel." I see him asking himself the question every corporation, every college, every church, every institution of any kind, has to ask every so often, so as not to get diverted, so as not to spread itself too thin. The question is: What business are we in? We can't do everything. What are *we* here to do? Jesus tells the woman: I have to feed my own people first. ". . . It is not right to take the children's food and throw it to the dogs."

Now, you might think Jesus could have found a nicer way to put it. Actually, he is using a kind of slang expression. It is not obvious to us from this distance, but his is a playful response. If you are offended by it, the Syrophoenician woman appears not to have been. She doesn't say, "How dare you call me a dog?" She doesn't protest Jesus' understanding of his priorities. She isn't put off. But she does not turn tail and run, either. She stands her ground, comes back at Jesus with a rebuttal that echoes his own playful remark. "Sir," she says, "even the dogs under the table eat the children's crumbs."

This woman is quick-witted and as tenacious as a bulldog. She has a child who needs healing. Somehow, she knows who Jesus is and what he can do. She knows that even a "crumb" from the hand of Jesus will be enough. That's what she asks for. She gets that and more. Taken, apparently, with the women's determined spirit and nimble mind, Jesus tells her, "For saying that, you may go — the demon has left your daughter." According to Matthew, Jesus says, " 'Woman, great is your faith! Let it be done for you as you wish.' So she went home, found the child lying on the bed, and the demon gone."

*   *   *

Well, there you have it: the time Jesus lost an argument. An interesting story, to say the least. But, what has it to do with us? Perhaps you are wondering about that. As I have pondered this episode in recent days, I have actually been surprised at how many meanings it has. There's time, this morning, for me to suggest just two.

One has to do with the woman who, it seems to me, could be a good role model for the likes of you and me. She is bold, determined, not easily discouraged — persistent. She knows what she wants, what her daughter needs, where and from whom she can get it, and she is relentless, one might even say shameless, in her pursuit. What a contrast she must have seemed, in Jesus' eyes, to the religious authorities whose only purpose in life was niggling criticism, fault-finding. I can also imagine Jesus thinking, If only my disciples had this woman's gumption, her nerve, her tenacity, her quick-wittedness — her "chutzpah"!

If you will pardon me for saying so, what this woman had, you and I could probably stand to have more of. There are things we want — or ought to want — and I am not talking about the stuff money can buy. Most of us have more than enough of that already. But when it comes to meaning and purpose in our lives, to joy and peace in our hearts, to a commitment to something other than our own comfort, to deep, abiding relationships with God and with one another — when it comes to things such as these, most of us need help. If we were to seek such things from Christ the way this woman sought his help for her daughter, who knows?

And, there are demons around, too, aren't there? We don't call them that today, but that's what they are. Societal demons that would entice our children and adolescents to believe that violent behavior is normal, that their bodies are what make them beautiful or ugly, that their worth is defined by what they have and not by who they are.

There are personal demons: encouraging cynicism, selfish indifference, resentment, bitterness, anger. What if we were to ask Jesus to deliver us from these — I mean really ask — in the manner of the Syrophoenician woman?

She could serve as a role model for us modern-day followers of Jesus, and for the church. By and large, churches are made up of people of good will and good intentions. We want the right things. We want a clean and safe environment, communities free of prejudice and discrimination, our society to be just and compassionate. We want the hungry to be fed, the homeless to have a roof over their heads, the ill and infirm to be cared for. We want the nation's children to grow up in safe places and to be taught in good schools. But do we want all these things the way the woman wanted her daughter to be healed? With her kind of passion? Are we willing to speak up the way she did? Are we prepared to persist as she persisted? As Christians, we want our children and young people to come to know and love Jesus. But do we want it enough to make church school, and youth activities, and worship, priorities? — not only for them but for ourselves. We ourselves want to become more mature in our faith. But do we want it enough to devote Sunday mornings to both study and worship?

Here, in this congregation, we are engaged in an innovative and challenging effort called the Urban/Suburban Partnership. It's a ministry that will not be without frustration and disappointment. Some things we try may not work. Our partners may not always be easy to get along with. Are we prepared to stay with it despite all that, hang in there the way the Syrophoenician woman did? As John Gardner reminded us sometime back, there are no easy victories. The Syrophoenician woman understood. I hope you do, too.

*   *   *

Here's the other thing I'd like to say about this story: it appears to have been a pivotal moment in the ministry of Jesus. It seems to have been the occasion for his decision to embark on a wider mission. Maybe you think Jesus was clear about God's will from the start, didn't have to struggle with that, didn't have to grow. It wasn't like that. Don't make him into some cardboard character devoid of humanity. Luke says plainly that he "grew" — and this is one clear instance of it. His encounter with the Syrophoenician woman enlarged his understanding of why he had come. He did not forsake Israel, but he broadened the scope of his ministry. I say so because, when you read on in Mark's Gospel, you discover that, after his encounter with the Syrophoenician woman, Jesus went further into Gentile territory. He healed a deaf man while he was there. He taught the people. And one day, when they had been with him for a long time, and had not eaten, there was a miraculous distribution of bread. Mark says: Jesus "took the seven loaves, and after giving thanks he broke them and gave them to his disciples to distribute; and they distributed them to the crowd. . . . They ate and were filled; and they took up the broken pieces left over, seven baskets full."

The woman said, Just give me the crumbs. She got a lot more. But so ever after have her people — Gentiles, like most of us here this morning. Not just crumbs. Bread! Did you hear what the apostle Paul said in his letter to the Ephesians when it was read earlier today? "Remember that you were at (one) time without Christ, being aliens from the commonwealth of Israel, and strangers to the covenant of promise, having no hope and without God and the world. But now in Christ Jesus you who once were far off have been brought near. . . . "

And so, we are able to be here today. Like the Syrophoenician woman, we are here because we have some sense of what we need and where and from whom to get it. And because of that woman, because of the time Jesus lost an argument — we are able, not merely to sit under the table waiting for some crumbs to fall, we are able to sit at the table as children.

I don't know if you are familiar with it, but there is an old communion prayer that has its inspiration in the story we have been pondering together. I am going to pray it now, as we prepare to partake of the sacrament.

Prayer:

We do not presume to come to this thy Table, O merciful Lord, trusting in our own righteousness, but in thy manifold and great mercies. We are not worthy so much as to gather up the crumbs under thy Table. But thou art the same Lord whose property is always to have mercy. Grant us therefore, gracious Lord, so to eat the flesh of thy dear Son Jesus Christ, and to drink his blood, that we may evermore dwell in him, and he in us. Amen.

---

1. Chad Myers, *Binding the Strong Man* (Maryknoll, NY: Orbis Books, 1988), p. 203.

~

There By the Grace of God Go I

Readings: Isaiah 6:1-8   January 28, 2001
          I Corinthians 15:1-11
          Luke 5:1-11

But by the grace of God I am what I am, and his grace toward me has not been in vain. On the contrary, I worked harder than any of them — though it was not I, but the grace of God that is with me.

— I Corinthians 15:10

You, no doubt, have heard it said. Perhaps you have said it. "There, but for the grace of God, go I." The expression is said to have originated with one John Bradford who, upon seeing a condemned criminal being led away, was heard to say: "There, but for the grace of God, goes John Bradford." It is hard to know just what he may have meant. I suppose, like John Newton, whose hymn we will sing later on, Bradford may have been alluding to some dramatic, divinely-initiated rescue from a wayward life:

> Amazing grace, how sweet the sound,
> That saved a wretch like me. . . . "

But, as Barbara Brown Taylor cautions, "There, but for the grace of God go I" can be one of the cruelest things we have learned to say on the subject." That's because the one saying it "assumes the absence of grace in another's life. . . ."[1] It supposes that God is present in some lives, in some circumstances, and not in others.

You may have noticed that Paul, in his Letter to the Corinthians, is saying something quite different. Not, "There *but for* the grace of God, go I." More like: "There *by* the grace of God go I." "By the grace of God," he writes, "I am what I am. . . ."

150

*   *   *

What Paul is, he says, is an apostle. Which is to say, a leader within the Christian community. It is something he never expected to be, something he knows he does not deserve to be.

You may remember how it happened. Paul was, at the time, the enemy of the church. He was on his way to Damascus, intent on rounding up as many Christians as he could find and bringing them in chains back to Jerusalem. But before he could get where he was going, somewhere and somehow along the way, Christ appeared to him in a vision, and asked Paul to stop his persecution and become a follower. It is that experience to which Paul is alluding when he writes, "Last of all, as to one untimely born, he" — that is, Christ — "appeared to me."

It was grace — a gift, unexpected, undeserved. An experience of unconditional love. Paul never got over it. It became the way he told his life story: "By the grace of God I am what I am. . . . " The grace of God, Paul soon came to realize, is at the heart of the gospel. It became his theme song, the central message of his preaching, the note that he sounds again and again in his letters: "For by grace you have been saved through faith, and this is not your own doing; it is the gift of God. . . . " Theologians define it as "the free, unmerited favor of God." What it means, says John Calvin, is that we "have in heaven instead of a Judge, a gracious Father."

Jesus told a parable about it. The story of a son who demands his inheritance, deserts his father, travels to a distant country, and proceeds to squander all that has been entrusted to him "in dissolute living." Eventually, the son decides to come home. He expects, at best, a chance to work himself back into his father's good graces. What he gets, instead, is unconditional love. The father throws a party because, he says, "This is my son, who has come home."

We are not told how the son responded. Jesus means the spotlight to fall not on the younger son, and not on his elder brother either who, you may remember, complained so bitterly about his father's generosity. The spotlight is shining on the father who loves both his sons, not because of what they do, but because of who they are and who he is.

Paul does tell us what his response was: ". . . By the grace of God I am what I am, and his grace toward me has not been in vain. On the contrary," Paul adds, "I worked harder than any of them — though it was not I, but the grace of God that is with me." What Paul means to say, I think, is that his life has taken on a new and different orientation. His had been a performance-driven life. His sense of worth, his stature, was something he had to achieve. The favor of God was something he had to try to earn. His sins were blots on his personal resumé that, somehow, he had to try to make up for, or work off. His experience of the grace of God changed all that.

I don't mean that Paul became a completely different person. Whoever it was who first explained what happens to a curmudgeon upon conversion may have had Paul in mind. Do you know what happens when a curmudgeon is converted? He, or she, becomes a Christian curmudgeon! That was true of Paul. He was still susceptible to the same sins and weaknesses. He continued to have a short fuse. He was opinionated prior to the Damascus Road experience, and he was opinionated afterwards. He worked as hard as ever — harder than any of the others, he says. What was different — completely different — was his orientation. It was one of sheer gratitude. He was no longer trying to earn "brownie points." He wasn't attempting to win God's favor. He realized he didn't have to. Paul had encountered, in Jesus Christ, the true gift of grace. Knowing himself to be loved, he could love himself, he could love others without having to change them. Instead of always having to prove himself worthy, he could live freely and gratefully, and that's what he did.

*   *   *

Here is what I am wondering about: Have you learned what Paul came to realize? Do you know that you are loved unconditionally? Do you believe it? Trust that it is really so? Have you opened your hand to receive God's free gift of grace? Or, are you still thinking that you have somehow to earn God's favor? I am asking you about your life-orientation: Is it like Paul's after his conversion? Or, are you more like Paul before he experienced the grace of God?

I ask these questions because the good news of the grace of God is not easy to believe. I mean really believe as in "trust." It is not easy even for those of us who have been brought up on it, nourished by it. There, by the grace of God, go I? It's so counter-cultural. It's un-American. I suspect there are many who sing "Amazing Grace" with great fervor, but whose real theology is not unlike that of the mechanic in Massachusetts, who repaired my car years ago and sent me on my way with the words, "Try to live so the Lord will take a liking to you." We are a people who pull ourselves up by our own bootstraps. We get our status, our sense of worth, the old-fashioned way: we earn it! And we are supposed to believe that, in God's eyes, we already have status, we already are somebody?

It *is* what we are asked to believe! Such, precisely, is the aim of the Christian faith: to have you understand, accept, know in both head and heart, feel, trust — to have as your life orientation: "By the grace of God I am what I am. . . ."

*   *   *

If and when you get there, what difference does it make? Is there any practical effect? I think there is.

It means a huge difference in the matter of self-esteem, for one thing. Self-esteem is something we all want. I almost said, "It is something we all want to *achieve*. That's what the culture says you have to do — achieve it. If you work hard enough, perform well enough, get far enough, become rich enough — you gain self-esteem. What the Gospel says is: you already have esteem. God esteems you. God loves you unconditionally. As one of God's beloved, how can you not accept yourself, respect yourself, value yourself?

You must have some sense of how absolutely damning the achievement, performance-driven orientation of our culture is to many. It is hard for some to have much of a sense of personal worth when the society we live in pretty much equates worth with usefulness, success, wealth — things like that. It makes it hard for the child who does not excel in school, the child who is less than perfect. It makes it hard for the adolescent who is not a star performer. It makes it difficult for the person who has become physically disabled, for those who are aging, who are becoming frail, whose minds don't work as well as they once did. A friend of mine, a recent retiree, reports the greeting he received soon after moving into a life-care community. "I know that you used to be somebody," he was told, "but now you are just one of us." To know, "by the grace of God I am what I am," is to know you are somebody whatever your condition.

It is also to understand that other people are "somebody." Other people don't have to prove their worth. They are loved by God, their worth is given, and they deserve your respect. They can be rich or poor, smart or not so smart, straight or gay, male or female, black or white, Christian or Jew or Hindu or atheist — none of these externals gives them their value. They are God's beloved, whether they know it or not, the recipients of God's grace, whether or not they realize it. And, as one who does know about the grace of God and is grateful for it, you treat these others as the beloved ones they are, without having to change them.

Here's another practical consequence of a grace-orientation. To say, "There, by the grace of God, go I" is to trust that even the hard times are not beyond the realm of grace. It is to believe that even the painful things that come along can become a sacrament. Do you remember the definition of a sacrament? A sacrament is "a means of grace." You may recall it's what Paul discovered about his "thorn in the flesh." Nobody knows for sure what Paul's thorn was. Whatever it was, he viewed it as a hindrance, and he prayed to be rid of it. The answer he got back, he says, was: "My grace is sufficient for you, for my power is made perfect in weakness." Not only was the "thorn" not going away, it was going to serve as yet one more door through which the grace of God would enter Paul's life.

Nobody I know of goes looking for trouble. but it comes. Every life has its "thorns" — some more than one. No life is free from adversity. To some, the trouble seems unfair: "What did I do to deserve this?" To some, it is simply bad luck. To some, it looks like evidence that God's back has turned, or that maybe there is no God at all. But for the person whose life is oriented around grace, even the presence of a "thorn" can become a sacrament. Such a one knows that grace is as active in the things that threaten, as in the things that thrill, because it's not the circumstances, but the presence of God that makes for grace.

There is one more thing I'd like to say about a life oriented around the grace of God: it's not fearful of the future. None of us knows what the future will bring, none of us can know. But, if your life is oriented around the grace of God, you do know who will be there, and you trust that all will be well.

A few weeks ago, we lost one of the truly masterful preachers of the gospel when David H. C. Read died at age 91, and entered the church triumphant. The grace of God was a constant theme in his preaching, and in his life. The first volume of his memoirs, about his years up through the Second World War when, for four years, he was a prisoner of war, he entitled, *This Grace Given.* The second volume which he finished in his 76th year, he called, *Grace Thus Far.* I pulled that second volume off my shelf the other day, and on the last page this is what I found: "Grace thus far for me. I am immensely grateful for its presence and guidance, . . . for the dark parts of my pilgrimage as well as for the joys. . . . Grace thus far. . . . That's how I see it; there is no end to the pilgrimage. I don't envisage a future of my own planning, and as I grow older, I am more and more fond of the text that says, 'Though our outward humanity is in decay, yet day by day we are inwardly renewed.'" Read went on: "I believe that the grace that has come to me thus far has far more to give, and that the pilgrimage that we have on this earth is a preparation for a continuing journey in the life to come."[2]

That's what it can mean to believe in God's grace. That's the kind of hope you can have, if you are able to say, There, by the grace of God, go I. John Newton thought so too, apparently. He wrote:

> Through many dangers, toils, and snares,
> I have already come;
> 'Tis grace has brought me safe thus far,
> And grace will lead me home.

1. *The Living Pulpit*, Volume 4, #1, p. 10.
2. David H. C. Read, *Grace Thus Far* (Grand Rapids, MI: Wm. Eerdmans Publishing Co., 1986), p. 130.

~

A Church for Children
to Grow Up In

Readings: Acts 2:41-47   May 5, 2002
            Matthew 28:16-20

> **Day by day, as they spent much time together in the temple, they broke bread at home and ate their food with glad and generous hearts, praising God and having the good will of all the people. And day by day the Lord added to their number those who were being saved.**
> — **Acts. 2:46-47**

This morning's sermon topic — "A Church for Children to Grow Up In" — is a direct consequence of what happened here last Sunday. If you were with us then, you know what a marvelous experience it was as the three children's choirs combined to present the cantata, "The Tale of Three Trees." Eighty-nine enthusiastic, energetic, engaged children excited to be part of this church, and pleased, as one of their adult leaders observed, not only to be participating in but helping to lead the worship of the congregation.

Afterwards, I began to imagine these children growing up — as they will, right before our eyes. And I started thinking about the on-going experiences of church that I hoped these children would have. I took paper and pen and began to jot down some characteristics of the church I hoped these children would grow up in, so that they would continue to experience it as life-giving and perhaps even transforming. I commend that as a useful exercise, and I would be interested to know what would make it onto your list, and if yours would be anything like mine. But, for now, let me tell you what I came up with — my picture of the church I hope our children will grow up in.

*   *   *

Heading my list is the hope that our children will grow up in a church where God is at the center. Which means a place where the worship of God is primary. A place where finite lives come into contact with the infinite, and human frailty meets up with divine mercy. A place where they will experience the claim of God on their lives. A place where the good news of God's love in Jesus Christ will never fail to be proclaimed, and where in the words of the hymn sung moments ago, they will learn of the "God whose giving knows no ending. . . ." I hope our children will grow up in a church where God is at the center, and where the worship of God on Sunday morning is the most important activity of their week.

*   *   *

Second on my list is the hope that our children grow up in a growing church where they themselves are helped to grow. I don't mean a church growing in numbers so much as growing in its understanding of what it means to be the church of Jesus Christ, what it means to call him "Lord" and to follow him in daily life. The church I hope our children grow up in is one that expects its members to come to a mature faith and will help them do so, one that encourages its members to love God with their minds as well as with their hearts, and that helps them explore the perennial religious questions of meaning and purpose, of guilt and grace, of life and death. I hope it will be a church, as well, that is ready, willing and able to wrestle with contemporary theological issues or ethical dilemmas.

I hope the church our children grow up in will be one that welcomes those who come to it not knowing what or even if they believe. A church like the one a friend of mine says she was fortunate to find at a time in her life when, as she puts it, she was "longing for God," but burdened with all kinds of questions. Seeking the counsel of a pastor near her home, she told him, "I am not sure what I believe, or even if I believe anything." "I accept that," the pastor answered. "Would you like to try to figure things out with some other people who are trying to do the same thing?" "Oh yes," she said. "Well, then," said the pastor, "you are welcome here."[1] It was in that community that my friend came to faith and eventually heard the call to ministry herself. I hope our children will experience the church as a community into which inquirers can come and discover others who are willing to walk with them on their spiritual journey.

*   *   *

That leads to the next thing: the hope our children will experience the church as a hospitable place, as a community that reflects the hospitality of Jesus who sat at table with saint and sinner, and went out of his way to befriend the marginalized. I hope our children will grow up in a community that says, "all are welcome here," and actually means it.

I hope the church our children grow up in will be a caring community. A place they can turn to when they need help, where they will find people to share their joys and their sorrows, people who will pray for them when, because of their own doubt or despair, they cannot pray for themselves, where, when the hard times come, as they inevitably will, there will be others to share the burden.

I hope the children grow up in a church that cares for its members, but not just for its members. I hope the church they grow up in will have a social conscience that causes it to reach out to its neighbors near and far. I hope it is a church that cares about hungry and homeless people, about the ill and the infirm, about children growing up in poverty, about victims of warfare and violence, and about those who, for whatever reason, are made to feel unworthy and unwanted.

I hope our children grow up in a church that teaches them to care, that introduces them to places of need and enables them to experience something of what it means to find their lives by losing them in service to others. I hope our children will grow up in a church that has its eyes open to human suffering, and in so far as it can, seeks to alleviate it, and where it can't, identifies with the sufferers.

*   *   *

Which brings me to something else: I hope our children will grow up in a church that is marked by generosity. Generosity of spirit, so that it is not one of those churches that claims to be in sole position of the truth, or one that insists all its members must adhere to one particular theological perspective. I hope it will be a church that encourages listening to one another and respectful conversation.

I hope our children will grow up in a church that is generous in that way — and in another way. I hope it will be a church that is generous with its own resources, and where its members are encouraged to give of themselves, to offer time, talent, and money. I hope our children, as they grow up, will be helped to resist the temptation to use God's good gifts merely for their own selfish purposes. I would like our children to grow up in a church where, at budget time, the main item of discussion is not how much money we need to keep for ourselves, but how much we can give away, how much we can share with others whose need is so much greater than our own. I hope our children will experience the church as a community with an open heart, open hands, and open pocketbooks, a community that is not content to do little, piddling things on behalf of Jesus Christ, but dares to conceive of ways it can really make a difference and commit itself to doing them. Oh, how I hope our children will grow up in a church marked by a spirit of generosity.

*   *   *

Here is something that until recently I might not have considered important, but today I do. I hope our children will experience the church as truthful. This is something we used to not have to worry about so much. Indeed, there was a time, and some of us are old enough to remember it, when people believed statements made by most of our institutions: governments, corporations, educational institutions, the news media. That is no longer true today. "It is," as another puts it, "pretty much assumed that press secretaries and public relations directors are hiding something we need to know. . ."[2] As has become painfully clear in recent days, the church is not exempt. The anger of Roman Catholics has to do not only with the abuse that has occurred, but with the denials, the cover-ups, and the failure of church leaders to confront the problem.

So, I hope our children will grow up in a church they can trust to be truthful. A church that can admit its failures and confess its sins the same as it expects its members to do. A church that can acknowledge error. A church that can admit what it does not know or is not sure about. A church whose members can be truthful with each other, can, as the Apostle Paul urges, "speak the truth in love," and where pastors can be trusted to say what they really believe and to really believe what they say. I hope our children will experience the church as a truthful and trustworthy community.

*   *   *

Recently I read about a church in Ethiopia that is named "The Place Where Jesus Lives."[3] That, at the end of the day, is the kind of church I hope our children can grow up in. A church where Jesus Christ is a living presence. A church that loves Jesus and knows itself to be his body in the world today, that seeks to serve the world as he served it, to give its life away as he gave his life away. A church that is gracious, open to the future, secure in its faith, bold in its vision, undaunted by its foes, unbounded in its love, energized by its hope, a church that has the courage of its convictions, that is willing to take risks on behalf of the gospel. A church that is ready and willing to do the right thing, knowing that the right thing is often a costly thing.

*   *   *

The sermon you have heard from me this morning is different from most of mine. Typically I start with a passage of Scripture and "milk it for all it is worth." I haven't done that today. But the lessons read earlier have not been absent from my thinking. Indeed the one from Acts, the picture Luke gives us of the church that came into being a few weeks after Easter, seems very similar to the one I have said I would like our children to grow up in. It's a picture of a church worshipping together, welcoming all who would be part of it, a people learning together, praying for and caring for one another, and manifesting a spirit of generosity. A community alive with the presence of Christ and the power of the Holy Spirit.

If our children do grow up in a church similar to the one I've described, maybe they will be as excited to be part of it at age thirty or fifty, or eighty, as they are today. And wouldn't that be wonderful? In any case, that's the kind of church I hope our children will grow up in, and that you, along with the officers we ordain and install this morning, will help enable this church to be.

1. Joanna Adams in *"Faith and Doubt,"* Trinity Presbyterian Church, Atlanta, Georgia, January 31, 1999.
2. Barbara Wheeler, *"Who Needs Organized Religion?"* Speech delivered on September 29, 2000.
3. *Journal for Preachers*, Easter, 2002.

~

Forty and Counting

Readings: Jeremiah 1:4-8   June 23, 2002
              II Timothy 1:8-14
              Mark 9:33-37

But the Lord said to me, "Do not say, 'I am only a boy'; for
you shall go to all to whom I send you, and you shall speak
whatever I command you. Do not be afraid of them, for I am
with you to deliver you, said the Lord."
                                                        — Jeremiah 1:7-8

Do not be ashamed, then, of the testimony about our Lord or
of me his prisoner, but join with me in suffering for the gospel,
relying on the power of God, who saved us and called us with
a holy calling, not according to our works but according to his
own purpose and grace.
                                                        — II Timothy 1:8-9

About six weeks ago I learned that plans were underway to observe
the fortieth anniversary of my ordination and my fifteen years of service
to this congregation. I was informed that my consent was not being
requested and that my advice would not be required. It was, I was told, out
of my hands. But since nothing was said about relieving me from the
responsibility of preaching today, I went in search of a text. I thought
almost immediately of that verse in the Book of Psalms where the poet
declares, "The boundary lines have fallen from me in pleasant places."
Thanks in no small measure to a supportive spouse and family, to committed and capable colleagues, to assistants who have served me with a
marvelous mixture of proficiency and patience, adaptability and devotion,

and because of the faithful congregations it has been my privilege to serve, as with the psalmist, so with me: "the boundary lines have fallen for me in pleasant places." That would easily have been my text.

Eventually, however, I was drawn to two others: an old favorite from the Book of Jeremiah, along with a word from Paul, that battle-tested veteran, to Timothy, his young assistant.

*   *   *

Ever since spending a seminary semester with the book that bears his name, and despite his reputation as a crabby, cantankerous, contentious prophet, Jeremiah has been a favorite of mine, as he seems also to have been of Jesus. What appeals to me is Jeremiah's combination of courage and hopefulness, his passion for righteousness and justice, his pastoral heart, his willingness to speak truth to power, his honesty in prayer, and that rare ability of his to discern the hand of God in human affairs. Of most relevance for today, I have long heard in the description of Jeremiah's summons to ministry echoes of my own call.

Like Jeremiah, I tried initially to fend off the call to ministry, and for much the same reason — self-doubt. I wish I could tell you that I've gotten over it. I haven't. There are many Sunday mornings when it seems utterly ludicrous that I should be so bold as to stand in this pulpit and speak God's word. Just because I have done it, or sought to do it, for forty years doesn't mean it has gotten easier, or that I am any less awed by the responsibility of it. But what I can say, and delight to say, is that the promise made to the prophet has proven to be one upon which I could rely as well. Don't give me that "I am only a boy" excuse, is what Jeremiah heard the Lord say. Don't tell me you do not know how to speak. You shall go where I send you. You shall speak what I command you. Put your fears aside, "for I am with you to deliver you." As it was for Jeremiah, so it has been for me: in ways I dare not try to explain, but cannot ignore, what I have been asked to do, I have been given the strength to do and, when required, the courage to do. Along with that experience has come a growing recognition of what Paul was trying to tell Timothy: what all of us have to rely on, you laity as well as us ministers, is "the power of God, who saved us and called us with a holy calling, not according to our works but according to (God's) own purpose and grace."

*   *   *

The forty-year period of my ministry has been a difficult and demanding time for both the church and the world. As I think back over it, a host of words and phrases flash through my mind like so many covers of Time or Newsweek: Cold War, Sputnik, Cuban Missile Crisis, Selma, Birmingham, the March on Washington, Vietnam, Kent State, the assassinations of the Kennedys, Martin Luther King and Malcolm X, the Sexual Revolution, the Drug Culture, Feminism, "God is dead," Apollo 7, Neil Armstrong's walk on the moon, Nixon goes to China, Watergate, the Information Age, the Berlin Wall, Apartheid, "Situation Ethics," a Global Economy, Impeachment, Religious Pluralism, Amendment B, and all through these years, the conflict in the Middle East, and finally, of course, September 11. These suggest just some of the tragedy and tumult through which we have come.

The challenge for me has been to preach and teach so as to make vital connections between the resources of faith and the experiences of life, to provide Sunday worship that has relevance for Monday work, to bring the worlds of the Bible and the newspaper, or CNN, or the internet, into conversation with one another, in short, to facilitate the encounter between the living Christ and the culture of our time and place.

As a Pastor and as a participant in denominational, ecumenical or interfaith activities, I have tried to keep the church faithful to its traditions, while helping it to adjust and respond creatively to changing circumstances and accommodate itself to new understandings of its ancient truth.

Especially in the last fifteen years, it has been my duty and my delight to lead this resourceful congregation and encourage you to put your resources to work in ways that make a difference — both here in this congregation and in the world beyond, whether in West Philadelphia or East Africa, whether among the seniors of the Main Line or the children of Appalachia.

In all this, and throughout the years, I have been helped enormously by the likes of you. It was in my very first parish, a little country congregation, where I began to learn that there were lay people who would stand with me if I did the right thing. In all the years since, and in each of the five congregations it has been my privilege to serve, there have been members who not only gave support and encouragement, but whose faithfulness far exceeded my own, and who sometimes were way ahead of me in knowing what loyalty to Christ required of his followers and of his church, and who pushed and prodded me to catch up. One of my ministerial mentors in the early years told me: "Your lay people will help you, if you let them." How grateful I am to have learned that early on and to have experienced it all these years.

*   *   *

Both the world and the church have changed much during these forty years, and so have I. It would be tragic if I had not. For we are meant to grow as persons and as Christians, and to grow is by necessity to change. It was, I believe, Cardinal Newman who said: "To live is to change, and to have lived long is to have changed often." I am thinking it may be of interest, and perhaps even of some help, for you to know what some of my growing edges have been.

One has to do with my understanding of God. As I have gotten older, my image of God has gotten bigger. Given the scientific knowledge we have acquired over recent centuries, and given our exposure to people of other faiths, I don't see that there is any other option. Oh, I suppose we could, ostrich-like, stick our heads in the sand, or park our brains, along with our cars, outside when we come to church. But I cannot do that. What it has meant for me is not abandoning faith, but getting a bigger God. My experience has not been unlike that of the astronomer I read about recently. After a few years of working with the Hubble Space Telescope he said this not long ago: "I have always believed in God. But when I see these awesome things, it's just that much more confirmation for me that, wow, this is an even greater God than I ever thought before."[1]

Another growing edge of mine has to do with Jesus. Not long ago James Carroll, a religion writer, wrote an op-ed column entitled "The Purpose of Religion." He began by discussing the Roman Catholic theological document, Dominus Jesus, a Papal encyclical which reiterates the old Catholic position that there is no "salvation" outside of the Catholic Church. Instead of engaging that old question Carroll shifted the paradigm. "Suppose," he wrote, "we Christians have got it wrong?" Suppose, he went on, the primary purpose of Jesus' coming is not salvation — saving us from judgment and damnation — suppose, instead, the reason for Jesus' coming is revelation — showing us that God loves us and that we belong to God? The salvation model suggests that Jesus' role is to change God's mind, but Carroll argues just the opposite: Perhaps it is our minds that need changing: from fear of God and anxious guilt, recognizing and to receiving God's love.[2]

In any case, that's how, more and more, I have come to see Jesus, and seeing Jesus in that way it has had an enormous impact on my view of the relation between Christianity and other religions. I no longer believe, if I ever did, that Christians have exclusive rights to God, or that God has nothing to do with people of other faiths. I know that some Christians hear Jesus say, "I am the way, the truth and the life, no one comes to the Father but by me," and assume not only that Jesus is the only way to salvation, but that Christianity is the only true religion. But Presbyterian theologian Shirley Guthrie recently asked an important question. Who is this Jesus who says, "I am the way?" He is the one who also says, "I have other sheep that do not belong to this fold. I must bring them also." Who is this who says, "I am the way?" He is the "friend of sinful, unbelieving, or dif-ferent-believing people who were excluded and rejected by law-abiding, morally respectable members of the religious establishment." Who is this Jesus? He is the one who "believed that caring for needy, suffering human beings is more important than conformity to the requirements of moral and theological orthodoxy."[3]

It is because of the God Jesus helps me to know that I cannot limit the scope of salvation. The hymn says, "There's a wideness in God's mercy that is wider than our minds." I am sure that is the case. Rather than pre-sume to say who is in and who is out, I am content to testify to God's amazing grace. I am more willing than ever, not only to acknowledge but appreciate the extraordinary diversity of God's people.

Just one more example of how I have changed: I have come to believe that religion, or faith, is more about the future than about the past. And that is a good thing, for the future is where the action is going to be. It is where all of us are headed.

There are in our own Presbyterian denomination those who want to return to the past, and to some imagined idyllic past, at that. What they want to return to never was to begin with. But more importantly, to retreat to the past is not an act of faith, but an act of fear. The Bible summons us into the future. We have our own race of faith to run, the Scriptures tells us, and they want us to get on with it.

The Gospel of Mark has a verse that has long intrigued and challenged me. Jesus and the disciples are headed for Jerusalem, and Mark says: "They were on the road, going up to Jerusalem, and Jesus was walking ahead of them; they were amazed, and those who followed were afraid."

How like Jesus to be out in front! And how like his disciples to be afraid to follow. Jesus has always been out ahead, and I believe he always will be. He is out ahead right now, and by way of the Holy Spirit, he is calling his church to catch up with him, to come with him. One of the things I hope to contribute to, in whatever additional time on this earth is to be mine, is a Presbyterian Church that will follow into the future where the Spirit of Christ is wanting to lead it. There will be no future for a church that is unwilling to change and unready to follow its Lord to new places.

*   *   *

When, five years ago, I went off to Cambridge for a sabbatical, I wanted among other things to write a personal memoir. My mother had died a short time before, and I wanted to record a bit of our family's story for my children and grandchildren, and I also wanted to do some reflecting on what had then been thirty-five years of ministry. I entitled the finished product, "An Unexpected Journey" because, after looking back on it, that's what it seemed like — as if I had been to places and done things I had neither foreseen nor planned. About that unexpected journey I wrote these words: "Like the ancient Hebrew patriarch, Abraham, who was also led to unexpected places, I have been blessed by the One who has led me. To what additional unexpected places or experiences I will be led in the future I do not know, but I go on, grateful for what has been and confident of the trustworthiness of the One who goes ahead of me."

The other day I received a gracious congratulatory note from Don Kocher who many of you fondly remember as our very first Associate Pastor for Senior Adult Ministry. "Congratulations on your fortieth anniversary;" Don wrote. "I am having my fiftieth this month," he said. "Would I do it all over again?" he asked. "Of course!" So would I, and, in case you are wondering, I am planning to stay with it a while longer. Like the man in Robert Frost's famous poem — I, too, have a few more miles to go before I sleep.

1. Howard Bushouse in *The Baltimore Sun* newspaper, sometime in June 2002.
2. Peter J. Gomes, "Redemption Yields to Revelation," *You Can Do This!* (Harvard University: The Memorial Church, 2001), p. 213.
3. In *The Presbyterian Outlook*, February 11, 2002.

~

"A Time To . . . ?"

Readings: Ecclesiastes 3:1-9   January 15, 2003
             Romans 13:11-14

For everything there is a season, and a time for every matter under heaven. . . .

— Ecclesiastes 3:1

Some of you, any of you who are Baby Boomers, especially, may recall the musical version of these words made popular by The Byrds: "Turn! Turn! Turn!" The song was a big hit in the 1960's, and the text remains a favorite of many. "For everything there is a season, and a time for every matter under heaven. . . ."

It has never been a favorite of mine. I have always heard it as encouraging a passive response to life, a religious version of "Play the hand that life deals you." There is, of course, a sense in which we all have to do that: respond to what we are given, take life as it comes. But there is also our calling, our responsibility, to influence events, to help shape life and not merely be shaped by it. So, the third chapter of Ecclesiastes has never warmed my heart.

Recently, however, I have learned that it is possible to view this text in a different light. Early last month I was in St. Louis with twenty-five other pastors with whom I meet twice a year for two or three days. One morning we were addressed by Dr. William Danforth, Chancellor Emeritus of Washington University. In the course of his talk, Dr. Danforth proposed an alternative reading of Ecclesiastes 3. What if, he asked, we were to interpret the text actively, instead of passively? "If for everything there is a season," Danforth said, "ought we not to be asking, 'What is the

167

season we are in now? If there is a time for everything, what is *this* a time for?' " What, in other words, is our time inviting, or even demanding, from us?

Danforth's question reminded me that the New Testament has two words which our Bibles translate as "time." One is the Greek word "chronos," from which we get "chronology," and which refers simply to clock or calendar time. "The time is eleven o'clock": that's "chronos." But the New Testament knows there is another kind of time, and its word for this second kind of time is "kairos," meaning an opportune time, a moment when there is an opening or an opportunity for a breakthrough to occur, for change to happen — a time which, if seized, could make a difference. It's what Paul has in mind in Romans 13 when he says, "You know what time it is, how it is time for you to wake from sleep."

Ever since hearing Dr. Danforth's talk, I have been haunted by his question. What is *this* a time for? I have wondered if this could be, in any sense, a "kairos" moment? I have come to think this might be such a time, especially for people of faith such as ourselves. And I want to suggest to you now two ways in which I believe this is a moment to be seized and made use of.

*   *   *

First of all, I believe this is a time for people of faith to affirm what Jonathan Sacks has called "the dignity of difference."[1] That's the title of his recent book. Sacks is the Chief Rabbi of the United Hebrew congregations in the United Kingdom. He reminds us that "one belief, more than any other" is responsible for the age-long slaughter of individuals, the wars of all the centuries and the more recent spate of terrorists attacks. "It is the belief that those who do not share my faith — or my race or my ideology — do not share my humanity."[2]

Sacks reminds us that we are now in a era when "difference has become part of the texture of daily life. At work, in the street and on the television screen, we are regularly confronted with people whose faith, culture, accent, race, skin color and customs are unlike ours." Says Sacks: "The critical question" is whether we will make room for the other, the stranger, in other words, "acknowledge the dignity of difference."[3]

Religion and religious people will either be part of the solution or part of the problem. In the past, we must sadly confess, religion and religious people have been part of the problem. One has only to recall the Crusades, the Inquisition, the pogroms, the Salem Witch Trials, to say nothing of the use of the Bible to justify slavery, or present day homophobia. As Sacks puts it: "Nothing has proved harder in the history of civilization than to seek (the image of) God . . . in those whose language is not mine, whose skin is a different color, whose faith is not my faith and whose truth is not my truth."

There are even Christians who have difficulty believing that other Christians who do not believe or behave exactly as they do will be saved. Perhaps you recall that account of heaven, popular in the early days of the ecumenical movement, where St. Peter is taking a newcomer around. In one room there are a lot of people dancing and drinking. "Who are they?" asks the visitor. "Oh, those are the Southern Baptists, making up for lost time." In another room there is loud, noisy conversation: "Who are they?" is the question. "Those are the Quakers, also making up for lost time." And yet in another room there are people just beginning to have a good time. "Those are the Presbyterians," St. Peter says; "they are learning how to have fun." As they turn the corner, at the end of the corridor there is a room in which a lot of people are looking very serious. "We must be very quiet here," St. Peter says; "we mustn't disturb them, for these are the Catholics and they think they are the only ones here."[4] It would be nice to believe we have outgrown that story, but there is evidence aplenty that we have not. We need to. Not only to realize that our particular version of Christian faith and life is not all there is to the Christian tradition. But, without forfeiting or diminishing our Christian faith one iota, we need to recognize that we are not the only ones beloved by God, and that people of other faiths may also possess some of the truth of God.

Today is Trinity Sunday, a day when we are encouraged to think about God, about the nature and being of God, the splendor, the transcendence of God. It is the perfect day for me to encourage you, as well as myself, to think bigger thoughts of God. We can believe, as I do and presumably you do, that "God was in Christ reconciling the world to himself," without consigning people of other faiths to outer darkness. We must not be so arrogant or ignorant as to think that our way is God's only way. Trinity Sunday is a perfect occasion for us to acknowledge that our ideas of God are not God. To equate our understanding of God with God is idolatry. "For my thoughts are not your thoughts, nor are your ways my ways, says the Lord. For as the heavens are higher than the earth, so are my ways higher than your ways and my thoughts than your thoughts."

What is this a time for? I believe it is a time for a new "generosity of spirit."[5] I believe it is a time for people of faith to outgrow puny, parochial, provincial notions of God, and time for us to recognize the humanity we share with all of God's children. A time, as Sacks puts it, to really and truly understand "that God transcends the particularities of culture and the limits of human understanding . . . , a time to believe in and commend to others a God who is above us all, teaching us to make a space for one another."[6]

Sacks asks, what would it be like to have such a faith? "It would," he says, "be like being secure in one's own home, yet moved by the beauty of foreign places, knowing that they are someone else's home, not mine, but still part of the glory of the world that is ours."[7]

*   *   *

My second thought about the "kairos" moment we are in is related to, but different from, the first. I believe this is a time for rediscovering and reclaiming the notion of the common good, or as we Pennsylvanians call it, the "commonwealth" — a time for a declaration of interdependence, of mutuality.

Here, in our own society, the gap between rich and poor is wide and growing wider. The gulf between city and suburb remains. The inequalities in our own state with regard to public education are a disgrace.

In the wider world, the disparities between the rich nations and the poor nations are enormous. According to a study by the World Bank, one out of every four persons in developing nations lives — or struggles to live — in absolute poverty, on less than one dollar a day.[8] In an address given during the recent meeting of the General Assembly of our denomination, former Senator Paul Simon pointed out that of the twenty-two wealthiest industrial nations in the world, the United States is first in wealth and twenty-second — dead last — in terms of aid given to combat hunger and poverty. And we wonder why we have enemies.

What is the time we are in? It is the moment for us to realize we cannot flourish while others perish. It is, I believe, a moment for people of faith to hear the cry of the needy, and to remember the admonitions of Amos and Micah, of Jeremiah and Isaiah, to be, in God's name, advocates for justice and agents of mercy.

Four years ago, during all the fuss about the dawn of the new millennium, the *New York Times Magazine* asked Peter Gomes, minister of

Harvard's Memorial Church, to nominate what he thought was the greatest sermon of the last millennium. Gomes reports how he recalled many of the great preachers of the years 1000 to 1999, people such as St. Thomas Aquinas, Luther and Calvin, Wesley and Edwards, Moody and Brooks, Fosdick and Sheen, Tillich and Barth, King and Graham. But the sermon he chose was from none of these. Can you guess what it was? It was the sermon preached by John Winthrop, a layman, aboard the ship Arbella before it landed the Puritans in 1630.

Winthrop's sermon was a call to mutuality. His argument went like this: "If we do not restrain our individual appetites and ambitions, and put the good of the whole before the good of the self; if we are unable to share abundance with those in need; if we are unwilling to take our public responsibility more seriously than our private convenience, then this new society we are seeking to create will be no better than the one from which we are trying to escape. We will be an embarrassment to ourselves and to the world."[9]

That's a paraphrase. Here are Winthrop's very own words: ". . . We must be knit together in this work as one . . . ; we must delight in each other, make each other's condition our own, rejoice together, mourn together, labor and suffer together, always having before our eyes . . . our community as members of the same body, so shall we keep the unity of the spirit in the bond of peace."[10]

The greatest sermon of the millennium? I don't know. But this I do believe: Winthrop's words are as relevant today as they were in 1630, and his vision of a community of mutuality, of a people who remain responsible for each other and bear each other's burdens, is one we need to recover. The prospects of peace depend on it. Faithfulness to the God of the prophets, to the God made known supremely in Jesus Christ, requires it.

Such a vision is not likely to come from the politicians. According to Robert Putnam — he of *Bowling Alone* fame — our political leaders actually missed the kairos moment provided by the tragedy of 9/11. "In the aftermath of (that) tragedy," Putnam writes, "a window of opportunity . . . opened for a sort of civic renewal that only occurs once or twice a century." We might have been called upon to sacrifice; instead, we were encouraged to shop. That crisis, Putnam says, "revealed and replenished the wells of solidarity," but so far those wells remain untapped.[11]

They need not remain so. "For everything there is a season, and a time for every matter under heaven. . . ." The season we are in is one where the wells of solidarity could be tapped. This, I believe, is a time for people of faith to see as a "kairos" moment, the opportune time for us to recover and reclaim a commitment to the common good, and lead others to do likewise. Like the Apostle Paul, I believe this is a moment for us to wake from sleep.

1. Jonathan Sacks, *The Dignity of Difference* (London, New York: Continuum, 2002).
2. Ibid., p. 45.
3. Ibid., p. 61.
4. Peter J. Gomes, *Life Before Death* (The Memorial Church, Harvard University, 1999), pp. 136-137.
5. Sacks, Ibid. p. 65.
6. Ibid.
7. Ibid.
8. *Christian Century,* June 14, 2003, pp. 24-25.
9. Peter J. Gomes, *There Is a Plan* (The Memorial Church, Harvard University, 2000), p. 134.
10. Ibid., pp. 134-135.
11. Quoted in *Context,* June 15, 2002.

~

On Being Shaped by the Supper

Readings: I Corinthians 11:17-29   September 7, 2003
              Luke 14:7-14

**Whoever, therefore, eats the bread and drinks the cup of the
Lord in an unworthy manner will be answerable for the body
and blood of the Lord. Examine yourselves, and only then eat
of the bread and drink of the cup. For all who eat and drink
without discerning the body, eat and drink judgment against
themselves.**

— I Corinthians 11:28-29

For a good many years now it has been our custom to begin the new
year in the life of the church with a service of Holy Communion. I am
aware, by the way, that what I have just said fails the test of liturgical
correctness. Liturgically the new year begins on the first Sunday of
Advent, not on the Sunday after Labor Day. Yet today does have the feel
of a new beginning, a fresh start, and practically speaking, today *is* when
we embark on a new year in our life and work together. So it seems
altogether right and proper that we should gather at the Lord's Table and
share in the Sacrament of the Lord's Supper.

All well and good, according to the Apostle Paul, as long as we do it
right. You heard what he told the Corinthian congregation, his warning
about an improper observance of Holy Communion. "Whoever . . . eats
the bread or drinks the cup of the Lord in an unworthy manner will be
answerable for the body and blood of the Lord. Examine yourselves," Paul
advises, "and only then eat of the bread and drink of the cup. For all who
eat and drink without discerning the body, eat and drink judgment on
themselves." If that doesn't get our attention, I don't know what will.

*   *   *

Paul was peeved at the Corinthians — something you surely sensed as you listened to my reading of the Epistle Lesson. His ire was directed at the way in which they were observing the Lord's Supper. We, for our part, will have to exercise care in identifying the reason for Paul's anger.

He warns about taking communion in "an unworthy manner." Over the years I have known people who, thinking Paul was referring to personal righteousness, refused to participate in communion because they "were not good enough;" they felt "unworthy." The truth is, and Paul knows it as much or more than the rest of us, none of us is worthy. We are all, each in his or her own way, like those Jesus refers to in today's Gospel Lesson. Maybe not physically, but spiritually, we are all among "the poor, the crippled, the lame, and the blind." It is precisely those who are not worthy, and who know themselves as such, whom Jesus invites to his table. "I have come," he said, "to call not the righteous but sinners." So, personal righteousness is not the issue.

What has Paul upset about the Corinthians is the quality of their life together, how they are with each other. "When you come together," he tells them, "it is not for the better but for the worse." Let me see if I can help you understand what he meant.

The early Christian communities — like the one in Corinth — did not have separate buildings in which to worship. They gathered in the homes of their members — often in the home of one of their wealthier members. In Corinth, the Lord's Supper was celebrated as part of a common meal — an early version of the church potluck supper. What appears to have happened was that the wealthier members, who did not work late into the day, arrived early for the meal, and proceeded to gorge themselves with food and drink most of the wine, even to the point of intoxication. So, when the working folks arrived there was little left. Now, according to one scholar, this was very much in line with the "conventional social mores" of the time where distinctions of rank and status were observed.[1] When, in other words, there were affairs to which many were invited, it was customary for the more privileged members of the community to receive more and better food than the others. Something like the difference between first class and coach passengers on airplanes. Paul regards such practices — however normal in the culture — to be an outrage when practiced in the church where all are equally guests at the Lord's Table, and where there are to be no distinctions, where as Paul says in another place, "there is no longer Jew or Greek, there is no longer slave or free, there is no longer male or female; for you are all one in Christ Jesus."

But there is even more to it. Paul has this notion that when Christians come to the Table they come, not as separate individuals, but as a part of a community. We come as members of a "body." That's Paul's favorite metaphor for the church: "the body of Christ." What is "unworthy," according to the Apostle, is when some members of the body come to the table thinking only of themselves, without regard for the needs of others. It was to counter such self-serving behavior on the part of the Corinthians, that prompted Paul to portray the self-giving of Jesus with those immortal words that we repeat at every service of communion. "The Lord Jesus . . . took . . . bread, and when he had given thanks, he broke it and said, 'This is my body that is for you. . . .' In the same way, he took the cup also, after supper, saying, 'This cup is the new covenant in my blood.'" How can we come to the Table of the One whose self-giving is so transparent, who, even now, offers himself to us in the bread we break and the cup we share — how can we come to his Table thinking only of ourselves? That's Paul's question.

Perhaps now you can get what he means by eating and drinking in an "unworthy manner." The test for the proper observance of communion is not anybody's personal righteousness, nor is it whether the minister gets the words exactly right, or whether the elders and deacons are clothed conservatively and appear appropriately somber, or whether there is song or silence when the elements are being served. Paul says the test for a proper observance of communion has to do with "discerning the body." Understanding, in other words, that we are part of a community. Being mindful of the sorrows and joys of others who come to the Table. Making sure there is room for all. Watching out for any who may be strangers, newcomers, and extending a word of welcome. Being especially concerned for any among us who are in greater need — whether because of age, or illness, or disability, or grief, or joblessness, or discrimination, or anything else that tends to marginalize people.

We care about and care for one another in these ways not because we are nice people, not because we want to be politically correct, or even humanitarian. We act this way when we come to the Table because we are the body of Christ. Which means we do not limit our care and concern to those within this congregation. We remember that there are parts of the body in West Philadelphia, and in Chester, and in South Africa and Kenya, in Cuba, and in Iraq — there is an old and fairly substantial Christian community in Iraq. And we know that a proper discernment of the body means being conscious of these brothers and sisters as well.

*   *   *

Over the years I have attended my share of potluck suppers in various churches, and I am glad to say I have not ever witnessed anything quite like what Paul says happened in the Corinthian congregation. So I am not suggesting a direct parallel between them and us.

Yet, we do live, as they did, in a culture that pays a lot of attention to social distinctions. There are exceptions — such as during the aftermath of 9/11 or following the blackout that occurred this summer — times when, even in our secular communities, we come together and pull together. But most days the notion of "rugged individualism" is alive and well.

As for our religious life, Sally Brown, a professor up at Princeton Seminary, suggests that individualism is rampant there these days, as well. She says the hymn "I Come to the Garden Alone" could be the anthem of twenty-first century Anglo-Protestant spirituality. In that hymn, she says, it is all about "me and Jesus." "He walks with me, and he talks with me, he tells me that I am his own . . ." — the anthem, Brown says, of twenty-first century Anglo-Protestant spirituality.[2]

"Private, personal meetings with God have their time and place," says William Willimon. But church on Sunday is not the time or the place. "On Sunday," we are called forth from our rugged individualism and yoked to the Body."[3] We do not come to the garden alone; we come to the Table together.

We are all a part of our society, our American culture, and we cannot help but be influenced by it. But, here's the thing. Here's what the Apostle Paul wants to impress upon us. We are part of another and a distinctive kind of community called "the body of Christ." And we have this very special thing we call "the Sacrament of the Lord's Supper." It is meant to be the thing that shapes us, reorients us. Even on those Sundays when we are not celebrating communion, the Table is always here, in full view, the cross behind it, reminding us, in Bonhoeffer's words, of "the man for others." We have a Table. We do not have an altar. We have a Table — a visible reminder every time we gather here that we are family, "members one of another," as Paul puts it.

*   *   *

Outside our little cottage in the Adirondacks hangs a hummingbird feeder which my spouse is zealous about keeping filled. On that feeder are four places for birds to feed. But you know what? There is never more than one bird there at a time. If one is there and another comes along, the one that was there first invariably chases the other one away. I don't know if hummingbirds are like that everywhere, but the ones at our place are — utterly selfish. They have no sense that they are members one of another. As I pondered Paul's description of the Corinthians behavior, I could not help but think of the hummingbirds at our feeder.

But there is, as you know, another species of birds that acts differently — the Canadian geese who will soon be heard honking their way south. They seldom fly alone. They usually fly in their famous V-formation. Scientists say that in doing so they can actually fly seventy-one percent farther than they could alone. The bird ahead creates lift that makes it easier for the bird just behind. Canadian geese even have a system of rotating leadership so that the burden of being in the lead is shared. And if a bird becomes ill and has to drop out of the formation, another member of the flock will always stay behind to help.[4]

Paul was peeved because the Corinthians were acting like hummingbirds. He has this notion that Christians are to behave more like the Canadian geese. He thinks, and so do I, that we will — if we will just permit ourselves to be shaped by this supper of which we are now happily to partake.

1. Richard B. Hays, *First Corinthians, Interpretation* (Louisville: John Knox Press, 1997), p. 196.
2. In Ted Wardlaw's Inaugural sermon as the President of Austin Seminary, *"A Telling Presence."*
3. William Willimon, *Sunday Dinner* (Nashville: The Upper Room, 1981), p. 105.
4. Thanks to Michael L. Lindvall for this reminder in *The Christian Life, a Geography of God* (Louisville: Geneva Press, 2001), p. 85.

~

Follow the Money

Readings: Deuteronomy 15:7-11   October 19, 2003
             Luke 12:13-34

**But God said to him, "You fool! This very night your life is
being demanded of you. And the things you have prepared,
whose will they be?" So it is with those who store up treasures
for themselves but are not rich toward God. . . . For where
your treasure is, there your heart will be also.**
                                            — Luke 12:20-21, 34

Earlier this Fall I was asked if, in these final months as your Pastor, I
was feeling under an obligation to tell you everything I thought you needed to hear. I said, No, that is not something I feel either a need or a desire
to do. Yet, when I began preparing for today, the run-up to Commitment
Sunday, and when I realized this would be my last "sermon on the
amount," as one of our members is fond of calling it, I confess that I was
tempted to fire all the ammunition that I had stored up over all the years.
That temptation, you will be glad to know, I was finally able to resist.

Actually, I fretted some for a while about the timing of this sermon
and wondered if I should not postpone it until another day. I noted that we
were having baptisms today, and I realized there would be many visitors,
as indeed there are. I thought maybe I should provide for our guests a
more appealing fare, one less likely to give them indigestion. In addition,
there are the thirty-five new members we are welcoming today. It might
be better, I thought, and certainly more considerate, if they were not subjected to a stewardship sermon on their very first Sunday as full-fledged
members. But that temptation, too — of avoidance — I was able to brush
aside.

178

You know why? Because what I am talking about this morning and asking you to think about, this business of stewardship, is not on the periphery of Christian faith and life, but pretty close to the center. If you do not believe me, you need to get better acquainted with the Bible. Someone has calculated that there are, in the Bible, over nine hundred references having to do, in one way or another, with our topic. Even more telling is the fact that about one-fifth of the teaching of Jesus has to do with money or material possessions. You would never know it on the basis of what preoccupies so many in the church today, but Jesus is far more interested in teaching us about the burden of money than he is in talking about the vices of sex. Jesus has a lot to say about what money means, about its danger, as well as its potential, and about the relative importance it has in our lives.

The twelfth chapter of Luke's Gospel, from which we read earlier, is a good example. There Jesus warns of problems associated with money: how the desire for it can make us greedy, how the lack of it can make us anxious, and how the possession of it can interfere with our relationship with God. That's the bad news. But there is good news. Because for all the problems associated with it, when rightly used, Jesus says that money has enormous potential. By giving "alms" we are obviously helping neighbors, but, he tells us, we are also accumulating "treasure in heaven." You are not going to believe this, but according to Jesus the right use of money can actually bring you closer to God — because, he says, "where your treasure is, there will your heart be also."

*   *   *

Perhaps I have gone too far, too fast for some of you. Let me back up, for a moment, and walk you through our gospel lesson a little more slowly, more carefully.

It begins, you remember, with a plea from an unnamed person for Jesus to resolve an "ugly dispute [that] is all too familiar":[1] a family squabble over an inheritance. Jesus refuses to get involved, and says: "Take care! Be on your guard against all kinds of greed; for one's life does not consist in the abundance of possessions." Or, as another translation has it: "Life is not defined by what you have, even when you have a lot."

It is hard to think of a more counter-cultural text. If you watch television, if your children or grandchildren watch television, you know what I mean. For every twenty minutes of entertainment you get ten minutes of advertising telling you and your children: you are what you have, and the more you have the happier you will be. All those Christmas catalogues that are already showing up in our mailboxes say the very same thing. It is nonsense, but the advertisers think if they say it often enough and persistently enough we will believe them. Having possessions is what it is all about. Or, as the old bumper sticker had it: "Whoever has the most toys wins."

It is, according to Jesus, a lie, and, as he often does, he makes his point by way of a parable. The story is about a farmer, a "rich" farmer to be precise, whose land produces "abundantly:" far more corn, barley, wheat, or whatever, than his barns can accommodate. What to do?, the rich man wonders. But only momentarily. Soon, he decides to tear down the old barns and construct new and bigger ones. And once the bountiful harvest is safely stored, the farmer assumes he "has it made" and decides to retire, "take his ease," as the text puts it, "eat, drink, and be merry." But no sooner has he settled back in his lazy-boy recliner, martini in hand, than he has a massive coronary and dies. Or, as Jesus puts it, God says to him: "You fool! This very night your life is being demanded of you. And the things you have prepared, whose will they be?"

Here it behooves us to be careful. We must not make the man in the parable into an evil villain. He is not. He has done nothing illegal. There is no hint of theft or graft. No mistreatment of his employees is suggested. There is nothing here of insider trading, or funny accounting, the kinds of things about which we have heard all too much in recent years. There is no reason whatsoever to impugn the farmer's character. There is, indeed, much to commend. He has an entrepreneurial spirit. He is prudent. He saves for a rainy day. He makes just one major mistake. He fails to reckon with his mortality. His problem is not just his self-absorption, but his self-deception. He assumes he is in charge of his life, and he is not.

As in many of the parables of Jesus, so in this one: we are being told what we would rather not hear: we are not the master of our fate and the captain of our soul. Like the rich farmer in the parable, we like to think we are in charge of our lives, but we are not. Our lives are in God's hands. If we fail to understand this basic truth about life, there comes a moment when the truth can no longer be denied. That moment can come at any time or at any place: when a fire breaks out in a Chicago skyscraper, or when an accident occurs on the Schuylkill Expressway, or when the Staten

Island ferry rams into a pier, or while we are in our beds fast asleep. In Eugene Peterson's rendering of our parable, God shows up and says: "Fool! Tonight you die. And your barn full of goods — who gets it?"[2]

By calling the farmer "Fool," Jesus brings to mind the saying in Psalm 14: "Fools say in their hearts, 'There is no God.'" The farmer is a fool because however much he goes to church or synagogue, he shows himself to be a practical atheist. He has defined himself by what he has, not by who — or rather whose — he is. He is a fool because he has forgotten the basic principle of stewardship. "Not," as another puts it, "this penny ante stuff we do every fall, the appeals to give more to the church so that the church can pay more bills, and hire more staff, and do more things. That's not what stewardship is. Stewardship is the fundamental understanding that your life is not your own and that all that you have and all that you are, are God's . . . ."[3] In other words, your life is a gift to be received and used and accounted for.

*   *   *

To help his followers, to help us begin to get it, Jesus goes on in the twelfth chapter of Luke's Gospel to talk about "the birds of the air who neither sow nor reap, who have neither storehouse or barn," yet God feeds them. "Of how much more value are you than the birds!" he says. He tells of the lilies which neither toil nor spin, who are clothed in a way that not even Solomon in all his glory can come close to matching. If God takes such loving care with a mere flower — a piece of grass that is here today and gone tomorrow — "how much more will he clothe you," says Jesus. All this anxious striving is for naught, he tells us. You cannot gain even one hour of life by worrying about it. Instead of wasting your time that way, realize what you have, understand your life as a gift from God, and all that you have as a blessing. Once again, I am drawn to Peterson's rendering of Jesus' words. "What I am trying to do here," he has Jesus say, "is to get you to relax, not be so preoccupied with getting so that you can respond to God's giving. People who don't know God and the way he works fuss over these things, but you know both God and how he works. Steep yourself in God. . . . Don't be afraid of missing out. You're my dearest friends! The Father wants to give you the very kingdom itself."[4]

How are we to understand the nature of this "kingdom" God wants us to have? It's not a promise of material prosperity or of physical health and well being. To be given "the kingdom of God" is to know you are loved by the One who put you here. It means the assurance that there is no place you can go, and no predicament you can get into, where God's grace and mercy cannot meet you. It means knowing as the Apostle Paul puts, that whether you live or whether you die, you are the Lord's. To have the kingdom of God is to trust the providence of God in this life and in the life to come.

And, you know what? Once you've got that, once you have understood that your life consists, not in the abundance of your possessions, but in the goodness and grace of God, once you have got that, the matter of giving and generosity is no longer a problem. You can afford to be generous, you can give freely and with an open hand, because you know you are and always will be the recipient of God's generosity.

*   *   *

All these years that I have been your pastor I have often asked you to give. Most recently I asked you to support our Fund for Worship, Music and Mission. And many of you have done so, some of you very generously. And here I am again this morning, encouraging you to give. I make no apologies for doing so.

For one thing, this church deserves your support. This church is carrying on the ministry of Jesus Christ, and it cannot do so without your financial contribution. It requires your time and talent, too, but it also requires your treasure.

I wish every one of you could have heard what the new members said about this place this past Tuesday evening when they met with the Session. How they praised our Church School, our Youth Ministry, our ministries of Fine Arts, the quality of our worship, our hospitality, our pastoral care, our ministries in the community and in the wider world. I wish you could have listened as they expressed their delight in becoming part of this community. This is a church that makes a difference in people's lives. Our new members sense it. You long-time members know it. Just don't take it for granted. There is no guarantee of on-going strength and vitality. I'm encouraging you to give because this church deserves it.

But here is the main reason I am once again asking you to pledge your support, and to do so as generously as you can. Because "where your treasure is, there your heart will be also." Jesus is a realist. He knows: our hearts follow our money. Some people think it is the other way around, but it isn't. Some of you will remember the advice given the Washington Post reporters who were investigating the Watergate break-in back in the 1970's: "Follow the money," they were told. It appears to be what the FBI is attempting to do right now, right here in Philadelphia. Jesus said it first: "Follow the money" — not just to catch and convict the "bad guys," but to see what your own priorities and values are. Check out your checkbook, and you will know. And, if you really want to grow spiritually, undertake the discipline of generosity. Because, "where your treasure is, there will your heart be also."

*   *   *

I conclude with an ecclesiastical version of an old story. Three people, one from the Church of the Redeemer, one from St. Luke's Methodist, and one Bryn Mawr Presbyterian member, are all stranded on a desert island in the South Pacific. The Episcopalian and the Methodist light fires, wave flags, draw big signs in the sand, hoping desperately to be rescued. The Bryn Mawr Presbyterian member meanwhile does nothing. The others, annoyed, say: "Why are you not helping us attract attention? Do you not want to be rescued?" The Presbyterian replies: "I am a member of the Bryn Mawr Presbyterian Church. The Stewardship Committee will find me."[5]

And so, if it has to, it will. Do not make that necessary. Go home today. Think about what you have heard. Think about what any Christian steward knows: how all that we are and have is a gift from God. Then, do what any Christian steward does: make as generous pledge as you possibly can, and bring it with you next Sunday and join with the rest of us in making your commitment, a glad offering to God knowing, that "where you treasure is, there will your heart be also."

1. Fred B. Craddock, *Luke, Interpretation* (Louisville: John Knox Press, 1990), p. 163.
2. Eugene H. Peterson, *The Message* (Colorado Spring, CO: NavPress, 1993).
3. Jon Walton, *"Marks of the Christian Life: Much Given, Much Required,"* The First Presbyterian Church of the City of New York, October 28, 2001.
4. Peterson, Ibid.
5. Peter Gomes tells a different version of this story in *What We Forgot To Tell You* (Cambridge, MA: The Memorial Church, Harvard University, 1999), p. 14.

~

A Preview of Coming Attractions

Readings: Isaiah 61:1-4
I Corinthians 12:12-31
Luke 4:14-21

January 18, 2004

When he came to Nazareth, where he had been brought up, he went to the synagogue on the Sabbath day, as was his custom. He stood up to read, and the scroll of the prophet Isaiah was given to him. He unrolled the scroll and found the place where it was written: "The Spirit of the Lord is upon me, because he has anointed me to bring good news to the poor. He has sent me to proclaim release to the captives and recovery of the sight to the blind, to let the oppressed go free, to proclaim the year of the Lord's favor."

— Luke 4:16-19

This morning, courtesy of Luke's Gospel, we are present at the beginning of Jesus' ministry. Last Sunday we learned that, by the age of twelve, Jesus has begun wrestling with the question of his identity — Who am I? — and with the question of his calling, his vocation — What am I to do with my life? That wrestling continues for the next eighteen years, about which we know nothing. Then one day, when Jesus is roughly thirty years of age, he lays down his carpenter's tools and goes out to the Jordan River to be baptized by John. Following his baptism there is a rather lengthy retreat in the wilderness — a total of forty days, we are told — after which Jesus returns to Galilee. When we catch up to him today he is back in his hometown of Nazareth. On the Sabbath he goes to the synagogue, the one he has frequented all his life. Not unlike the politician who returns to his

184

boyhood home to announce that he is running for some office, Jesus has come home to Nazareth formally to launch his ministry.

*   *   *

As you must know, beginnings are important. First impressions tend to linger. A teacher's initial meeting with students, a new CEO's first speech to employees, a president's inaugural address, a pastor's first sermon, can set a tone, suggest an agenda, send a signal regarding what is to come.

I was acutely aware of this some seventeen years ago when I was beginning my ministry here. I was very deliberate and very intentional about choosing the text and the theme of my first sermon. The sermon was entitled "Great Days," and the text was the forty-third verse of the tenth chapter of Mark's Gospel: ". . .Whoever wishes to be great among you must be your servant." A key part of that sermon went this way: "As today we begin a new partnership in ministry, both you and I want this to be a 'great' church." But, I went on, there is greatness as the world tends to measure it: in terms of size and wealth and power, and then there is the greatness Christ wants us to have. I asked the congregation to "remember that what distinguishes the followers of Jesus Christ is their aptitude for service." Service was the theme with which I launched my ministry among you.

As I was pondering Luke's story about the beginning of Jesus' ministry the other day, I got to wondering what I would do if I were able to start my ministry all over again. Knowing what I now know, and having had my forty plus years of experience, what text would I use as a launching pad? How about the one we came upon back in Advent? "You brood of vipers! Who warned you to flee from the wrath to come?" . . . That probably would not be the best way to begin one's ministry — or end it, either. So, don't worry: I won't be saying that to you come September.

But, seriously, what text? There are so many possibilities. If I wanted to set an evangelical tone, the choice might be the one in Acts where one of his jailers asks Paul, "What must I do to be saved?" For a pastoral emphasis, perhaps Jesus' words in Matthew: "Come to me, all you that are weary and are carrying heavy burdens, and I will give you rest." Micah 6:8 might be a good choice: ". . . What does the Lord require of you but to do justice, and to love kindness, and to walk humbly with your God." Or, maybe in these anxious, post 9/11 days the seventh verse of the fourth chapter of Philippians would be the perfect choice: ". . . The peace of God, which surpasses all understanding, will guard your hearts and minds in Christ Jesus."

Do you see what I am getting at? A different signal could be sent, a different tone established, depending on the choice of text. And there are so many possibilities.

*   *   *

Jesus did not have as many choices. There were no Gospels, of course, no Acts of the Apostles, none of the letters of Paul or Peter or John. Jesus had only what we know as the Old Testament — actually only a small portion of that. Luke tells us that when Jesus "stood up to read, . . . the scroll of the prophet Isaiah was given to him." Still, within that book alone there is an abundance of marvelous texts. Luke says: Jesus "unrolled the scroll and found the place where it was written: 'The Spirit of the Lord is upon me, because he has anointed me to bring good news to the poor. He has sent me to proclaim release to the captives and the recovery of sight to the blind, to let the oppressed go free, to proclaim the year of the Lord's favor.' Then," says Luke, Jesus began to say to them, 'Today this scripture has been fulfilled in your hearing.' "

Do you see what Jesus is doing? Do you get it? This is a kind of inaugural address. Jesus is laying out his program. He is telling his friends and neighbors where those eighteen silent years have led him: to the side of the poor, to the blind, to the captives, to the oppressed — to all the marginalized. Jesus is defining himself, sharing his understanding of his vocation, his conviction regarding his calling. He is describing the work to which he is committing the rest of his life.

Our bulletin cover calls this the second Sunday in ordinary time. Personally, I prefer the old description: the second Sunday after the Epiphany. Do you know what the word "epiphany" means? You should know. An epiphany is an uncovering of what has been hidden, a manifestation, a disclosure, a demonstration.

There are several epiphany stories in the Gospels. The one everybody knows is the one about the magi. They come searching for a king, and when, at last, they get to the manger the baby's true identity is uncovered, made manifest: He is Lord of lords and King of kings.

But there are other stories by means of which we learn who Jesus is and what he does. And this story from Luke is one of them. What it discloses is the direction Jesus' ministry will take. It gives us a taste of what is to come, a preview of coming attractions. So we are not surprised when, in the days following, Jesus begins to mingle with lepers, eat with sinners and outcasts, embrace the poor, befriend women, console the suffering, open eyes that are blind, bless children, speak approvingly of the hated Samaritans, and, at the very end, while hanging on his cross, welcome a convicted criminal into the kingdom of God. We are not surprised because, back there in the synagogue at Nazareth, Jesus sent the signal that his ministry would take him to the dispossessed, the people on the margins, those most vulnerable.

Nor are we surprised by his response when John the Baptist, in prison and uncertain about Jesus, sends to ask: "Are you the one who is to come, or are we to wait for another?" Do you recall the response Jesus sends back? "Go and tell John what you have seen and heard: the blind receive their sight, the lame walk, the lepers are cleansed, the deaf hear, the dead are raised, the poor have good news preached to them. And blessed is anyone who takes no offense at me." As if to say, didn't anybody tell you, John, about my very first sermon? Had you not heard what happened when, after you baptized me, I went back to Nazareth to begin my ministry?

*   *   *

Maybe you are wondering, so what? What does this have to do with us? The answer is short and simple: everything. It has everything to do with us. The kind of ministry Jesus undertook back there in Nazareth we are expected to carry on here and now. This is part of what it means when we say that the church is the body of Christ. Jesus is no longer physically present. But his church is. And it is our job, as it should be our joy, to embody his kind of ministry, to live out his passionate concern for the least, the left out, the lost.

Few have understood this so well as the one whose life and work we remember and honor tomorrow. Martin Luther King, Jr. will always be remembered within the context of the struggle for racial justice and, to be sure, his contributions to the cause of civil rights and equal opportunity were enormous. But King was not just a social reformer. He was first and foremost a follower of Jesus Christ, a lover of the gospel. When he "exhorted the nation to a higher standard of justice, his message gained its power precisely from its rootedness in biblical imagery and language."[1]

As one who knew him well says: "King believed and taught that the life and teaching of Jesus are not just radical but relevant and redemptive."[2] He understood the nature of the ministry Jesus articulated on his inaugural day. King knew that there are still the poor hungering for good news, there are still captives to be released, there are still the blind who cannot see, there are still the oppressed looking to be set free. There is still the work of justice, peace and mercy to be undertaken. King understood, as should we — that the ministry of Jesus is the unfinished business, the on-going work, the high and holy vocation of the church.

It is one of the great joys of my life to be part of a community of faith that has understood all this, as well. It is one of the things that has given me such encouragement, satisfaction and delight during these years we have been together. How you have opened your eyes to see the marginalized and the dispossessed of our time. How you have opened your ears to hear their cries, opened your hands and given your time so as to help, opened your pocketbooks so as to support our outreach, our worldwide ministries, our partnerships with the people and institutions of West Philadelphia, our ministries with the hungry and the homeless. And — this, too, I have witnessed — how many of you work in other ways and through other institutions to keep on with the agenda our Lord laid out back there in the synagogue of Nazareth.

Jesus took it on as his agenda because he believed it was and is God's agenda. And now we take it as our agenda because it was and continues to be his: to reach out, in his name, to the most vulnerable, and to do so as graciously and as generously as we can, and with as much intelligence and imagination as we are able to muster. It is a major part of our purpose, one of the primary reasons churches such as this exist. What a responsibility! What a privilege!

*   *   *

A friend and sometime colleague of mine in one cause or another, Eileen Lindner, tells a story with which I shall conclude. "Eileen is a life-long child advocate and speaks and lobbies and makes a lot of wonderful noise on behalf of children. She, with all of us, is dismayed when children suffer. So she was compelled by the story of the mother of one of the youngsters killed in the school shooting at Paducah, Kentucky, a few years ago. When the mother heard that there had been a shooting, she prayed, 'Please God, not my child: And if my child, please may he live.' When [the mother] arrived at the school, she learned that her child was one of the ones who had died. Medical personnel asked the terrible but necessary questions about harvesting and using the child's organs, and the anguished mother agreed."

"Months later Eileen read a follow-up story." Somehow the mother learned the identity of the person who had received her child's heart. "It turned out to be a minister whose life was saved by the heart transplant. [The mother] contacted him, and they visited and talked and wept together and prayed and talked some more. As [the mother of the donor] rose to leave, she made an unusual but understandable request. Could she please put her ear to [the recipient's] chest and hear her child's heart beating, giving life."[3]

Eileen says the story reminded her of the church, a church she continues to love, as we do, too, despite all its failures and foibles. "The church, the body of Christ, in which beats the heart of God's child, Jesus Christ. The church to which God on occasion bends down to listen for the heartbeat."[4] What joy there must be in heaven when God does bend down to listen and discovers there is indeed a place where the heartbeat of his beloved Son may still be heard. May it always be so in this place, within this community of faith.

1. Daniel Born in the *Christian Century,* January 13, 2004, p. 32.
2. James Earl Massey, *Sundays in the Tuskegee Chapel* (Nashville: Abingdon Press, 2000), p. 172.
3. Thanks to John M. Buchanan for this story from our mutual friend in his sermon, *"Godneighbor,"* Fourth Presbyterian Church, November 2, 2003.
4. Ibid.

~

A Sower Went Out

Readings: Isaiah 55:1-3a, 6-13   February 8, 2004
          I Thessalonians 1:1-8
          Luke 8:1-8, 16-21

. . . So shall my word be that goes out from my mouth; it shall not return to me empty, but it shall accomplish that which I purpose, and succeed in the thing for which I sent it.
          — Isaiah 55:11

When a great crowd gathered and people from town after town came to him, he said in a parable: "A sower went out to sow his seed. . . . "
          — Luke 8:4-5a

I don't know about you, but I am feeling really good about the way this year has begun.

I am not talking about the weather. Obviously, I am not talking about the weather! It's been too cold, and there has been altogether too much ice and snow and rain. I am not talking about the weather.

And I am not talking about the things that have been preoccupying the news media: the suicide bombings, the job losses at Kodak and Cigna, the kidnapping and murder of that eleven-year-old girl down in Sarasota, the Jacksons, Michael and Janet. I am not feeling good about any of that.

What has me feeling good is how, courtesy of Luke's Gospel, on recent Sunday mornings we have been able to be with Jesus at the beginning of his ministry. What a privilege it has been, and still is, to have Luke as our guide.

Three Sundays ago he took us to the synagogue in Nazareth, Jesus' hometown. We were there when Jesus launched his ministry. We heard his inaugural sermon, the one where he laid out his agenda: to bring good news to the poor, release to the captives, freedom to the oppressed.

Everybody said it was a wonderful sermon. That is, until they realized how Jesus meant to include the excluded. That made them angry and they proceeded to run Jesus out of town. You remember that.

Last Sunday Luke took us to the Lake of Gennesart, otherwise known as the Sea of Galilee. We watched from the shore as Peter and his companions caught so many fish that their nets were breaking. What was even more astonishing was how, when they came ashore, those fisherman — Peter, James, and John — just up and quit the fishing business and became disciples, followers of Jesus. How good it was to be there and see that. It has been such a privilege to be with Jesus in the early stages of his ministry.

*   *   *

I wish I could tell you the exact place to which we have come today. Luke is not saying. Maybe even he doesn't know. One village looks pretty much like another. And Jesus has been going rapidly from town to town. "Proclaiming and bringing the good news of the kingdom of God," and moving on. Let's see, if this is Sunday it must be — well, it's somewhere in Galilee. That's all I know.

A couple of things have happened since we were last together. One is that the inner circle around Jesus has grown to twelve. Peter, James, and John have been joined by nine others. Moreover, there are some women among Jesus' followers: Mary Magdalene, Joanna, and Susanna, to name the most prominent ones. It has caused a few eyebrows to be raised. An entourage of female followers, women without husbands, providing financial assistance to Jesus and his disciples. You can imagine how the tongues of the pious have gone to wagging about the presence of these women.[1] Jesus, however, seems unperturbed.

Wherever it is we have come to, today, we are certainly not the only ones. "A great crowd" has gathered. Everybody is hoping to get a glimpse of Jesus, hear what he has to say. . . . And there he is! He is motioning for quiet. . . . I wish the crowd were not so big. It is hard to see Jesus. Fortunately, his voice carries well. If we cannot see him, we can hear him. . . . That's Jesus now, isn't it? His voice?

"A sower went out to sow his seed; and as he sowed, some fell on the path and was trampled on, and the birds of the air ate it up. Some fell on the rock; and as it grew up, it withered for lack of moisture. Some fell among thorns, and thorns grew with it and choked it. Some fell in the good soil, and when it grew it produced a hundred fold. Let anyone with ears to hear listen!"

Is that it? It looks as if that's it, all there is going to be. . . . That's Jesus, and those are the twelve, on their way again. Off to another village. And we are left with — well, not much — just this parable.

*   *   *

Now, I confess that I have "a leg up," as they say, on the rest of you. I wasn't surprised just now when Jesus told the parable. The reason is that, a few days ago, I sat down with Luke for a private conversation. He told me that Jesus is getting in the habit of teaching by way of parables. Just telling a story and leaving it to his listeners to figure out the meaning for themselves.

Some people don't like it, Luke says. They want somebody to tell them exactly what they should think, what they should believe, what they should do. They want answers; no ambiguity; certainty. They don't want to have to think for themselves. But Jesus says they have to get involved, take some responsibility. They have to share the burden of preaching. So everywhere he goes he is telling these parables. If I could have warned you, prepared you for what Jesus was going to do today, I would have. But we haven't been together since last Sunday.

So, here we are. Jesus is gone. He has moved on. We are left with this parable. What does it mean? What do you think?

*   *   *

I'll tell you what I think. I am wondering about all those different places into which, or on which, the sower throws the seed. The seed — the seed must be the word of God. Don't you think so? I can't think what else it could be. The seed must be God's word. And the different places — the path, the rock, the thorn-infested ground, and the good soil — must represent the various ways in which people respond to God's word. Does that make sense?

As a preacher I find something appealing about such an interpretation. If my sermon doesn't go over well, doesn't lodge in your hearts and minds, I can say that the problem is not the sermon but the listeners, the congregation. So much unreceptive soil resting there in the pews! That's very comforting to the preacher. Maybe too comforting!

Yet you don't have to be a preacher to get the point of the different kinds of soil. You know, as well as I do, that some people are like a beaten-down path. God's word doesn't have a chance. They are not bad people. They are just not interested. They sit out under a starlit sky and, *unlike* the psalmist, they do not say: "When I look at your heavens, the work of your fingers, the moon and the stars that you have established, what are human beings that you are mindful of them . . ." They don't say or feel anything like that. No sense of mystery. No astonishment. No wonder. They just take it all for granted. Like a path onto which seed is thrown and the birds come along and eat it all up.

And you know people who are like rocky ground. Not much depth. I think I spotted some people like that on Christmas Eve at the eleven o'clock service. I don't know who they were. I had never seen them before, and I haven't seen them since. But that night I could hear them — all the way up here. All through the prelude: chatting about this and that. It wasn't any of you, I am glad to say. You know better. Here we were, trying to get ourselves ready to ponder the mystery of the incarnation, to give thanks for the gift of God's very own self in the baby born in Bethlehem, and these two or three people were just telling one another: "Oh, as soon as Christmas is over, we are going here, and then we are going there. We'll be seeing so and so." You remember them. No sense at all that they were on holy ground, sitting in sacred space. I thought to myself: if anything takes root and grows in that soil, it will be a miracle. There are people like that: not much depth.

And the ground overgrown with thorns? People who are so busy, whose lives are filled with so much clutter. So many things to do. So many places to go. So much stuff to accumulate. Laboring, as Isaiah says, for that which is not bread. Some people call it "the rat race." It reminds me of what Jesus said to Martha: "You are worried and distracted by many things. . . ." So many things. So many worries and distractions. And pretty soon the things of God just get the life choked right out of them.

And then there is the good soil. Let's not overlook the good soil.

This past week I got an e-mail message from a young woman in Chicago who, when she was a student at Bryn Mawr College, worshiped with us. She said: "I want you to know that I am one of those souls walking around with your words spinning in my head and in my heart." Well, you can imagine how that made me feel. "Good soil," I said to myself.

She's not alone. There are lots of people like that. People who, when they are absent from worship, I wonder if they are sick. Every time the doors are open, they are here, always in the same pew. There are people like that. Faithful people. Every week they show up to help with the Middle School Breakfast Club. Or every Tuesday or Wednesday evening they are here to help with the tutoring program. Or, year after year, they teach in the Church School, or sing in the choir. Or they may not be here. They may be out in the community, quietly making a difference there. "Good soil" people who produce a hundred fold.

I suppose Jesus could be wanting us to think about these different soils. He might be wanting us to ask ourselves which of them is most like us — you, me. Or maybe he is hinting that there could be something in us of all four kinds. I mean, on occasion we are like a hard path. Some days we are rocky ground. Other days our lives are overgrown with thorns. And sometimes . . . why, sometimes the word of God falls into our heart and lodges there and the results are just amazing. Maybe that's the point of the parable. Could that be?

*   *   *

Yet, here is another idea. I wonder if, instead of being about the soils, the point of this parable is not the sower. "A sower went out to sow his seed. . . ."

What gets my attention, and yours, too, surely, is the way the seed is sown. Very unusual. Dumb, you might even say. A farmer just throwing seed anywhere and everywhere. Not paying attention to where it lands. Not worrying about the seed that will end up being wasted. What a crazy farmer!

I wonder: Could Jesus be talking about God? Are we supposed to think that this is what God does? Throw his word around with the abandon of the sower? Just throwing it here, there, and everywhere? Is Jesus wanting us to realize that's what God does with his grace, his love, his goodness and mercy? Not worrying about whether or not any of it is going to be wasted. Just flinging it all over the place. Wouldn't it be something if God were like that?

What does Isaiah say? "For my thoughts are not your thoughts, nor are your ways my ways, says the Lord. For as the heavens are higher than the earth, so are my ways higher than your ways and my thoughts than your thoughts."

If the sower is supposed to represent God, you can say that again! God's ways are not our ways. We wouldn't do it the way the sower does it in the parable. We would be more prudent, more careful, more calculating. I mean, you know and I know there are some places where it is a waste of time and money to sow the seed. There are some people, some situations, where it will be a waste of effort. But then I remember — and maybe you do, too — how that's what some people said about Jesus. Why is he not more careful about where he sows the seed of God's word? Why is he associating with those sinners and tax-collectors? Those lepers? Those women, especially the ones with a questionable reputation? Why is Jesus wasting so much time on them?

You know, I don't think this parable is about the soils so much as it is about the sower. I think maybe it's about a God who flings the word of his love and goodness all over the place, and does so with the confidence, as Isaiah puts it, that God's word will not return to him empty, but will succeed in the thing for which God sends it. Or, as the parable says: some of the seed will find good soil, where it will grow, and produce a bumper crop. I'm thinking you could be one of those in whom the word of God does not return to God empty, but prospers in the thing for which God sends it. In you, for instance.

*   *   *

I have just this one last thought. It seems to me that this parable speaks in a particular way to the church. Especially today's church.

There are just a lot of questions about how effective the church is, these days. It's hard to see how we are having much of an impact. We do all this outreach, we support all these overseas ministries, and sometimes we wonder if we are getting anywhere at all. We wonder if what the church says and does makes any difference. Especially when the latest Gallop poll reports that now only about one third of Americans see religion increasing its influence in public life.[2] It is so easy to get discouraged.

That's why I wonder if this is not in a special way a parable for the church. I wonder if Jesus isn't saying: Get over it, and get on with it. Some of the seed you plant may not take root and grow. So what? Quit worrying about it. You are God's people? Then why don't you do what

God does? Sow the seed. Preach the gospel. Even better try to live the gospel. And trust the promise: Some of the seed you sow will find good soil and the harvest will amaze everybody — maybe you most of all.

1. John P. Meier, *A Marginal Jew*, Volume 3 (New York, London, Toronto, Sydney, Auckland: Doubleday, 2001), p. 79.
2. *Christian Century*, February 10, 2004, p. 13.

PART FOUR

Sermons on the Issues of the Day

~

The Christian Faith and Euthanasia

Readings: Genesis 1:26-31   November 7, 1993
                Romans 14:1-12

So then, each of us will be accountable to God.
                                        — Romans 14:12

Earlier this fall I said that any congregation which is serious about
Christian nurture has to be ready and willing to explore the complex and
often ambiguous issues with which people are confronted today. I am
devoting this morning's sermon time to one such matter. It involves decisions that some within this congregation have already had to make. Many
more will likely be involved with such questions in the future.

*   *   *

Let me say, at the outset, that this sermon is not intended as any kind
of final word. My purpose is not to *stop* conversation, but to get it *started*.
Whether or not you agree with me doesn't matter. That you think about
these issues from a Christian perspective does.

I should also say that my topic is more inclusive than the sermon title
might suggest. The word "euthanasia" is a combination of two Greek
words meaning "a good death." These days, the word refers to the taking
of the life of a terminally ill or dying person for reasons of compassion —
either by *doing* something to cause death, called "*active* euthanasia," or by
not doing something that might prolong life, called "*passive* euthanasia."

The topic, as I conceive of it, has many dimensions: physician assist-
ed dying — of which Dr. Kevorkian is the most prominent, if also one of
the least ethical, examples; the freedom to refuse medical treatment, or to

stop treatment once it has begun; the responsibilities of physicians, nurses, hospitals, and nursing homes; the involvement of family members; the role of the courts; and the question of how, as a society, we should allocate health care resources. In other words, I have in mind the broad range of issues concerning what is sometimes called "the right to die."

*   *   *

So far, I have been talking about these matters in an abstract and impersonal way. But these issues come to our attention because they involve real people. It's time to meet a few of them.

Dr. and Mrs. Henry Pitt VanDusen, for example. Some of you may recall hearing, some twenty years ago, about their double suicide. Dr. VanDusen was a Presbyterian minister and a former President of Union Theological Seminary in New York. At the time of their suicide, he and his wife were both elderly, both physically enfeebled, and both intellectually alert. They left a letter saying that their infirmities had become intolerable, and that their decision to end their lives was an expression of Christian stewardship, thoughtfully and prayerfully made. . . . What do you think? Is it possible for such a decision to be called "Christian"?

Another "for instance." Diane was diagnosed as having acute leukemia. After exploring her options with her physician and her family, she not only decided to refuse treatment, but asked her doctor if he would help her end her life when *she* determined the time had come to give it up. After many discussions with Diane and much personal soul-searching, the physician gave Diane a prescription for barbiturates, exacting from her a promise to consult him before taking enough of them to commit suicide. Months later, the two of them met for what was to be the final time. Of that encounter, the physician writes: ". . . It was clear that (Diane) knew what she was doing, that she was sad and frightened to be leaving, but that she would be even more terrified to stay and suffer. . . ." Two days later her husband called to say that Diane had died.[1] . . . What do you think? Should Diane's doctor be condemned or commended?

Charles Lukey was a pastor. He died a few years ago of a rare disease that, as one man describes it, involves "a galloping degeneration of the nerve cells." When the crisis came, Lukey wrote a letter to his friends. "What," he asked, "does the Christian do when he stands over the abyss of his own death and the doctors have told him that the disease is ravaging his brain and that his whole personality may be warped, twisted, changed?

Then, does the Christian have any right to self-destruction, especially when he knows that the changed personality may bring out some horrible beast within himself?" Answering his own question, Lukey said: ". . . it comes to me that, ultimately and finally, the Christian has always to view life as a gift from God, and see that every precious drop of life was not earned but was a grace, lovingly bestowed on him by his Creator, and it is not his to pick up and smash.

"And so," Lukey went on, "I find the position of suicide untenable, not because I lack the courage to blow out my brains, but rather because of my deep abiding faith in the Creator who put the brains there in the first place. And now the result is that I lie here blind in my bed and trust in the loving, sustaining power of the great Creator who knew and loved me before I was fashioned in my mother's womb. But I do not think it is wrong to pray for an early release from this diseased and ravaged carcass."[2]

That is a courageous and profound statement of faith! . . . What do you think? Could someone else have made a different choice and been equally faithful in doing so? Or did Lukey make the only possible *Christian* decision?

A final example. Elizabeth is twenty-eight and suffering from severe cerebral palsy. She is a quadriplegic, and wholly unable to care for herself. She also suffers from degenerative arthritis and is in continuous pain. She wants to die. The guess is that by force-feeding her, Elizabeth could live another fifteen or twenty years. Right-to-life advocates believe she has a duty to live. Elizabeth has gone to court to secure permission to forego medical treatment or life support through mechanical means.[3] . . . What do you think? Does Elizabeth have the right to say when her life no longer has quality or meaning? Or, is she obligated to wait until her body revolts against the medical technologies that are keeping her alive?

*   *   *

Time was when questions such as these had neither to be asked nor answered. Life and death decisions were made *for* us, not by us. The tragedy was that many people died before their time, prematurely.

Today, the situation is different. Children and young people still die before their time, as some in this congregation know only too well. But now there are many older people who feel they have lived *beyond* their time. Medical technology is able to prolong life and cure disease, but it can also keep "alive" those who are severely brain-damaged, or the comatose, or those, like Elizabeth, who no longer want to live.

The result is that today, what people fear, sometimes, is not the approach of death, but its postponement — they fear that their dying will be prolonged beyond what is reasonable, or that their lives will be extended when their dignity and purpose have long since disappeared. It's because of this new situation that we are facing the issue of euthanasia and the related questions I mentioned earlier.

*   *   *

The question is how, given this new situation, we can make wise, compassionate, faithful moral choices. As Christians, what should we keep in mind as we encounter these new and difficult dilemmas? As I have thought about it, there are some things I come to see as important.

First, we need to remember the Biblical warning about human frailty and human sinfulness. We are limited in wisdom. We are imperfect people, with mixed motives and hidden agendas. So, as regards these life and death decisions, caution is called for, not recklessness. Ethicists are right to worry about "the slippery slope" — a way of saying that once we start down a certain path, something like gravity will pull us further along. Applied to euthanasia, the worry is that once we allow physicians, or others, to end the lives of people like Diane or Elizabeth, it won't stop there, and before long we will be intervening to end the lives of the senile, say, or of handicapped newborns, or the lives of those whose care is judged to be too expensive.

This cautionary note is important, but for me, at least, it doesn't end the discussion, or relieve us from the responsibility and burden of deciding in individual instances. So what other guidance is there?

There is, of course, the Biblical admonition to "choose life," along with the commandment *not* to kill. But, at the time when Moses urged his people to "choose life," the definition of life was simple: If you were breathing, you were alive. That simple definition has long been obsolete. Is someone alive who is breathing only because he or she is hooked up to a machine? Again, is the command not to kill absolute? What about killing in self-defense? What about war? What about capital punishment? In these cases, many Christians make exceptions to the rule. Is euthanasia another possible exception? These Biblical injunctions are important, but they don't end the discussion either, they don't relieve us from the burden of decision-making.

So where are we? With regard to these life and death dilemmas, where we are, and where we will always be, I think, is somewhere between two poles, of a theological kind: one we might call "finitude" and the other, "freedom."

At the one end, near the pole labeled, "finitude," the emphasis is on acceptance, on playing the hand that life deals you, not complaining about the quality of the cards, but playing them to the best of your ability — in other words, accepting whatever comes, be it good or bad, joyful or sad, and seeking in and through your acceptance to honor God. Of the people we met earlier, Charles Lukey heroically represents this response.

At the other end of the spectrum, near the pole labeled "freedom," the emphasis is on taking responsibility. This passage read earlier, from Genesis, seems to encourage this response. For, there it is said that human beings are created in God's image and are given "dominion." When, in other words, we take responsibility for our lives, we are not usurping a divine prerogative, but only assuming our God-given power and responsibility. The VanDusens are representatives of this response.

Somewhere along this spectrum, between finitude and freedom, between acceptance and responsibility, Christians will take their place as they are confronted by these life and death decisions. Rarely will we confront a clear moral choice. Most of the time the choice will be ambiguous. And my contention is that there may well be more than one acceptable decision from a Christian perspective. As a Christian community we should, of course, support a Charles Lukey when he chooses to live out his life, come what may. But, should we not also respond compassionately to a Diane or an Elizabeth, not condemning, but valuing a different kind of courage and faithfulness?

Which is where the lesson read earlier, from Romans, comes into the picture. The issue Paul was dealing with seems trivial when compared with the questions we are thinking about. But his warning against making one's own decisions normative for everybody else, applies nonetheless. Each of us, says Paul, is accountable to God. But even though we all are equally serious about our accountability, we may not all arrive at the same decision. And Paul pleads with us to refrain from easy judgments about the difficult decisions others make.

One final thought: I am persuaded that this new situation in which we find ourselves should cause us to re-examine our understandings of both life and death.

Those who oppose "the right to die," for example, are often heard to speak of the "sacredness" of life. Life is a precious gift, to be received with gratitude and treated with utmost respect. But, while life is precious, for people of faith it is not the only thing of value in this world. Something more important can cause us to put our lives on the line. It is the clear teaching of the New Testament that something more important caused Jesus to put his life on the line: namely, the kingdom of God and obedience to his heavenly Father. "No one takes my life from me," Jesus said, "but I lay it down of my own accord." The question is, may people like the VanDusens, or Diane, or Elizabeth also lay down their lives if and when they decide that their lives have become unbearably painful and without meaning? My own answer is Yes, that *can* be a faithful decision. And as a pastor, I have supported people in making such a decision.

We also need to think anew about death — about how to define or recognize it. A hospital chaplain by the name of Gerald Oosterveen writes: "It is time for the Christian community to see death in a broader context than mere biological or brain death. . . . A human being is more than the total of his or her functions, more than heartbeat and breathing and brain flow combined. Life is relationships with God and human beings." He goes on: "As the evidence mounts that a loved one will never again have a meaningful relationship with another human being on earth, is that person not dead? . . . Have we, as committed Christians, the right to bring to the bedside every possible machine, drug or procedure that cannot change the ultimate outcome but only prolongs the dying process?" If, "Oosterveen concludes, "we truly believe that 'this world is not our home, that we are only passing through,' how can we justify delaying the going-home of a dying person? Do we," he asks, "love our loved ones enough to let go? And do we trust God enough to let our loved ones enter into God's presence?"[4] I would add: As Christians, should not our perspective on these matters be different from those who hold onto life because they have nothing else to hold onto?

*   *   *

We are faced today with choices our grandparents did not have to make. It's obvious that I cannot offer you a few easy solutions on how to deal with these questions, something to laminate in plastic and carry in your wallet. As regards those two poles I talked about earlier, I myself gravitate — not without fear and trembling — to the responsibility side. But you will have to determine your own position. What I want to do, above all, this morning, is remind you that you are not alone as you make these life and death decisions. Whether you are deciding for yourself or another, whether you are patient or physician, family member or friend, attorney or pastor, God is with you in your struggle. Be confident of that. Do the best you can. And know that God's grace and mercy surround you.

1. Timothy E. Quill, M.D., *Death and Dignity — A Case of Individualized Decision Making,* The New England Journal of Medicine, March 7, 1991, pp. 691-694.
2. James W. Crawford, *Worthy to Raise Issues* (Cleveland, Ohio: The Pilgrim Press, 1991), p. 41.
3. Howard Moody, *Life Sentence*, Christianity and Crisis, October 12, 1987.
4. Gerald Oosterveen, *Decisions at Life's End,* Presbyterian Survey, November 1993, p. 19.

~

One House With Many Rooms

Readings: Jonah 3:10-4:11   May 8, 1994
          John 14:1-12

In my Father's house there are many dwelling places. . . .
— John 14:2a

Some years ago, I remember seeing a so-called "Christian" bumper sticker showing a single index finder held aloft, accompanied by the words, "one way." The implied message was: there is only one way to God — the Christian way, perhaps even a particular version of the Christian way — and all other approaches are dead ends.

There is an opposite attitude which I have never seen expressed on a bumper sticker, but which I have heard in casual conversations many times. It's a religious version of "all roads lead to Rome." This point of view suggests that while all religions are not alike, they all serve a similar purpose, and who are we to judge which is better than the others?

These extreme points of view serve to bring into focus the topic I invite you to think about this morning: How are we, as Christians, to relate to people whose experience of the holy is different from our own? As those who believe in Jesus as Lord and Savior, what are we to think of those who are deeply religious, but not Christian?

I am well aware that a sermon dealing with such questions may fall into the category of "fools rush in where angels fear to tread." But the time has come when these matters must be addressed. My experience as your pastor has taught me that you have the intellectual, emotional, and spiritual maturity to deal with difficult questions. I dare to hope that your experience with me has given you some confidence that I don't address such matters without careful thought and prayerful preparation.

* * *

Let me begin with a word as to why the Christian attitude toward people of other faiths has become an unavoidable issue.

Primarily because of a revolution in communication, the world has shrunk to a "global village." Where once it took months to travel to distant places, and few ever did so, today no place is more than a day or two away by airplane, and many of us think nothing of making the trip. Where it used to take a long time for news to reach us of an earthquake in Asia or a war in Africa, it now takes only minutes. We see and hear about people our grandparents may not have known even existed. We have come to realize that the world is diverse in many ways, including religious belief, and we sense that Christians have no corner on decency, integrity, or piety.

Meanwhile, it's becoming increasingly obvious that there is a religious dimension to the conflicts we read and hear about daily. In places like Northern Ireland, the former Yugoslavia, the Sudan, the Middle East, and India, religious intolerance is part of the problem, and religious understanding will surely have to be part of any solution.

Here in the United States, religious diversity is increasing rapidly, mostly because of immigrants from Asia, the Pacific and the Middle East. There are Hindu and Buddhist temples, Muslim mosques, and Jewish synagogues, of course, in virtually every American city. There are already more Muslims in the United States than Episcopalians. And there are many smaller religious groups: Sikhs, Jains, Zoroastrians, and others. Many Christians now have personal encounters with people of other faiths: in the work place, at school, and in neighborhoods. More and more, that will be the case: we will be interacting with people whose traditions, experiences, and world-views are different from our own.

In recent years the major challenge confronting Christianity has been secularism: a view of life that discounts the reality of God and pushes religion to the margins. In the years to come, the challenge may be entirely different: not secularism, but religious diversity. What will be our response as Christians? How will we relate to whose faith is different from our own?

* * *

In an earlier sermon, I made reference to a book by Diana Eck entitled, *Encountering God*. Today I wish to recommend it as a profound and sensitive treatment of the questions before us. Eck says that, as Christians, we have three alternatives in dealing with people of other faiths. One is "the exclusivist response" which she describes this way: "Our own community, our tradition, our understanding of reality, our encounter with God, is the one and only truth, excluding all others." The "one way" bumper sticker represents this approach.

A second possibility, says Eck, is "the inclusivist response," an attitude that says: "There are, indeed, many communities, traditions and truths, but our own way of seeing things is the culmination of the others, superior to the others, or at least wide enough to include the others under our own universal canopy and on our own terms." The late Roman Catholic theologian Karl Rahner represented this approach when he referred to good people of other faiths as "anonymous Christians."

Eck commends yet a third approach, "the pluralist," which she describes this way: "Truth is not the . . . possession of any one tradition or community. Therefore the diversity of communities, traditions, understandings of the truth, and visions of God is not an obstacle for us to overcome, but an opportunity for our energetic engagement in dialogue with one another. It does not mean giving up our own commitments; rather, it means opening up those commitments to the give-and-take of mutual discovery, understanding, and, indeed, transformation."[1] The conversations we have had in recent years with area Jewish synagogues are modest examples of this third approach.

I join Professor Eck in commending this "pluralist" approach: Not because it is the easiest; it may well be the most difficult. I commend it because I believe it is what a mature Christian faith demands. While I have no intention of trying, verbally, to bludgeon you into going along with my view, I do want you to realize that mine is not an arbitrary attitude, but one which takes *Christian* beliefs seriously. So, let me say a word now about each of three important aspects of our faith as they relate to the question before us: the Bible, Jesus, and the Holy Spirit.

*   *   *

Within the *Bible*, a tension exists between exclusivism and universality. You can find passages that picture God as a tribal deity, interested in only one nation, or one group. But you can also find passages that speak of God as the Lord of all, and as caring about all. Honesty bids us to acknowledge that tension, while noticing that the movement is in the direction away from exclusivism and toward universality.

Within the Old Testament, the Book of Jonah is a prime example. The story was written to counter the notion that God loves the Jews and nobody else. Jonah, a Jew, was sent to preach to the people of Nineveh — a foreign city, full of Gentile unbelievers. The assignment was so distasteful to Jonah that he sought to escape it by fleeing from God — which he discovered it was impossible to do. Reluctantly he went to Nineveh and a marvelous thing happened. The people listened and repented, and God had mercy on them. Jonah was outraged. Whereupon God came to him and said, in effect: "Jonah, can't you understand that I care about all my children, not just the people of Israel? And if I care for them, can't you care for them, too?"

The tension between exclusivism and universality is present in the New Testament, too, even, in some cases, within a single book. So, in John's Gospel we hear Jesus saying, "No one comes to the Father except through me." But he is also reported to have said: "I have other sheep that do not belong to this fold." In the Book of Acts, Peter says of Jesus: "There is salvation in no one else." But later on in Acts, the Holy Spirit is said to have instructed Peter differently, so that he declares: "I truly understand that God shows no partiality, but in every nation anyone who fears God and does what is right is acceptable to God."

In the Bible there is a tension between exclusivism and universality, and if we want to, we can throw proof texts back and forth to attack another's view or defend our own. Perhaps this is a good time to remind ourselves that the Bible contains many images of God, that they are not of equal value and importance, and that, in the end, as Eck says, we are all responsible "for the image of God that we are content to believe in."[2] I choose to believe in the universal God whose love extends to all, not the tribal deity whose concern is limited to a few.

*   *   *

But what about *Jesus*? What did he think about those of a different faith? Maybe, as one scholar says, "He didn't think about the question at all."[3] He was preoccupied with what he knew of God's truth, and concerned to reveal it to all who would hear and see. We don't have any direct teaching from Jesus on the matter before us.

We do have the example of Jesus to think about. As Eck puts it: "He kept company with everyone in the world of his day. He freely and boldly crossed the barriers that might separate one ethnic group from another — Samaritans, Jews, Romans. In fact, many who are exemplars of faith and recipients of loving mercy in the Gospel narratives are those we might call 'people of other faiths': the Roman Centurion, the Syro-phoenician woman, the Greek Cornelius, the Good Samaritan." It appears, says Eck, that "Jesus did not see 'Christianity' and 'Judaism,' or the other 'isms' we use to categorize people of faith today. He saw faith."[4]

Yet, Jesus did make judgments about the quality of the faith he encountered. He argued with the Pharisees, censured the rulers of the temple, and sometimes lamented the puny faith of his own followers. The key to his approach seems to have been, "By their fruits you shall know them." Says theologian Harvey Cox: Jesus "seemed singularly uninterested in the doctrinal content or ritual correctness of the different religions he encountered. He was, however, terribly concerned about the practical outcome of people's spiritual commitments. He once told a pagan Roman he had not found such a faith as his anywhere in Israel."[5]

From Jesus we learn to look for disclosures of God where we don't expect them, including in people we are all too ready to dismiss as unworthy — the poor, beggars, prisoners, strangers! If we are to find God in them, why not also in the devout Hindu, Jew, native American, or Muslim?

The disclosure of God's love in Christ is precious to me. I have said before and say again that, were it not for "Jesus Christ and him crucified," I would find it hard, sometimes, to believe in God at all. I rejoice in the grace and truth disclosed in Christ and want to share this revelation with others. But I do not wish to limit God's disclosure to Christ, to say that there are not other ways by which God is revealed, or arrogantly to assume that those who don't believe as I do are consigned to outer darkness. I can't do it. Indeed, it is because of what Christ reveals of God's extravagant love, that I am bold to believe there is *not* just "one way."

As for the *Holy Spirit*, was it not Jesus who taught that, like the wind, the Spirit "blows where it chooses"? In the Gospels there is Jesus' puzzling reference to blasphemy against the Holy Spirit as the "unforgivable sin." Over the years, many have worried that there is some mysterious thing a Christian could say or do that might turn out to be unforgivable, though nobody has ever quite been sure what it is. But what if this particular sin is not some word or deed, but an attitude — an attitude that rejects the sovereignty of the Spirit? What if the "unforgivable sin" is a refusal to trust that the Holy Spirit is at work not only in Christians, but in the life and traditions of other people and other faiths? This is *not* to say that all religions are the same, or that one is as good as another. It *is* to say that the Holy Spirit is not confined to the places we know and the people we love. Ultimately, we have to choose to believe in a Holy Spirit who is exclusive or inclusive. The Bible, Christ, and my own experience lead me to say, "I believe in a Holy Spirit who is at work in many places and in all kinds of people."

*   *   *

I am late in coming to my text: "In my Father's house there are many dwelling places." We usually associate these words with funerals and the promise of life beyond life. But perhaps they also have something to say regarding the questions we have been thinking about. Is it possible that, with regard to the human experience of God, there is one house with many rooms?

The Greek word for house is "oikos" from which comes "oikoumene," and the English "ecumenical." It's worth remembering that there was a time, not so long ago, when different branches of the Christian tradition viewed one another as heretics and outcasts. In this century, we have begun to learn that people of different Christian traditions belong to one and the same household. Is it not time now to expand the concept of ecumenicism even more, to confess, not begrudgingly but joyfully, that what we know and experience of God is far from exhausting the reality of God? And would it not be a great and good thing if we dedicated the twenty-first century to interfaith dialogue — the kind of dialogue where we both say what is important to us and listen to hear what is important to others? As Christians, we have something wonderful to share. But may we not also have something to learn?

The questions I have asked you to think about today are complex, and I have only scratched the surface in dealing with them. As I have had occasion to say before, so I tell you now: This sermon is not intended to end the discussion, but only to get it started. I hope you will join in.

1. Diana Eck, *Encountering God* (Boston: Beacon Press, 1993), p. 168.

2. Ibid., p. 48.

3. Gerald S. Sloyan, *Interpretation: John* (Atlanta: John Knox Press, 1988)

4. Eck, p. 93.

5. Harvey Cox, *Many Mansions* (Boston: Beacon Press, 1988), p. 14.

~

The Wreckers and the Reconcilers

Readings: Acts 21:37-22:16   November 12, 1995
Luke 9:46-56

**When his disciples James and John saw it, they said, "Lord,
do you want us to command fire to come down from heaven
and consume them?" But he turned and rebuked them.**
                                              — Luke 9:54-55

As Luke, the author of the Book of Acts, tells it, Paul was visiting
Jerusalem on his way to Rome. In a meeting with church leaders, the
apostle was informed of a rumor concerning him which was making the
rounds. Paul was said to be encouraging Jewish Christians to disregard the
Mosaic law and to let certain religious customs go unobserved. In an
effort to prove the rumor false, Paul agreed to participate in the Jewish rite
of purification and, subsequently, to attend a temple service. While he was
in the temple, his enemies caught sight of him and began loudly to accuse
him of "teaching everyone everywhere against our people, our law, and
this place." Soon, a mob psychology took over, and had it not been for the
intervention of the Roman authorities, Paul might have been murdered.
After order had been restored, the apostle asked for permission to speak.
Luke reports: ". . . When there was a great hush, he addressed them. . . ."
It constituted a moment of reflective civility, following an ugly incident of
violence.

This story came to mind in the wake of the assassination of Yitzhak
Rabin. One effect of his murder has been to make a good portion of the
world stop and think. Unfortunately, in the case of Mr. Rabin, the period
of reflection has come too late to save his life. But, perhaps it can be a sav-

ing moment for the rest of us if we use the time to ask not only how, but *why* the assassination happened, and what we might learn from it. Moreover, because a kind of religious fanaticism seems to have influenced the assassin and those who supported him, directly or indirectly, and because there is evidence of a kind of religious zealotry in our own society today, we also need to think about the proper expression of religious convictions. It is my hope that this sermon will contribute, in a small way, to your reflection on these matters.

*   *   *

Perhaps the place to begin is with the reminder that peacemaking is hard, costly work — especially in places where the divisions run deep, the hostilities have a long history, and the level of suspicion is high. It is easy to talk of peace, to dream of a world of peace, but doing what is necessary to make peace possible is difficult and dangerous. One needs only to recall names such as Gandhi, Hammarkjöld, Sadat, and Martin Luther King, to realize that while peacemakers may be "blessed" in the eyes of God, they are often maligned as "traitors" and trouble-makers by their fellow human beings. If not maligned, peacemakers are often ignored, or given pitiful support by the rest of us.

The Bible informs us time and again that the main resistance to peace-making comes from — guess where? The human heart, with its desires, its difficulty in forgiving, its determination to have its way. "Those conflicts and disputes among you, where do they come from?" asks the apostle James, and he replies: "Do they not come from your cravings that are at war within you? You want something and you do not have it; so you commit murder. And you covet something and cannot obtain it; so you engage in disputes and conflicts." James was merely echoing Jesus who said, ". . . it is from within, from the human heart, that evil intentions come. . . ." Why is it so difficult to effect reconciliation, resolve differences, make peace? Because human selfishness and pettiness are involved.

Whether in the Middle East, or Bosnia, or Northern Ireland, or as regards the racial tensions and religious differences in our own country and communities, the wreckers have an easier time of it. They have human frailties and human fears on their side. It takes courage to be a reconciler, to take risks for peace, to overcome ancient hatreds, to recognize that "new occasions teach new duties." It was Mr. Rabin's willingness to do these things, amidst great opposition, that makes his death so tragic. Surely King Hussein drew the correct conclusion when, at Mr. Rabin's funeral, he said it was time now for all people of good will to speak out, loud and clear, in support of the reconcilers, on behalf of every effort to make peace.

* * *

A second thought: the assassination of Mr. Rabin is yet another reminder of the power of "poisonous rhetoric." For months, he had been assailed, by opponents of the peace process, as a "traitor" and a "murderer." Some right-wing rabbis allowed as how religious law would not look unfavorably upon his execution because he had given away Israeli soil. While one cannot prove a direct link between violent rhetoric and violent acts, it is the height of credulity to believe that there is no connection. The connection certainly occurred to Jesus, which is why, in the Sermon on the Mount, he equates insulting another human being with murder, and elsewhere warns that, "on the day of judgment, you will have to give an account for every careless word you utter."

I have mentioned, on other occasions, my worry about the decline of civility in our own society — not just among the likes of Rush Limbaugh or Howard Stern, but among public officials and candidates for high office, among protesters or advocates of one policy or another, among spectators at sporting events, and even among children and adolescents on school playgrounds and in classrooms.

In a recent *Inquirer* column, the writer Chaim Potok struck what seems to me to be exactly the right note. He wrote: "This is a time when one must be especially careful about the power of language — that mysterious and otherwise blessed invisible bridge that binds us. It would help us a good deal now if we worried about the law of unintended consequences and considered words as sticks of dynamite, as nitroglycerine." He concluded by warning: "A constant quantity of raging words turns, after a time, into the cruel quality of a speeding bullet, (or) a ghastly explosive."

The most recent tragedy could turn out to be redemptive if it causes us, first to recognize, and then, to remove abusive, disrespectful language from our vocabularies, and to commit ourselves to civility in both public and private discourse.

* * *

Which brings me to the issue of fanaticism, especially of the religious variety. Yigal Amir, Mr. Rabin's assassin, has said that he acted on "God's orders." Moreover, the primary opposition to the peace process from both Jewish and Palestinian extremists has been motivated, to no small degree, by religious zealotry. In our own society there is a kind of excessive religious zeal which is ready to trample on the rights, the feelings, and the convictions of others in order to impose its understanding of God's will on the entire society. Religious convictions have been used to justify acts of violence at Planned Parenthood offices and the murders of physicians who performed abortions. Sad to say, even within the Presbyterian Church, there are those who are hard at work to root out, or destroy the reputations of those who do not share their views.

We need to understand what we are dealing with. As David H. C. Read once put it: "Because religion is the strongest kind of motivating power in human beings, it can either lead to the most sublime achievements of the human spirit, or, when twisted, lead to the most vicious kind of fanaticism." There are many examples of the latter within the Bible and throughout human history.

In the Second Book of Kings we are told of Jehu who said, "Come with me, and see my zeal for the Lord," and who then proceeded to one bloody massacre after another. In the speech of Paul, heard earlier, the apostle confessed that his misguided zeal for God had once prompted him to persecute the church and send both men and women to prison and to their deaths. It was a sign of the genuineness of his "conversion," that, later, he could write the chapter in I Corinthians that begins, "If I speak in the tongues of angels, but do not have love I am a noisy gong or clanging cymbal." As for historical examples of religious fanaticism, how many wars have been fought in order to establish the authority of one form of religion or another, including that of Christianity?

We may be concerned about the zealotry of the religious right in Israel, or the fanaticism of Islamic fundamentalists, but our ability to influence either is not great. We might better address the excessive religious zeal in our own society, most of which goes by the name "Christian."

No one has ever cared more for the purposes of God; no one has ever been more devoted to the will of God, than Jesus. But the spirit of fanaticism was not in him. When his disciples tried to stop another from "casting out demons" because he was not one of them, Jesus said: "Do not stop him; for whoever is not against you is for you." When those disciples wanted to incinerate some Samaritans who refused to offer hospitality, Jesus rebuked them. When the Rich Young Ruler chose not to follow him, Jesus did not consign him to the lower reaches of hell. Rather, we are told, Jesus "looked on him and loved him." Jesus came among us, not as a crusading zealot trampling down the opposition, but as a servant who knelt to wash the feet of those who ended up denying and deserting him. It is true that Christ summons his followers to a costly commitment, but nothing we know about him suggests that he would approve evangelism by coercion or favor the use of political power to achieve spiritual ends or accomplish a moral agenda.

So how do we respond to religious zealotry? Not by descending to the same level, or by using similar tactics, but by showing another way, trusting that, in the end, graciousness, generosity, humility, and compassion will carry the day. This is not to suggest that we should be indifferent or complacent. For, in the current struggles, the future of faith and the character of the church are both at stake. Far more important than any particular issue now in contention is the question of whether the center can hold, or whether extremism of the right or left will prevail. A victory for zealotry in the short run will be counter-productive in he long run and likely produce a reaction, which may be as extreme in the opposite direction.

So, those of us who represent the center cannot but resist the zealots. But only in a way that reflects the mind and manner of the One we claim to follow. We can counter a humorless faith with one able to laugh at itself. We can meet arrogance with humility. We can oppose intolerance with compassion. We can resist a grim and gloomy zealotry with a joyful, confident faith. We can follow the advice of one who said, "Never let your zeal outrun your charity."

*   *   *

The best thing we can do is be the church. I mean: Be a community where all are welcome and none is neglected. Be a community where complex and contentious issues can be discussed and debated with care and sensitivity. Be a community where people with differing experiences and views can meet each other, respect each other, and learn from one another. Be a community of Christian conviction that is open to the insights and perspectives of other faiths. Be a community which, in the name of Jesus, cares for the destitute and the disadvantaged. Be a community which never lapses into despair, no matter how sick or sinful the world appears, but remains confident that change is possible and maintains hope in the ultimate triumph of God's will. Be a community which remembers that God has "given us the ministry of reconciliation" and which never forgets the saving power of a minority dedicated to the hard and costly work of peacemaking. Be a community, in other words, which understands that it will serve the purposes of God best, and help our weary world most, by refusing to join with the wreckers, and remaining solidly among the reconcilers.

1. *The Philadelphia Inquirer*, November 8, 1995.
2. In a sermon entitled, *"Enthusiasm — Not Fanaticism,"* and preached at the Madison Avenue Presbyterian Church on March 19, 1989.
3. Hosa Ballou, in Carroll & Simcox, *A Treasury of Quotations on Christian Themes* (New York: The Seabury Press, 1975), p. 220.

~

The Issue That Won't Go Away

Readings: Galatians 3:23-4:7   June 9, 1996
Mark 10:28-34

**As many of you as were baptized into Christ have clothed
yourselves with Christ. There is no longer Jew or Greek, there
is no longer slave or free, there is no longer male and female;
for all of you are one in Christ Jesus.**
— Galatians 3:27-28

Let me begin by ending the suspense that may have been created by
my sermon title. "The issue that won't go away" concerns the place of gay
and lesbian persons in the church, and particularly their eligibility to serve
as deacons, elders, and ministers. It's something all denominations are
having to confront, and about which there is considerable discord.

Presbyterians have been struggling with the issue since 1976 when the
General Assembly of the United Presbyterian Church appointed a task
force to study "Christian approaches to homosexuality." In 1978, after
receiving the report of its task force, the General Assembly rejected one
of the key recommendations and, in what came to be called "definitive
guidance," declared the ordination of "unrepentant" homosexuals to be
inappropriate. At the same time, congregations were urged to welcome
homosexual persons of faith into membership, and what was termed the
"sin" of homophobia was condemned — the treatment of gay and lesbian
persons with "contempt, hatred and fear." Despite obvious inconsistencies
in these pronouncements, subsequent General Assemblies reaffirmed
them. But neither the issue, nor the differences over it, have gone away.
As a result, in 1993, the General Assembly asked Presbyterians to devote

three years to study and dialogue. Here, at Bryn Mawr, a number of forums were provided for that purpose, and many of you participated in one or more of them.

Today's sermon is prompted by the approach of another General Assembly where the issue will once again be joined. I believe it is important that we consider, not only the questions involved, but the best way for the church to respond to them. It may be, as another has suggested, that the *way* the church deals with the issue will, in the long run, be as important as *what* is decided.

I am aware, of course, that you are not all of one mind regarding "Christian approaches to homosexuality." I know that some of you are not where I am as regards this issue. I wasn't always where I am today! I ask you to hear me out. If, having done so, you have questions or concerns, be sure that now, as always, I am ready and willing to listen to you, and to engage in constructive conversation.

*   *   *

Whenever the issue of homosexuality is raised in the church, one of the first questions is: What does the Bible say? There is a related question that should be asked, but isn't always: What is the Bible's authority with regard to these matters?

To the first question, What does the Bible say?, the answer is: not much. Homosexuality is just not a great concern of the Scriptures.

In the Old Testament there is the story of Sodom and Gomorrah. But a careful reading of that story reveals it to be an indictment, not of homosexuality, but of inhospitality. Wherever, in the rest of the Bible, there is a reference to the destruction of Sodom, it is in that vein. Ezekiel, for example, declares: "This was the guilt of your sister Sodom: She . . . had pride, surfeit of food and prosperous ease, but did not aid the poor and needy."

In the Book of Leviticus we are given a law prohibiting homosexual behavior on the part of males. Such behavior is labeled "an abomination." But those who use this text as an excuse for rejecting homosexuals fail to point out all the other things which the Levitical Code condemns which do not concern us at all. Eating pork, cross-breeding cattle, sowing two kinds of seed in the same field, wearing clothing made of two kinds of material, and the like. These and similar prohibitions, which seem silly to us, appear in the Levitical Code for one reason. At the time, the Hebrew people were a tiny minority surrounded on all sides by pagan culture.

They were concerned to preserve their identity as a peculiar people of faith. So, many things commonplace in non-Hebrew societies, including homosexual behavior, were prohibited. The question that has to be asked, is this: On what basis do Christians today ignore all these prohibitions except one — that concerning homosexuality? A selective literalism seems to be at work.

As for the New Testament, Jesus is not reported to have said anything about the subject. He said a great deal, as you know, about various sins and temptations. He spoke about the dangers of wealth, about a censorious spirit, about adultery, divorce, pride, hypocrisy. If homosexuality were as great an evil as some suggest, one would think Jesus might have mentioned it. But there is no evidence that he did.

Paul does speak to the issue, here and there, but again, it is not something that preoccupies him. While there is a reference in his letter to the Romans to female homosexuality — the only such reference in the Bible — a number of New Testament scholars have concluded that Paul was primarily concerned about a very specific form of behavior, namely, the solicitation and use of young boys as passive partners in male homosexual activity. Such exploitation of young boys was not uncommon in Paul's day, just as in our society it's not uncommon for teenage runaways who are female to be preyed upon and turned into prostitutes.

To summarize, the Bible has very little to say about homosexuality, and what it does say, isn't very helpful. It doesn't address the question of ordination at all. The Bible is concerned with homosexual *behavior*. It says nothing about homosexual *orientation* — for the simple reason that when the Bible was written nothing was known about that. It was assumed that everybody was naturally heterosexual. Now we know that matters are more complicated. Some people — estimates range from three to five percent of the population — are of a homosexual orientation. Why this is so is not clear. It may have something to do with genetics. Environmental factors may play a role. Whatever the cause, most authorities agree that there is no way to change it.

In addition to assuming that homosexuality was "unnatural," Paul also assumed that all homosexual *behavior* was exploitive. He seems not to have considered the possibility of caring and faithful adult homosexual relationships. All of which leads one highly regarded New Testament scholar to say: "Biblical judgments against homosexuality are not relevant to today's debate . . . not because the Bible is not authoritative, but simply because it does not address the issues involved."

*   *   *

Which is not to suggest that we are bereft of Biblical guidance. Many passages which have no direct bearing on the topic have much to tell us regarding how we might deal with the issue and the *people* related to it. If we had nothing else, we have the teaching and example of Jesus Christ, regarding which Bill Coffin has written: "The problem is not how to reconcile homosexuality with Scriptural passages that condemn it, but rather how to reconcile the rejection and punishment of homosexuals with the love of Christ. It can't be done." I agree.

It is important to remember that we are dealing, not just with an *issue* — homosexuality — but with human beings who happen, among other things, to be homosexual. They are persons, first and foremost. And within the community of faith, they are Christian persons. The ones I know trust Jesus Christ as Lord and Savior. They love his church as much as the rest of us. They are as morally sensitive as anybody else. Do they need forgiveness? Of course. Who doesn't? But what they don't need forgiveness for is who they are. What they need, as all of us do, is understanding and compassion — and a little help in their struggle for justice. For, homosexual people continue to experience hostility and discrimination. Some have been frozen out of their families. Many live in fear. All have experienced rejection.

The basic issue is how we treat our fellow human beings, about which the Bible has a lot to say. As we heard earlier, the second of the two great commandments is, "You shall love your neighbor as yourself." Like it or not, for those of us who are "straight," gay and lesbian people are our neighbors.

As for Paul, I submit that what he has to say in Galatians has far more bearing on the issues before us than the few specific, but obscure references he makes to homosexual behavior. The purpose of Paul's letter to the Galatians is to say that it is our faith in Christ that makes us Christians. ". . . In Christ Jesus you are all children of God through faith. As many of you as were baptized into Christ have clothed yourselves with Christ." Then, thinking of some of the major divisions of his day, Paul goes on, "There is no longer Jew or Greek, there is no longer slave or free, there is no longer male and female; for all of you are one in Christ Jesus." I can't be sure, of course, but my hunch is that, today, the apostle would add "heterosexual" and "homosexual" to his list of examples.

Paul does not pretend that distinctions among people do not exist. We could name a hundred things that make people different from one another: their color, their health, their wealth, their politics, their nationality, their age, their marital status — and their sexual orientation. Paul's argument is: whatever the differences among people, within the church they should not matter. "All of you are one in Christ Jesus." You are all God's children and you are all in need of God's saving grace.

I long for the time when our denomination will catch up to Paul's understanding of the church, as much as I long for the time when it will grow beyond Paul's understanding of homosexuality. I yearn for the day when people will not have to say what the novelist Reynolds Price has said: "The only thing that makes me rejecting of most forms of institutional Christianity is that they spend so much time condemning and excluding, whereas if you look at the gospels, you see that Jesus is entirely accepting of anyone who wants to come to him. . . ."[3]

With regard to ordination, I believe that the day will come when, in deciding who should be ordained, we won't ask about a candidate's sexual orientation anymore than we do about his or her wealth, or occupation, or color, or age. Someday we will reach the point where we are concerned only with the person's faith, character, commitment, and call from God. But, as I will suggest in a moment, that day is not yet.

Lest there be any doubt, let me say that, certainly, concerns about sexual *behavior* are important and relate to the question of character. Of course Paul is right in denouncing the exploitation of children. Of course pornography and promiscuity are concerns. But — and hear me now — these are as much heterosexual, as homosexual, issues. *Any* sexual behavior that exploits or demeans another human being is wrong. But this can, and does, happen in marriage as well as out of it, it happens among straights as well as among gays and lesbians.

Listen for a moment to the wisdom of the late theologian and ethicist Helmut Thielicke: "The primary moral problem," he said, "is not sex within marriage versus sex outside marriage, or sex within a heterosexual versus sex within a homosexual relationship. The problem is sex as a depersonalizing force versus sex as the fulfillment of a human relationship."[4] Bold as that statement may seem to some, I think Thielicke is right.

The issue we need most to worry about is how our sexuality can contribute to the fulfillment of personhood — one's own and others. Get that right, and a lot of other things will take care of themselves.

*   *   *

As indicated earlier, when the General Assembly meets in Albuquerque later this month, it will once again take up these matters, in particular the question of ordination. What will happen is anyone's guess.

From my perspective, a positive outcome would be a decision permitting ordaining bodies — Presbyteries, in the case of ministers, and congregations, in the instances of deacons and elders — to do what they have always done and ordain those who they believe are fit to hold office. Such a decision is possible, but unlikely.

The worst outcome, in my view, would be one which seeks to write into the church's constitution, as some have suggested, a requirement that, in order to be ordained, a person must be either faithful in marriage or celibate. Imagine, if that were to happen, the kind of examination *all* single persons might be subjected to.

If either of these two options receives the support of a majority, a substantial minority will be opposed, many out of deep conviction. On this issue, there simply is no consensus among Presbyterians, or among Christians generally. We are not ready, as a body of God's people, to make a final decision. Individually we may be; corporately we are not.

I am drawn, therefore, to the suggestion recently offered by Eugene Degitz of Princeton Seminary. Thinking of the discord this issue has wrought, Degitz suggests an analogy with a family in the midst of a quarrel. He writes: "When a nuclear family is at odds over some family matter, sometimes the best solution is to back away, buy time, affirm the best intentions of all members, and place a moratorium on decisions about the disputed issue. . . . This liberates a family from estrangement and self-destruction. The matter that has been 'tabled' can be decided later when calmer heads and clearer insights prevail."

"The Presbyterian family," says Degitz, "has been engaged in important and long overdue . . . conversations about human sexuality. Many helpful insights have come out of these discourses; much remains for us to learn about the mystery and complexity of human sexuality. These conversations and debates have also, on occasion, generated heat bordering on arrogance from both sides. . . . Common ground, at this moment, does not seem to be in the picture." So, says Degitz, perhaps this is "the time for an indefinite moratorium for the Presbyterian church family concerning pronouncements and decisions, but not discussion and learning, about human sexuality. . . . We Presbyterians need to continue to study, to think, to pray, to listen, to talk without the pressure of a 'final exam.'" He concludes, "If history is any guide, given enough hard work, persistent prayer and sufficient time, a solution will be found that is faithful to our Judeo-Christian heritage and that has consensus within the Presbyterian Church. . . ."[5]

The reference to "history" reminds us of other times and of other contentious issues, such as slavery, or the ordination of women, and reminds us that, on most such issues, it takes time for the church to discern God's will. That's the gift I hope the General Assembly will provide. In any case, the assumption that some decisive action will put this issue to rest is a pipedream. No matter what the General Assembly does or doesn't do, it is an issue that won't go away. Somehow, we have to learn to live with it, and with each other.

1. Robin Scroggs, *The New Testament and Homosexuality* (Philadelphia, PA: Fortress Press, 1984), p. 127.

2. William Sloane Coffin, *A Passion for the Possible* (Louisville, KY: Westminster/John Knox, 1993), p. 65.

3. Quoted in *Context*, by Martin Marty, Vol. 28, #9, p. 5.

4. My records do not indicate the source of this quote but I am sure it is from Thielicke's *Sexual Ethics*.

5. The *Presbyterian Outlook*, May 20, 1996.

~

Forgiveness

Readings: Psalm 130   **September 27, 1998**
             II Corinthians 1:23-2:11
             Matthew 18:21-35

Then Peter came and said to him, "Lord, if another member of the church sins against me, how often should I forgive? As many as seven times?"

— Matthew 18:21

Surely you have noticed how, in the wake of recent revelations and accusations of presidential folly, we not only find ourselves thinking and talking about perjury, obstruction of justice, impeachment, censure — legal and political matters — but also about sin, contrition, repentance, forgiveness — religious concerns. Listening to these theological terms being bandied about, I have wondered to what extent their meaning is understood. I have wondered how much appreciation there is for the ambiguities and complexities that arise once you get out of the dictionary and into a real life situation. So, I am seeing this as a teaching moment, and, this morning, I propose that we take one of these words and dig beneath the surface to see what's there.

The word is "forgiveness." I suggest we look into it not merely because the country is ultimately going to have to decide whether or not to forgive the President, but because we all deal in forgiveness, and with some frequency — either because we need to receive it, or because we are in a position to offer it. To paraphrase Hamlet, to forgive or not to forgive is often the question: within our marriages, families and friendships, in corporations, classrooms and churches, whenever somebody says or does something that offends or harms.

*   *   *

The Monday following the publication of the Starr Report there was a newspaper article about what had been said from pulpits the previous day.[1] The impression was that most preachers had urged forgiveness. They appear to have said that forgiveness is a good thing, and that in any case, Christians have no choice: they are required to forgive. There is, let us admit, considerable Biblical basis for such a sentiment. Luke, for instance, reports Jesus telling his disciples: "Whenever you stand praying, forgive, if you have anything against anyone; so that your Father in heaven may also forgive your trespasses." Again, according to Luke, Jesus urges us to "be merciful, just as your (heavenly) Father is merciful." And, of course, every Sunday we pray: "Forgive us our trespasses, as we forgive those who trespass against us."

What was it Mark Twain said? Something about it wasn't the parts of the Bible he did not understand that troubled him, but the parts he *did* understand! It seems clear: Christians have a duty to forgive.

And yet! Wait a minute! Isn't that what you want to say? It's not just that we find it hard to forgive, sometimes. Most of us do, even when what's involved is a first offense. But when somebody repeatedly offends? Peter may have been the first, but surely he is not the last to want to know, "How often should I forgive?" I can imagine that question being asked within the White House. Can't you? Forgiveness that has to be repeated is hard. But there is something else: you have to wonder if it doesn't give the offender permission to keep offending.

It happens. Ask victims of domestic violence or sexual abuse who have forgiven the abuser, only to be abused again. Here's something some pastors will have a lot to answer for. I mean those who have urged victims of abuse to forgive the perpetrators, instead of holding them responsible for their actions. I am not suggesting the offender can never be forgiven. I am saying that forgiveness can be pre-mature — a pardon offered too easily, too quickly. Sometimes withholding forgiveness might be the right thing to do, the most loving thing.

And what about something even more hurtful: murder, for instance, or acts of terrorism? You recall the three girls in West Paducah, Kentucky, who were murdered by a fellow student? The girls had not even been buried when some of their classmates, participants in a Christian prayer group, announced to the murderer, "We forgive you, Mike."[2] After the Oklahoma City bombing, a minister friend of mine told a congregation on Martha's Vineyard — interestingly enough, with President Clinton in attendance! — the minister told the congregation that it was the duty of all Christians to forgive Timothy McVeigh.[3] Is forgiveness supposed to be automatic? Unconditional? Is there some place for accountability? Contrition? Repentance? Are Christians not to concern themselves with issues of justice?

Despite what seems, on the surface, to be a pretty clear obligation on the part of Christians, once you start to think about it, there is a lot to ponder. I will warn you right now: even after this sermon, there will still be a lot to ponder. But maybe I can help a little. First of all, by trying to clarify what forgiveness is and what it is *not*.

*   *   *

It's easier to say some things forgiveness is not. So, let me start there.

Forgiveness is not the same as indifference. It's not over-looking the wrongful or hurtful act. It's not shrugging the shoulders as if to say, "Who cares?" With regard to the President, a fair number of people seem to be confused at just this point. Forgiveness, for them, seems to mean that neither sexual misconduct nor untruthfulness is worth bothering about. "What's the big deal? It's a private matter. Get over it." What such an attitude represents, I suggest, is not forgiveness, but moral apathy. And you cannot justify such an attitude by appealing to the example of Jesus. No doubt about it: he was a friend of sinners, but he was not indifferent to sin. On one occasion he told his followers: "Be on your guard. If another disciple sins, you must rebuke the offender, and *if there is repentance* you must forgive." Not now, but when you go home, take a look at what preceded today's Gospel Lesson. There you will find Jesus giving detailed instructions about how his followers should confront one believer who has offended another believer, and what they should do if the offender fails to acknowledge the offense. Ignoring wrong-doing, or dismissing it, is not forgiveness.

Nor, despite what you have heard, does forgiveness mean forgetting the offense. "Forgive and forget" is not only virtually impossible, it is the opposite of what forgiveness really means. Donald Shriver, a long-time teacher of Christian ethics, writes: "The most serious aspect of forgiveness is confronting the evil perpetrated by human agents. We do not forgive hurricanes and floods; we forgive human beings who could and should have acted differently. We hold them responsible, and we hold them under the judgment of memory, especially as long as (they) do not repent their actions. Even after they repent," Shriver says, "the evil we suffered may be too important to forget. . . ."[4] Christians are not called to "forgive and forget," but to remember and forgive.

Here is something else: to forgive is not to say there is no accountability, or that there are no consequences. There may or may not be punishment, but when we behave badly there are always consequences. I suggest the President as a case in point, whether or not he is eventually censured or impeached. Some chickens have already come home to roost. His power is diminished. His moral authority may be gone forever. He is the butt of crude jokes. Forgiveness may wipe the slate clean, provide another chance. But the effects of the President's behavior will linger. And forgiveness does not mean that some form of punishment cannot or will not happen.

Forgiveness does not mean that the option of punishment has to be abandoned. It does require that we abandon vengeance, the impulse to get even. That, I remind you, was the greatness of Lincoln, and a profound of sign of his spiritual depth. One might say that he imposed the punishment of war in response to secession, but throughout the long conflict, and afterwards, one heard not a hint of vengeance emanating from that great soul.

*　　*　　*

So, then, if forgiveness is not the same as indifference, if it is not a matter of forgetting, if it does not preclude punishment, what is it? Mostly, I would say, it is the mending of what has been broken. That's so whether it is divine or human forgiveness we are thinking of. Forgiveness means the restoration of a relationship, the overcoming of a rift, whether between oneself and God or between oneself and another human being There is more to it, but that's the heart and soul of it.

Here's how Fred Buechner puts it: "To forgive somebody is to say one way or another, 'You have done something unspeakable, and by all rights I should call it quits between us. Both my pride and my principles demand no less. However, although I make no guarantees that I will be able to forget what you've done and though we may both carry the scars for life, I refuse to let it stand between us. I still want you for my friend.'" Buechner goes on: "To accept forgiveness means to admit that you've done something unspeakable that needs to be forgiven, and thus both parties must swallow the same thing: their pride."[5]

From a human standpoint, the act of forgiveness involves a recognition of one's own frailty and empathy for the other's humanity. After Lee's surrender at Appomattox, Ulysses S. Grant wrote in his journal: "I felt . . . sad and depressed at the downfall of a foe who had fought so long and valiantly, and had suffered so much for a cause, though that cause was, I believe, one of the worst for which a people ever fought."[6] You can hear moral judgment in what Grant wrote: the cause which Lee gave himself to was a bad cause. At the same time, there is also empathy for a "foe who had fought long and valiantly, and had suffered so much. . . ." It is such an understanding of the humanity of one's enemies, that makes it possible to entertain the idea of living with them as fellow human beings. It's what has been so long in coming in places like Northern Ireland, Israel, the Balkans.

This morning's Epistle Lesson is a case study in forgiveness. In some of his other letters you get the impression that Paul is writing about forgiveness in a term paper kind of way. It's profound, but it is also pretty abstract. With the Second Chapter of II Corinthians, it's not abstract; it is pastoral and personal. Paul has been wronged, treated badly, lied about. The people responsible were in the minority, but they were a vocal minority. There was a rift in the congregation and Paul had decided to stay away for fear of making it worse. Instead of visiting Corinth, he had written a letter in which he had rebuked those who had mistreated him. The letter had awakened some of the leaders who had been ignoring the trouble. They got busy, called the troublemakers to account, and resolved matters. What we heard earlier is Paul practicing forgiveness. He does not overlook the wrong. He is not forgetting it. He doesn't say there should be no punishment of the ringleader. He says there has been enough punishment. It is time, says Paul, "to reaffirm your love for him." As far as the Apostle is concerned, the matter is over and done with. "Anyone whom you forgive, I also forgive," he says. We all need to forgive, Paul concludes, so that we don't end up in league with the Devil!

*   *   *

There is a lot more to think about. More than we have time for today. But don't reach for The Hymnal quite yet! What about repentance? How are repentance and forgiveness connected? The short answer is, paradoxically.

On the one hand, repentance seems to be a condition. To be forgiven, I have got to acknowledge my need for it and want it. As badly as the psalmist who said: "I wait for the Lord, my soul waits, and in his word I hope; my soul waits for the Lord more than those who watch for the morning. . . ." Why is the psalmist wanting God? Because he needs and longs for forgiveness.

On the other hand, it is the possibility of forgiveness that encourages repentance, perhaps even makes repentance possible. So, again, the psalmist: "If you, O Lord, should mark iniquities, Lord, who could stand? But there is forgiveness with you, so that you may be revered." In our Call to Confession here in worship, there is always a reminder that a gracious God awaits us, and therefore we may, with courage and confidence, confess our sins. As another puts it: "Christian faith does not say, Repent and you will be forgiven; it says, You have *been* forgiven, therefore, repent."

There are two sides to the repentance coin. But here is one thing certain: forgiveness has no meaning if the sinner persists in his sin, if the wrongdoer keeps on doing wrong. Like love and marriage, the horse and carriage, forgiveness and repentance go together.

*   *   *

Perhaps you can recall that moving moment just about two years ago when a thirty-three-year-old Vietnamese woman laid a wreath at the Vietnam Memorial in Washington. She was only nine years old when a photographer took her picture, running, holding her arms above her head, and screaming in agony and terror as napalm seared her small body. Nearly a quarter of a century after her ordeal, she stood at the Vietnam Memorial and said: "I have suffered a lot from both physical and emotional pain. . . . But God saved my life and gave me faith and hope. Even if I could talk face to face with the pilot who dropped the bombs, I would tell him, 'We cannot change history, but we should try to do good things for the present and for the future to promote peace.'" One veteran of that war who was there that day said: "We were just kids doing our job. For her to forgive us personally means something."[7]

Forgiving another can be, and usually is, hard to do. And there can be questions — legitimate questions — about the timing: Is this the time, or is it premature? Yet, in Jesus Christ, we have received unmerited grace. If we cannot find it within ourselves to pass that grace along, we are as ungrateful as that poor, miserable slave in Jesus' parable.

And listen! Without forgiveness there is no moving on. Without forgiveness we stay stuck. How many marriages end up in divorce, how many wars keep being fought, how many families and churches and friendships are wrecked, because of an inability or an unwillingness to forgive? My guess is there are some here this morning who are stuck at just that point. Short of forgiveness, there is no moving on.

Nobody, least of all Jesus, ever said that forgiveness is easy. But it *is* essential. I doubt if there is anyone here who, deep down, doesn't know as much.

1. *The Philadelphia Inquirer*, September 14, 1998.
2. As reported by Dennis Prager in *The Wall Street Journal*, December 15, 1997.
3. Ibid.
4. As reported in *Context*, a commentary on Religion and Culture (date uncertain).
5. Frederick Buechner, *Wishful Thinking* (New York: Harper & Row Publishers, 1973), pp. 28-29.
6. Donald W. Shriver, Jr., "What Is Forgiveness?" in *The Living Pulpit*, Volume 3, Number 2, 1994, p. 16.
7. *The New York Times*, November 12, 1996.

~

Two Men on a Bench

Readings: Genesis 1:1-27, 31-2:1   October 17, 1999
          Mark 12:28-34

In the beginning when God created the heavens and the earth. . . .

— **Genesis 1:1**

Last August the Kansas Board of Education voted six to four to remove evolution, along with the Big Bang theory, from that state's science curriculum. Some saw the decision as a victory "for religious Fundamentalists and their allies."[1] Scientists, by and large, expressed a combination of dismay and alarm. Ever since the Kansas decision, and as recently as last Sunday's *New York Times* and last Thursday's *Philadelphia Inquirer*, articles and editorials have been appearing, one after another, on the often troubled relationship between religion and science.

It's the topic I am taking up this morning — for several reasons. I have in mind our young people, now in middle or high school, and soon to be in college or university. I want them to know that they do not have to choose between the science they are learning in school and the faith they are being taught in church. I am mindful, as well, of you who frequently come to this house of worship, because you are seeking a relationship with God, but who have difficulty fitting the world of the Bible into the world you know about and experience every day, and who, therefore, hesitate to make a faith commitment. And I am thinking that most of us find ourselves standing, as it were, with one foot in the world of the Bible and the other foot in the modern scientific world, wondering what, if anything, these two worlds have to do with each other. Are they totally separate? Is the one in competition with the other? Is conflict between them inevitable and unavoidable? Is an uneasy peaceful coexistence the best we can hope for? Or, is there the possibility of something better, more constructive?

*   *   *

I suggest that, in thinking about these questions, we begin with the Bible, not only because the Bible is often the main battleground, but because a lot of people seem to be misinformed about the nature of this book. They think it contains scientific information. It doesn't. As Peter Gomes puts it: "It is not that the Bible has 'good' science or 'bad' science. It has no science. . . . To impose a constraint of science upon the Bible," says Gomes, "is to force it into a role for which it was never intended, and to which without violence to author, text, and reader, it cannot be adapted."[2]

Well, you say, what about the first chapter of Genesis? The so-called "scientific creationists" say it gives us an alternative to the theory of evolution. Are they mistaken? Yes, I believe they are. Genesis 1 is not science. It is not history. It is theology: "In the beginning God. . . ." The Old Testament scholar, Walter Brueggemann says we should think of Genesis 1 as a kind of doxology, as a hymn of praise.[3] It is a response to the wonder that the sun, the moon, the stars, the world, and, most of all, that you and I, exist. Genesis 1 answers the question, "Why is there anything at all?" Why? Well, because of God!

One of the very few genuine theological giants of recent times was a man by the name of Karl Barth. Among several of his works on my bookshelf is a collection of his correspondence. The other day, as I was thinking about this sermon, I recalled reading within that volume a letter Barth had written to his niece. She was in college at the time and apparently had been troubled by a teacher who insisted that since the Bible's account of creation can't be squared with the theory of evolution, one or the other must be wrong. This is what Barth wrote: "Has no one explained to you in your seminar that one can as little compare the biblical creation story and a scientific theory like that of evolution as one can compare, shall we say, an organ and a vacuum-cleaner — that there can be as little question of harmony between them as of contradiction?"[4]

In other words, we are talking, here of two different things. Like the organ, Genesis 1 is an instrument of praise. It directs us to the God who is the source of all that is, the One to whom we owe our gratitude and our loyalty. Like the vacuum cleaner, science is a practical tool which helps us understand the workings of all that has been given to us. What I want to hear in the Bible is the organ music that directs my attention toward God. If I want to be informed about biology, or physics, or astronomy, I have to turn elsewhere. The Bible is one thing; science is something else.

*   *   *

But where does that leave us? Does it mean that religion and science have nothing to do with each other? Are we left straddling a great divide?

Some would say so. Here, for instance, is the Harvard geologist Steven Jay Gould: "Science and religion should be equal, mutually respecting partners," he says, "each the master of its own domain, and with each domain vital to human life in a different way."[5] There are theologians who say much the same. Religion, they maintain, answers the question, "Why?" Science, on the other hand, answers the question, "How?" "Science is about understanding our world," says one. "Religion is about understanding the meaning of the world."[6] Different questions and separate and distinct worlds: religion here, science over there.

But recently people from both sides of the divide have been suggesting the possibility of something beyond a mere peaceful coexistence. This morning one of our members is being recognized as a person who, in his life and work, demonstrates that scientific endeavor, science teaching, and technological development are all part of God's calling. The honor comes from The Presbyterian Association on Science, Technology, and the Christian Faith. It is a fledgling organization, made up of scientists and theologians, whose purpose is to to challenge and assist the Presbyterian Church (USA), to take seriously the implications of science and technology as they affect the life and work of the church, and to challenge and assist Presbyterian scientists, engineers, and other technical professionals to take seriously the insights of the Reformed theological tradition for their scientific and technical vocations. Here, in other words, within the church is an organization that seeks to bridge the gap between religion and science.

From the other side, too, there seems to be a thawing of what another calls the "500 year-old cold war between science and religion."[7] Recent scientific discoveries have prompted more and more scientists to ask religious questions and these discoveries have even led some scientists to faith. Here, for example, is one who writes: "The more I examine the universe and study the details of its architecture, the more evidence I find that the universe . . . must have known that we (human beings) were coming."[8] Here is a physicist declaring that the present-day cosmology "leaves us with a choice: either the universe was created by an Intelligent Designer, or it is a massive and incredible coincidence the likes of which we can hardly imagine."[9] Here is a prominent astronomer saying: "Science cannot answer the deepest questions. As soon as you ask why is there something instead of nothing, you have gone beyond science. I find it quite improbable that such order came out of chaos. There has to be some organizing principle. God," says this scientist, "to me is a mystery, but is the explanation for the miracle of existence. Why there is something instead of nothing."[10]

One of our members, Paul Burgmayer, is a scientist. He has written: "For a long time, I would have said that my science world view impeded my Christian faith. . . . As I now see it, God reveals himself to us through nature in an infinite number of ways that nonetheless obey certain basic laws. For a scientist, these laws are one important sign of God's presence and covenant with us. There is an exquisite beauty in the depth to which these laws are obeyed throughout the universe."[11] That almost sounds like an echo of Psalm 19 and the Hayden anthem sung earlier. "The heavens are telling the glory of God." Not only the heavens but the earth!

*   *   *

Nobody, least of all me, can be certain how the relationship between religion and science will play itself out in the twenty-first century. One thing we need to be alert for, so as to resist, is dogmatism from either side. There are, warns A. N. Wilson, "bigoted scientific materialists who never tire of explaining that you have no right to say that you believe in anything which cannot be verified on scientific grounds — which would," Wilson goes on to say, "give you no right to say why you like Beethoven's last quartet; no right to say that you are in love with anybody, or anything else; why you miss somebody when they die; no right to say most of the interesting things that human beings have ever said."[12] In my experience it is not generally the scientists themselves, but some of their small-minded secular friends who think the only truth worth knowing is factual truth. And my guess is that religious dogmatism is the greater danger, especially that of the anti-intellectual variety. Reason is not the only road to truth.

Christian faith rests on the foundation of revelation, most of all the revelation of God's love in Jesus Christ. Yet, churches had better heed the warning of the philosopher Immanuel Kant: "A religion which, without hesitation, declares war on reason, will not, in the long run, be able to hold out against it."[13]

Fortunately, we are a part of a tradition that has always sought to love God with the mind, along with heart, soul, and strength. We are not biblical literalists. We welcome light from all sources. We believe it is part of the human enterprise to probe and question, and to seek truth wherever it may be found. We do not view science as the only arbiter of truth. At the same time, our tradition is one that is grateful both for science and for scientists. I am personally delighted that the Presbyterian Association on Science, Technology, and the Christian Faith has come into being. As their pastor, I want the scientists of this congregation, and those whose work is informed by science, to know that their church respects and honors their work, even views theirs as a godly, religious enterprise.

As part of my preparation for this sermon, I met earlier this past week with several of our scientists. In the course of our conversation, they suggested there is something religion could well learn from science. As one of them put it: "Science is always 'pushing the envelope,' continually daring to seek answers." Science never stands still. It was their thought that religion, on the other hand, often is content to stand pat. It's not an altogether accurate perception. If, as I hope you will, you come out to hear this year's Theologian-in-Residence, Jack Rogers, you will learn that the church has indeed changed its mind, from time to time. But almost never without a huge struggle and a good deal of anxiety. So, I would agree with our scientists: an openness to fresh disclosures of truth is indeed something religion can learn from science.

As for science, we must keep in mind the distinction between knowledge and its application. While we are generally grateful for what science discovers and makes possible — not only the vacuum-cleaner, but vaccines, and much else — we also recognize that science is increasingly presenting us with moral dilemmas. To clone or not to clone. To mess around with genes, or not to do so. Because, in our time, scientific knowledge is so great and technical skill so immense, the possibilities for good and evil are also immense. We can do so many things, heretofore undreamed of things. The vexing question has increasingly become, Of course we can do this or that, but should we? Is it wise to do so? And these are questions which we, with the wisdom of the Bible, the teaching of Jesus, the guidance of the Holy Spirit, and the insights of our theological tradition, ought to be ready to engage and help to answer.

*   *   *

At the start of this sermon, I offered a number of images having to do with the relation between religion and science: conflict, competition, separation, peaceful coexistence. Here is one more, the one I would like you to take with you. It's the image of two individuals sitting on a park bench, engaged in conversation — an image that came to mind because of two real people.

I learned about them years ago when I went to seminary at Princeton. Soon after arriving there, I was told how, some years earlier, two residents of the town, each distinguished in his own field, used to be seen sitting together on a park bench, engaged in deep conversation. One was in residence at the Institute for Advanced Studies; the other was a seminary professor. They were both refugees from Nazi Germany, sharing a concern for their homeland and for friends whom they knew to be suffering. But they also shared an intellectual curiosity and an attitude of reverence. One was the renowned physicist, Albert Einstein. The other was not famous. His name was Otto Piper. He was a brilliant New Testament scholar and respected theologian. Einstein the scientist, Piper the biblical scholar, physicist and theologian, sitting together on a park bench, engaged in respectful conversation, each seeking to learn from the other. That, it seems to me, is an image not only of what is possible, but an image of what would bring delight to the God whose works both the scientist and the person of faith are seeking to know.

1. *Time*, August 23, 1999. p. 59.

2. Peter J. Gomes, *The Good Book* (New York: Wm. Morrow & Co., 1996), p. 318.

3. Walter Brueggemann, *Texts Under Negotiation: The Bible and Postmodern Imagination* (Minneapolis: Fortress Press, 1993), p. 29.

4. Jürgen Fangmeier and Hinrich Stoevesandt, editors *Karl Barth Letters 1961-1968* (Grand Rapdis, MI: Wm. B. Eerdmans Publishing Co., 1981), p. 184.

5. In *Time*, Ibid.

6. Russell Roberts, *"Can Theology and Science Live Together?"* in *Alumni/ae News*, Princeton Theology Seminary, Winter/Spring 1993, pp. 5-7.

7. Barbara Brown Taylor, *Origins: The Evolution of Praise*, The Princeton Seminary Bulletin, Spring 1999, p. 171.

8. Freeman Dyson, *Disturbing the Universe* (New York: Harper & Rowe, 1979), p. 250.

9. In *Context*, July 1, 1998, p. 7.

10. Allan Sandage in *Context*, June 1, 1991.

11. In *Scitech*, May 1999, p. 4.

12. In *Books and Culture,* September/October, 1999. p. 23.

13. Quoted by Hans Küng, *Does God Exist* (Garden City, NY: Doubleday & Co., Inc., 1980), p. 125.

Where Else?

Readings: Psalm 61:1-5   **September 16, 2001**
              Isaiah 40:1, 11, 27-31
              Romans 8:35-39, 12:1-2, 9-21
              John 6:66-70

Simon Peter answered him, "Lord, to whom can we go? You have the words of eternal life."
— John 6:68

I expected you to be here today. I knew this is where you would want to be: in your spiritual home, in the company of your faith family, in this place where the symbols of font, table, and cross remind us of God's love in Jesus Christ. I knew this is where you would come today: to let the somber music of the organ wash over you, to be encouraged by the anthems, to hear the words of scripture, to pray — whether in song, or in spoken words, or in silence. This is the right place to be. For, in the words of the hymn, here is where:

> We share our mutual woes,
> Our mutual burdens bear.
> And often for each other flows,
> The sympathizing tear.

I knew you would be here today. And, as you might imagine, I have thought long and prayed hard about what I should say to you. My hope is that the few things I am led to say will be helpful to you, faithful to the gospel, and, as we prayed moments ago, acceptable to the One in whose name I dare to speak.

*   *   *

There are, to begin with, a few things you will want to know. Some of our families have loved ones who undoubtedly have perished. We are doing all we can to put our arms around them. One of our members managed to get out of the World Trade Center alive. A sister of another member escaped from the Pentagon. Others who were initially feared lost are safe. For these mercies, we are grateful. We are also appreciative of the condolences that have come to us from some of our overseas partners in mission. Two of these are especially poignant: one from Spiwo Xatile in South Africa, and the other from Doug Baker in Belfast, Northern Ireland. In the category of "Ripley's Believe it or not," the Protestants and Roman Catholics in Ireland even found it possible to issue a joint message of condolence and concern!

*   *   *

Our own emotions are rubbed raw. And there are so many of them: anguish and anger, disbelief, dismay and doubt, a new sense of our vulnerability, a renewed awareness of our fragility.

I want you to know that our faith gives us permission to take these reactions to the throne of grace, including the ones you may consider the worst or most dangerous of them: the rage, bitterness, and hostility. If you have reservations about this, if you think God does not permit such honesty, if you assume that only polite and innocuous prayers are welcome in heaven, I urge you to read the psalms, scan the Book of Lamentations, or turn to a prophet such as Jeremiah. In reading such you will find the kind of profound faith that is able, not only to be honest in prayer, but a faith that fully expects God to take seriously the one who is offering complaints, crying out with laments, or posing hard questions. I encourage you not to withhold from your prayers those things that are breaking your heart and tearing at your soul.

*   *   *

One of the first questions I was asked on Tuesday morning was: "Why does God allow something like this to happen?" It was pure coincidence, but earlier that morning I had been reading a book by Philip Yancey. In a chapter entitled, "Faith Under Fire," Yancey tells of having received a phone call from a television producer following the accidental death of Princess Diana. "Can you appear on our show?" he was asked.

"We want you to explain how God could possibly allow such a terrible accident." Yancey says his immediate response was: "Could it have had something to do with a drunk driver going 90 miles an hour in a narrow tunnel? How, exactly, was God involved?"[1]

We human beings desperately want things to make sense. When bad things happen, we try to explain, find reasons, justify. The result is often an amazing accumulation of clichés, half-truths, outright falsehoods. Pastors hear them all the time, and grieve all the more for the suffering who often assume, somehow, that God is responsible for their trouble, either paying them back for a real or imagined wrong, or simply working out some inscrutable divine purpose. The classic Biblical example of such reassuming is found in the Book of Job. Job's friends insist on a quid pro quo relationship between sin and suffering. Job listens but is unimpressed and unpersuaded. He says: "Your maxims are proverbs of ashes, your defenses are defenses of clay." The truth is, as finite human beings, we cannot know the answer to our "why" questions.

I myself am inclined to believe that what happened on Tuesday morning is a spectacular demonstration of human freedom run amok. Some human beings committed a monstrous evil. In their demented state they may have thought they were doing God's will. They were not. God does not hijack planes and fly them into skyscrapers, and God does not want anybody else to do that. What God does do, it seems, is give human beings freedom. We are not puppets on a string, and God is no divine puppeteer. We are free to make our own choices and to make of life what we will. It is a tremendous risk on God's part, for freedom can be misused, and when it is, terrible things can happen.

When they do, the best, and sometimes the only thing we have to fall back on is the clue that comes to us by way of the cross of Jesus Christ. In his suffering is the assurance that God identifies with ours. This is hard for many to grasp, but once in a great while somebody does. Like the German sculptor, about whom some of you may recall me telling you years ago. He was commissioned to carve a statue of Christ for a church, in the town of Käfertal. The church had been destroyed in World War II and was to be rebuilt. Before beginning his work, the sculptor came with a cot for sleeping and, for a week, proceeded to live in the rubble of the bombed out church, in order to recapture the feeling of the place when the bombs were falling on it and all around it. In the statue which he carved, there is a piece of shrapnel in Christ's shoulder, the kneecap is broken, and a chunk of metal protrudes from the Savior's side. The artist took the wood for the sculpture from a tree in which several pieces of shrapnel had been lodged, and he incorporated what had once been these instruments of death and destruction in his carving as a witness to the Christ who shares all our wounds and identifies with all our brokenness. Perhaps some artist will use some of the debris from the World Trade Center in a similar fashion.

In any case, such is the image of God I beg you to have and to hold in your minds, and to keep in your hearts. It's the image the prophet had in mind when he spoke of one who would "feed his flock like a shepherd; . . . gather the lambs in his arms, and carry them in his bosom, and gently lead those that are with young." Such is the God we see and meet in Christ, the One we sometimes call Emmanuel, God with us, and who, because of his victory over death, permits us to hope that death, destruction and demonic evil will not have the last word.

*   *   *

All that I have said thus far is after the manner of the prophet who spoke on God's behalf to say: "Comfort, comfort you my people, says your God." Now, I am led to say what you may not wish to hear, but which you need to hear, as do I. As Christians we need to remember who and whose we are, as we go forward. This is why I read earlier from the 12th chapter of Romans. Is it hard to do what Paul urges? You bet. But, listen! It's not just a few verses in Romans; it's the whole New Testament. That's where the words come from that you typically hear at the end of our services of worship. I spoke them on Tuesday evening at the end of our service of worship, and somebody said to me that hearing those familiar words on that occasion was "a different experience." "Go forth into the world in peace. . . . Hold fast to that which is good. . . . Render to no one evil for evil. . . . Honor all persons." It was no easier for me to say such words than for those present to hear them. And what of this morning? Listening to the Beatitudes. Or saying the Lord's Prayer. Maybe that was a different experience, too. "Forgive us our trespasses as we forgive those who trespass against us. And lead us not into temptation, and deliver us from evil."

It is so much easier to worship Jesus than to follow him! Worshipping is easy. Following is hard. But, so far as I can tell, if, that is, the Gospels faithfully represent him, Jesus never asks for our worship. He calls us to follow. What, in the days ahead, might that mean?

I think it does not mean that, as a nation, we have to turn the other cheek. Whatever else the Sermon on the Mount is, it is not meant as a practical guide for a nation under attack. The criminal act of aggression deserves punishment. The perpetrators must be brought to justice. This nation, like any other, has the right to defend itself from an act of war.

But we must not give in to our worst impulses. We must be mindful of men, women and children who live in places where the terrorists have been harbored and even honored, and who have been as powerless as you and me to do anything about it. Maybe you saw the Op Ed piece in the *Inquirer* the other day that recommended the kind of military response which would bring about "the complete collapse" of the economies of certain "rogue states," "a total war,"[2] the author called it. Soon after reading the piece, I recalled a warning of Theodore Parker Ferris, the late and beloved Rector of Trinity Church in Boston. You can never get even with cruel and brutish people, he said; you can only get to be more and more like them. That's the temptation we must pray to be led away from, the evil from which we must be delivered.

Some of you know Tom and Cindy Stewart. Their son-in-law is among the missing and presumed dead. Yesterday I was privileged to read a newspaper article from a paper in Connecticut reporting an interview with Tom. "There is," Tom was quoted as saying, "a natural tendency to seek revenge. But we hope this nation will follow what our faith would tell us. We do seek justice, but not an eye for an eye. We pray," Tom said, "that our leaders will resist the temptation to strike back and become as evil as those who perpetuated this atrocity." I cannot convey the mixture of humility and pride this pastor felt upon reading such sentiments from a parishioner.

If the words, "one nation under God" mean anything, if those words are more than empty rhetoric, we cannot respond with excessive and indiscriminate violence. I cannot believe God will "bless America" if we do.

We could do well, it seems to me, not to forget the legacy that is ours from the Old Testament prophets, or ignore what they have to say. In catastrophic times they looked beyond the obvious for meaning. And when their lands were invaded, they did not merely pronounce doom on their attackers; they also asked, What are the sins of Israel? Are there things about ourselves which we must try to learn? Are there things which we need to change?

I do not fancy myself a prophet. But I do believe we need to wake up to the fact that not everybody perceives us as a good and benevolent nation. There are many, especially in the so-called undeveloped worlds, who look upon us as arrogant in our use of power, selfish in our materialism, oblivious to environmental realities, and bent on increasing our wealth at their expense. It behooves us to consider the extent to which these perceptions may be justified.

We need to remember what I fear many have forgotten: we live in an interdependent world and we need to realize there will be no lasting peace except one built on a foundation of justice. As Dick Shaull, one of our Parish Associates, wrote this week, "We can no longer expect to live in peace and enjoy our wealth if we perpetuate an economic order which is driving more and more people . . . into such despair that they see no other way than to strike out through terrorist attacks."

"What we can do," Dick says, "what the God who suffers with us, the God of the crucified and risen Christ may be calling us to do, is to recognize that we, in our vulnerability, are bound in solidarity to the rest of the world, and that we can . . . change our priorities and use our wealth, our knowledge, our built-in concern for the well being of others to collaborate with (our world neighbors) in an all out effort to overcome the causes of terrorism. And as we do this," Dick suggests, "the God who suffers with us will also be the source of tremendous vitality, of an offering of life which makes hope come alive once again."[3]

We listened earlier to the prayer of St. Francis, "Lord, make me an instrument of your peace." That remains our charge: to love, not hate; to build, not destroy; to help, not hurt. I pray we will not forget, not grow hard and cold, and not give up on the mission with which Christ has entrusted us.

*   *   *

Our sorrow is profound. Our distress is great. And I am not unmindful of the stress and strain all this may be putting on your faith. That is why I wanted you to hear that portion of John's Gospel where we are told that some found following Jesus too hard and drifted away. Jesus asked the twelve, "Will you also go away?" And Peter replied, "Lord, to whom shall we go? You alone have the words of eternal life."

To whom shall we turn with our sorrow? With our emotions rubbed so raw? To whom shall we commit the dead and the bereaved? To whom shall we turn for strength and wisdom in the days ahead? Where shall we look to find the grace and courage to think, speak, and act in ways that will, in Lincoln's words, reflect the better angels of our nature? I don't know anywhere else to go but to Jesus Christ. Do you? I didn't think so, and that's why I knew you would be here today.

1. Philip Yancey, *Reaching For the Invisible God* (Grand Rapids, MI: Zondervan Publishing House, 2000), p. 56.

2. *The Philadelphia Inquirer*, September 13, 2001.

3. Personal correspondence.

~

Marching As To War?

Readings: Psalm 33:6-22   October 20, 2002
          James 3:13-18
          Matthew 22:15-22

The war horse is a vain hope for victory, and by its great might it cannot save.

— Psalm 33:17

For where there is envy and selfish ambition, there will also be disorder and wickedness of every kind. But the wisdom from above is first pure, then peaceable, gentle, willing to yield, full of mercy and good fruits, without a trace of partiality or hypocrisy.

— James 3:16-17

I want to begin this sermon by saying what I hope will come out of it. My aim is to encourage, even to provoke, a conversation — a conversation I believe we need to be having with each other as the prospect of war looms over the horizon. You may wonder: Has there not already been conversation? Over lunch or drinks at the club? In the newspapers? On NPR and Crossfire, with Larry King and Jim Lehrer? And above all, in the Congress? There has been and there will be. But I have in mind a conversation of a particular kind, with a peculiar thrust, so that we will talk with each other not as political partisans, not as Democrats or Republicans, but as people who profess to be followers of Jesus Christ. I'm looking for a conversation among believers who want and expect their faith to impact their attitudes and influence their actions when it comes to the troubling questions of every day life and to the perplexing problems of the world. As I imagine it, the conversation will be undertaken with a recognition that there are many questions and few easy or obvious answers, so that pontificating will have no place, while rigorous thought, honest speech, and careful listening will be required.

*   *   *

Now for my contribution to it. I want first to acknowledge a dilemma: that of being both a Christian and a citizen. When, on the one hand, we say, "I pledge allegiance to the flag of the United States of America and to the Republic for which it stands," and when we also confess, "Jesus Christ is Lord," an inevitable tension is created. We are pulled, as it were, in two directions. In a time such as the present that tension, that potential conflict of loyalties, can feel pretty intense.

It's such a tension that lies at the heart of the conversation Jesus is having in today's Gospel lesson with the Pharisees and Herodians about taxes. There is more that can and ought to be said about it than I have time for today. But let me say at least this much. When Jesus says, "Render to Caesar the things that are Caesar's," he is acknowledging the legitimacy, indeed the necessity, of government, as well as affirming the responsibilities all of us have as citizens. The alternative to government is likely to be anarchy. Sin makes government necessary. But sin also makes governments dangerous. That is to say, Caesar, too, is a frail human being who is entirely capable of faulty judgments and bad behavior. And so, Jesus goes on to say, Render "to God the things that are God's." By adding that phrase, he is reminding us of One who has a greater claim upon our loyalty, and before whom governments as well as citizens are accountable.

The implication is inescapable, I believe. When, as Christians, we come to a matter such as the one facing us now — the possibility that our beloved nation will launch a war — we cannot simply surrender our consciences to the state. Indeed, one of the principles of our Presbyterian heritage is that "God alone is Lord of the conscience." No small part of our obligation as Christians is discernment: to think, to think as Christians, to ask questions of right and wrong, of wisdom and foolishness, of truth and falsehood. And actually, this service, which we are to render to God, may also eventuate in the best of all service we can render to Caesar or to his modern counterparts. So this morning, we are seeking to bring Christian thought to the prospect of war with Iraq.

*   *   *

There is, of course, one response that would essentially end the conversation before it begins: the response of pacifism. There are now and always have been Christians who condemn any and all wars and refuse to participate in them. Most of the first Christians were pacifists. And pacifism remains an honorable and defensible choice — but only, I would suggest, for individuals. Few would argue that pacifism is a realistic option for a state. One of the primary responsibilities of the state, after all, is the protection of its citizens.

Among the first to recognize this reality was the great Fourth Century theologian, Augustine. "Recognizing that Christian tradition challenges any resort to violence," Augustine concluded "that wars of aggression and aggrandizement are never acceptable, but that there are occasions when the resort to force may be tragically necessary. . . ."[1] He formulated the theory of the "just war," a theory that ever since has served to guide the thinking of most mainstream Christians. The "just war" theory is, I wish to suggest, a useful aid in helping us today in thinking about the impending war with Iraq.

"Just war" theory says that, for any war to be morally acceptable, a number of conditions must be met. The war must be one of self-defense, against an act of aggression, and undertaken only as a last resort. The war must be authorized by a legitimate government, must have clearly articulated goals, and must have a reasonable chance of success. The war must be conducted with means proportional to the ends and with a minimum involvement of non-combatants.

When I apply these criteria to the war for which plans are underway, I am left with many questions and with serious doubts as to its moral justification. I am not, let me say, one who doubts the motives or good intentions of our leaders. They are, I believe, people of integrity who are doing what they think is the good and necessary thing. They may be right. They know things I do not. But I remain unconvinced that war with Iraq can be morally justified. Let me put my concerns in the form of questions.

Is the proposed war one of self-defense, a response to an act of aggression? Certainly not as those terms have been traditionally understood. There has been no attack from Saddam Hussein and, despite accusations, no evidence that he is allied with Al Qaeda. Proponents of the war say it is preventive. But justifying a preemptive war as self-defense is a stretch. Then, there is the question of precedent. Is a preemptive war the kind of moral example America wants to provide for the rest of the world? Is prevention of imagined aggression the rationale we want others to be able to use to launch wars of their choice?

Let's suppose a war against Iraq were to begin next week. Could we honestly say it is a "last resort"? Even if Iraq has "weapons of mass destruction," which not everyone agrees it does — Scott Ritter, for one, said in a recent speech at Princeton that it does not — but even if it does, have we exhausted all other means of disarmament? Deputy Secretary of Defense Paul Wolfowitz has recently conceded that any plausible threat from Iraq is as much as a decade away.[2] So is war required tomorrow? What is the hurry? A policy of containment has worked for twelve years. Why the rush to abandon it?

There are questions of legitimacy to be addressed, as well. True, the Congress has now given permission for war left up to the President to decide. But is that enough? For such a war to be morally justified is it not essential for more than one or two nations to think so? Why is it that so many of our friends remain unconvinced of war's necessity? Why is it that so many religious leaders around the world are voicing opposition and raising cries of alarm as to the consequence of such a war?

Additional questions cluster around the criteria having to do with goals, success, the means to be used, and the effect of a war upon non-combatants. The gamble seems to be that if a war is launched the Iraqi army will not resist and the Iraqi people will welcome the conquerors. Maybe. But maybe not. If, as some believe, the battle will take place in the streets of Baghdad, how many of our brave men and women will come home in body bags? If we unleash our weaponry from the sky, how many innocent Iraqis will become "collateral damage"? If Saddam has weapons of mass destruction, will war provoke him to use them? If Israel is attacked and responds as Ariel Sharon has promised, will the entire Middle East be engulfed in war? Last, but by no means least, will such a war diminish the likelihood of terrorism or increase it? Will the war make Islamic fundamentalism more attractive? Result in more recruits for Al Qaeda? If the recent elections in Pakistan are any indication, the answer is likely to be Yes.

Circumstances could cause me to change my mind, but as of today, I believe a war against Iraq would not be a just war, and I must raise my voice in dissent.

*   *   *

A year ago, following the tragedy of 9/11, the United States had the sympathy and experienced the compassion of most of the rest of the world. Now, a year later, much of that good will seems to have dissipated. There is concern in many places about what is perceived as American arrogance, our go-it-alone, we-know-best attitudes. In recent days I have been re-reading Reinhold Niebuhr, and listening anew to his warnings about national self-righteousness and moral pretension. I have been arrested by his warning that "powerful . . . nations are in greater peril from their own illusions than from their neighbors' hostile designs."[3] I have pondered his statement that, "the more we indulge in an uncritical reverence for the supposed wisdom of our American way of life, the more odious we make it in the eyes of the world, and the more we destroy our moral authority, without which our economic and military power will become impotent."[4] I have noted Niebuhr's observation that "nations . . . always find it more difficult than individuals to behold the beam that is in their own eye while they observe the mote that is in their brother's eye; and individuals find it difficult enough."[5] I worry that such is the case with the United States today. So focused have we been on getting the enemy that we are still avoiding the question of why it is we have enemies. There has been little or no recognition of, to say nothing of repentance for, past policies and practices that, in hindsight, are hard to justify, and which have bred resentment. We seem unwilling even to confess our gluttony when it comes to oil, our disproportionate consumption of the planet's non-renewable resources. We need, I believe, more modesty, more humility, than we have shown of late, more of that "wisdom from above" about which the lesson from James speaks.

I am hoping and praying that in the days to come we will have the wisdom and courage to be self-critical, not self-righteous. I want us to be proud of who we are as a nation, yet always to remember that we are only one nation among many. I am hoping and praying we will avoid unilateral action and resort to war only if and when other nations have agreed that it is necessary. Moreover, I am hoping and praying that more of our energies and passion will be turned outward toward the service of others, away from war and toward a cooperative effort to deal, in a serious way, with the problems of poverty and disease, hunger and human rights, economic development and environmental protection. Self-interest alone requires that we do so. The best defense against terrorism is, after all, a world where people can live in hope and not in despair.

The psalmist says: "The war horse is a vain hope for victory, and by its great might it cannot save." I offer that to you as a word from the Lord that even now it is not too late for us to hear and to heed.

*   *   *

As I mentioned a few weeks ago, this is a church that honors the freedom of the pulpit, and this is a pulpit that honors the right of those in the pew to think for themselves. So, let the conversation begin.

1. Donald W. Shriver, "Violence for Peace: An Oxymoron?" in the *The Living Pulpit*, October-December 1998, p. 4.
2. The *Christian Century*, October 9-22, 2002, p. 9.
3. Harry R. Davis and Robert C. Good, editors, *Reinhold Niebuhr on Politics* (New York: Charles Scribner's Sons, 1960), p. 277.
4. Ibid., p. 279.
5. Reinhold Niebuhr, *Moral Man and Immoral Society* (London: Westminster John Knox Press, Louisville, 1932), p. 107.

~

A Tract for These Times

Readings: Jonah 1:1-3; 3:1-5, 10; 4:1, 4-10   January 26, 2003
          Luke 4:16-30

And should I not be concerned about Nineveh, that great city, in which there are more than a hundred and twenty thousand persons who do not know their right hand from their left, and also many animals?

                                            — Jonah 4:11

I know all the things we say about the Bible, all the attributes we ascribe to it: how it is divinely inspired, a reliable guide for faith and life, a lamp to our feet, a light to our path, and so on. Still, I find myself being astonished, every now and then, at its timeliness. Sometimes it strikes me as being a great mystery: how these ancient texts we call Holy Scripture can speak with such power and relevance to us today.

Take, for instance, the Old Testament lesson assigned for reading this morning in all the churches — the old tale with a one-word title — Jonah.

                       *   *   *

A tale, a story, is what it is. Fiction, not fact. So don't waste your time wondering how any human being could be swallowed by a large fish — the text never mentions a whale, by the way — live in its belly for three days and three nights, and then get spewed out on dry land no worse for the wear. Do not worry your head about how that could happen. It did not happen. Jonah is in the category of make-believe. Like Alice in Wonderland or The Wizard of Oz. And like those stories, the truth of the Book of Jonah is not that of fact, but a truth of a far deeper, far more important kind.

You might think of the four chapters of Jonah as four acts in one drama. As the curtain goes up on Act One, the Lord is heard giving Jonah an assignment. He is told to go to the city of Nineveh and cry out against its wickedness.

Now when, in the Bible, prophets are told to do something, they almost always do it. They go where God directs them and say what God wants them to say. Not Jonah. God wants him to go to Nineveh. Jonah takes off in the opposite direction. The text does not say why. But when the story was first told everybody would have known.

Nineveh was the capital of the Assyrian Empire, now known as — guess what? Iraq! At the time the Assyrians were bitter enemies of the Jews. "The more things change. . . ." The Assyrians had invaded and looted the Northern Kingdom of Israel. The Assyrian regime was widely regarded as being tyrannical, a purveyor of violence. Did I not tell you? This is like reading this morning's newspaper. You want to know what the first readers of this story thought of Nineveh? Listen to this prophecy of the fall, the destruction, of Nineveh from the Biblical Book of Nahum:

> Woe to the bloody city,
> all full of lies and booty . . .
> All who hear the news of you
> clap their hands over you.
> For upon whom has not come
> your unceasing evil?

You can understand why Jonah wants no part of Nineveh. He goes to Joppa instead and boards a ship bound for Tarshish — modern day Spain — fleeing, not only Nineveh, but God — a fool's errand, he soon discovers. With the psalmist he learns: "If I take the wings of the morning and settle at the farthest limits of the sea, even there your hand shall lead me. . . ." Actually, in the case of Jonah, God whips up a great storm. Imagine scenes from the book or movie *The Perfect Storm*. Just an awful storm at sea.

On board the ship are sailors, of course. They are not part of Jonah's faith community. We are to imagine that they represent a number of different religions and come from a variety of countries. Jonah no doubt considers them to be "heathens." But they are peaceful men and pious in their own way. They imagine the storm to be the result of the anger of some god. They pray. They jettison cargo. But the storm continues to rage. The ship is in peril. Finally, Jonah admits he is to blame. Yet even then, the sailors act humanely. Even though Jonah has admitted being the cause of their troubles, even though he is not one of them, the sailors are reluctant to do him harm. Only when Jonah, in an act of moral heroism, insists that they throw him overboard, do the sailors rid themselves of the troublemaker.

It is an interesting aspect of the story, for the sailors — clearly the "outsiders" — are portrayed as having compassion for Jonah, while Jonah — the "insider," God's prophet, — has none for the Ninevites. One thinks of Jesus' remark that sometimes "the children of light" have much to learn from the so-called "children of darkness."

In any case, as Act One draws to a close, the sailors toss Jonah into the ocean. Whereupon God sends the great fish to swallow him.

We can dispense quickly with chapter two. It tells of Jonah's prayer. It's a bit strange because it is a prayer of thanksgiving for deliverance, even though Jonah is still imprisoned in the belly of the fish. But the prayer is soon answered. The Lord speaks to the fish and the fish spews "Jonah out upon the dry land."

As the curtain rises on Act Three, Jonah is once again told: "Go to Nineveh . . . and proclaim to it the message that I tell you." This time Jonah obeys. He goes to Nineveh where he preaches the shortest sermon on record, and surely one of the worst that has ever been preached. "Forty days more," Jonah says, "and Nineveh shall be overthrown." That's it. But the result is remarkable. Unheard of! Better than all the Billy Graham Crusades put together. Everybody, including the king, repents. The entire city. The king decrees that every living creature — not just the people, but all the animals, too — must cloth themselves with sackcloth. Imagine it: dogs and cats and even camels, all wearing sackcloth! "Who knows?" says the king. "God may relent and change his mind; . . . so that we do not perish." Which is exactly what happens. Seeing the repentance of Nineveh, God announces a reprieve from judgement.

As Act Four begins, Jonah is not a happy camper. He is angry — angry at God for being merciful. Angry that the Ninevites have not suffered judgment. Angry, too, because he so wanted to be right. Jonah is very angry. I knew it, he says to God. "That is why I fled to Tarshish . . . ; for I knew that you are a gracious God and merciful, slow to anger, and abounding in steadfast love, and ready to relent from punishing."

Jonah knew it — but he didn't like it — not if God's mercy included the Ninevites!

There he sits, sulking. The day is one of those days we complain about in July and August — and would give almost anything to have just about now. It's a hot, muggy day. And God, seeing how uncomfortable Jonah is, places a bush beside the prophet to provide him with some shade. Jonah is grateful. But it's all a trick. Because the next day, God sends a worm to attack the bush so that it withers. Then God sends a sultry wind and raises the temperature even higher. Now Jonah is really feeling sorry for Jonah.

That's when God and the prophet have the conversation with which the drama comes to a close. "Is it right for you to be angry about the bush?" God asks. You bet your life, says Jonah. "Angry enough to die." Then comes the punch line. The Lord says: "You are concerned about the bush, for which you did not labor and which you did not grow. . . . And should I not be concerned about Nineveh, that great city, in which there are more than one hundred and twenty thousand persons . . . and also many animals?" One can almost hear the father in Jesus' parable of the Prodigal Son asking the older brother, Is it not right to throw a party for your brother who was lost and now is found? Dearest Jonah, is there some part of my creation about which I am not to care? Is there any place over whose destruction the God of the entire universe should not weep?

*   *   *

This old story bears the name Jonah. But it is not about Jonah. It's not about the Ninevites. And it is certainly not about the fish. This story is about God. And the whole purpose of the story is to encourage bigger, more expansive thoughts of God. Well, maybe there is another purpose: and that would be to challenge the ways we humans use religion to exclude, how we humans assume our enemies are God's enemies, how in the name of God we condemn those who do not believe what we believe or act as we do.

Perhaps it will help you see what the story is getting at if I tell you when and why it came to be written in the first place. The date was around 400 BC. The Jews had only recently returned from exile. Following the lead of the scribe Ezra, many of them had become quite narrow theologically: believing that God was God only of the Jews, that salvation was for the Jews alone, and that one day God would annihilate all their enemies.

The author of the Book of Jonah wrote his story as a protest against such religious arrogance. For the author of Jonah, God is the God not of the Jews, but of all — even the hated Ninevites.

What is even more important for us who call ourselves Christians, disciples, followers of Jesus Christ, is his example. His is the spirit of the author of Jonah, not that of Ezra. As another puts it: "Jesus possessed an incredible ability to accept people as people — flawed and filled with greatness, faithful and faithless, weak and strong. . . . He accepted people as they were rather than demanding them to be what he wanted them to be."

"Jesus didn't condemn Matthew or the Roman Centurion for working for an oppressive regime. Instead, he tolerated their work as he worked on them. Lepers, beggars, Samaritans were shocked at the way this Palestinian Jew embraced them. . . . (He) didn't see them as lepers, beggars, Samaritans. He saw them as children of God."[1]

As Luke tells it, this was Jesus' way from the beginning. In his hometown synagogue, he confronted the prejudices he had grown up with, telling his friends and former neighbors: "There's a wideness in God's mercy, like the wideness of the sea." He tells his former neighbors: you think the good news of God's liberating love and bountiful grace is only for you. No! No! And to make his point he calls upon two stories from within the people's own faith tradition. There were many widows in Elijah's time, he says, but during that great drought and time of famine, to whom did God send Elijah? To a gentile woman, a foreigner. And in Elijah's time, there were many lepers in Israel. But who got cured? Naaman the Syrian. Another foreigner. "The love of God is broader than the measure of (your) mind" is what Jesus told them. They didn't want to hear it, and they ran him out of town.

Maybe you can begin to understand why I am calling the old tale of Jonah "A Tract for These Times." For there are many today who would employ religion as a divisive force. It's not a new thing, of course. Religion has often been used that way: "to draw boundaries, to define who is in and who is out; who's saved and who's not."[2] Religion has been used and is being used today "to define the other, the outsider, the enemy, the not chosen, the non-elect, the infidel. In that regard, religion has played a supporting role in some of history's worst atrocities."[3]

The Book called Jonah, and the man called Jesus, encourage a different Spirit, inviting us to leave behind the tiny, petty, parochial God who loves only a Jew, whose mercy falls only upon the righteous — to leave that god behind, and to embrace the great God who, in an inspired moment, the apostle Paul spoke of as "above all and through all and in all."

*   *   *

I conclude, this morning, with another story, an old Hasidic tale about the Exodus when the Israelites were freed from their long years of slavery and the Egyptians who tried to recapture them were drowned in the sea. According to one of the Rabbis, the angels were all rejoicing over the deliverance of Israel at the Red Sea: playing their harps, singing, dancing. "Wait," said one of them. "Look, the Creator of the Universe is sitting there weeping!" They went to God. "Why are you weeping when Israel has been delivered by your power?" "I am weeping," said the Maker of the Universe, "for the dead Egyptians washed up on the shore — somebody's sons, somebody's husbands, somebody's fathers."[4]

The God of that story sounds a lot like the God of the Book of Jonah to me. "Should I not be concerned about Nineveh, that great city, in which there are more than a hundred and twenty thousand persons who do not know their right hand from their left, and also many animals?" We are not told how Jonah responded to God's question. That's because his is not the response that matters any more. Your response is the one that counts now. What do you think, should God not be concerned about Nineveh?

1. John Wimberly, Jr., "Jesus: A Model of Tolerance or Intolerance," *The Living Pulpit*, January-March, 2003, p. 29.
2. John M. Buchanan, *"A Time to Return,"* Fourth Presbyterian Church, Chicago, Illinois, January 5, 2003.
3. Ibid.
4. Albert C. Winn, "A Way Out of No Way," *Journal for Preachers*, date unknown.

~

A Minor Prophet
Speaks a Major Word

Readings: II Chronicles 28:8-15   November 16, 2003
           Romans 12:9-21
           Matthew 5:21-24

**Then those who were mentioned by name got up and took the
captives, and with the booty they clothed all that were naked
among them; they clothed them, gave them sandals, provided
them with food and drink, and anointed them; and carrying
all the feeble among them on donkeys, they brought them to
their kindred at Jericho, the city of palm trees. Then they
returned to Samaria.**

— II Chronicles 28:15

Do not be overcome by evil, but overcome evil with good.
— Romans 12:21

Recently, I was meeting with one of our newer members. In the course
of our conversation he said: "In the church to which I used to belong, over
in New Jersey, the sermons were all based on the Bible, but they never
seemed to make their way out of the Biblical world and into ours. Coming
here," he said, "I found the sermons to be Biblical, as well, but they do
make a connection with what is going on in our time and in our lives." He
meant it, and I took it, as a compliment. That is what I try to do. It is very
much what I hope to do this morning.

Last Tuesday we observed Veterans Day, what was at one time known
as Armistice Day — because it was on November 11, 1918 that the

terrible slaughter of the First World War — the war to end all wars, it was said — was finally concluded. On Tuesday the President laid a wreath at the Tomb of the Unknown Soldier. There were stories on the television evening news, and pictures in the newspapers the following day, of people — veterans, friends, relatives — visiting the resting places of those who lives have been sacrificed in one war or another.

The twentieth century was the bloodiest ever. Wars claimed over one hundred million souls, nearly two-thirds of them civilians.[1] At the beginning of the twenty-first century we are still at it. The "War on Terror" has been going on now for over two years. The number of casualties continues to climb in Iraq and Afghanistan, and the waste of life goes on in Israel and the Palestinian territories, in Turkey and elsewhere. Here at home we live with an inescapable sense of vulnerability and the threat of additional terrorist attacks. It appears that there are more people than ever so filled with hatred, or anger, or despair, or whatever, that they are ready to kill, not only others, but themselves. There is no end in sight, no apparent light at the end of the tunnel.

I have been wondering if, as people of faith, as those who have pledged their love for and loyalty to Jesus Christ, the time might be right for us to think together about where we are, and more importantly, where we ought to be headed. What I am proposing is not easy to do: to step back, and reflect, especially on a day when we wake up to learn that seventeen more U.S. soldiers have died in Iraq. When we are in the midst of war, the tendency is to suspend thought, especially, as another puts it, "self-critical thought."[2]

Yet it is something worth doing, something I believe we need to do. What I am inviting you to think about goes far beyond Iraq. Whether, like me, you had reservations about invading that country, or whether you thought it was the right thing to do, we are there now and surely we all hope that, when we leave, the place will be better than when we arrived. But there is, I believe, a bigger question that we would do well to be thinking about — as citizens, as especially as citizens who claim a faith in God. Here's the question: How are we to behave in this difficult and dangerous time? What does our faith encourage us to be and to do? I am wondering if that ancient and obscure prophet about whom we heard in this morning's Old Testament reading might have a word for us and for our time.

*   *   *

I am guessing that, prior to today, you had never heard of Oded. He is one of those characters who makes a cameo appearance in the Biblical story and then is never seen or heard from again. He is identified only as "a prophet of the Lord" — which is say, one who speaks on behalf of God, who quite often speaks truth to power, and who does both without asking anyone's permission, and without regard to the consequences.

Oded shows up at the end of a war — a war between Israel and Judah, two kingdoms which had recently been one under David and Solomon. As we know from our own civil war, battles between brothers can be the bloodiest of all. According to the Chronicler this particular war had resulted in "a great slaughter," with Israel emerging victorious. We entered the story at the point where a long line of prisoners — two hundred thousand of them, the text says — were being marched to Samaria, the capital of the Northern Kingdom. The usual practice in those days was to turn able-bodied prisoners of war into slaves, and to put to death the rest. There was no Geneva Convention to limit the reprisals of the winning side.

So, this is the scene: the victorious army has returned home, accompanied by a host of captives. The expectation is that they will be made to pay for being on the losing side. "But," says the text, "a prophet of the Lord was there, whose name was Oded; he went out to meet the army that came to Samaria. . . ." The prophet acknowledged that that the defeated enemy had suffered for their wrongdoing. But, the response of Israel had gone too far. "You have killed them in a rage that has reached up to heaven," Oded said, and he went on to say that the Israelites were about to compound their guilt with a vengeful treatment of the captives. "You intend to subjugate the people of Judah and Jerusalem . . . as your slaves, but," Oded asked, "what have you except sins against the Lord your God?" In other words, are you so much in the right that you can punish others for being in the wrong? "Hear me," Oded said, "and send back the captives whom you have taken from your kindred. . . ."

We are told that the "chiefs" — the civilian leaders — listened. They told the victorious army: "You shall not bring the captives in here, for you propose to bring on us guilt against the Lord in addition to our present sins and guilt." The returning warriors were sent to their homes. The action that follows can only be described as magnanimous. Instead of being enslaved or executed, the captives were clothed, given sandals for their feet, provided with food and drink, and then escorted back to their "kindred at Jericho."

*   *   *

That's the story. Does it have anything to do with us? If you have noticed the sermon title you will know I believe this minor prophet has something of major importance to tell us. Actually, as I have pondered the story I have heard three things from Oded that I believe might be God's word to us.

The first is the prophet's concern for all the victims of war, including the enemies of his own people. The captives are people, too, in his eyes.

It is an unusual thing. You know what happens whenever there is a war. The people on the other side are often demonized, become the embodiment of evil. Chris Hedges is a veteran war correspondent who has written a book entitled *War Is A Force That Gives Us Meaning*. He says that war invariably produces a distinction with regard to the value of human life. "While we venerate and mourn our own dead," Hedges says, "we are curiously indifferent about those we kill. . . . Our dead. Their dead. They are not the same. Our dead matter, theirs do not."[3]

Oded, "a prophet of the Lord," offers a different perspective. He represents a God who recognizes the common humanity of those on both sides of the conflict. It is something that Martin Niemoller, many years later, came to realize, as well. Niemoller was a German submarine captain in World War II, and eventually a prisoner of war. After the conflict he became a minister and a prominent spokesperson for peace. Speaking on one occasion before an international audience he said: "It took me a long time to learn that God is not the enemy of my enemies. He is not even the enemy of his enemies." Maybe Niemoller had in mind the saying of Jesus that God "makes his sun to rise on the evil and on the good." Or maybe he had in mind the image of Christ on the cross praying for those who had put him there: "Father forgive them, for they know not what they do."

In Bruce Catton's book about our civil war, *A Stillness at Appomattox*, there is a scene where the opposing armies are bivouacked on either side of the Rapidan River in Virginia. Catton tells of two Union officers who, through their telescopes, watched the Confederate men on the other side of the river "lounging about in shirt sleeves, some of them smoking their pipes and washing their clothes, others playing ball." The two Union officers stared at them for a long time, getting their first look at Confederate soldiers off duty. At last they put down their telescopes, and one officer said to the other: "My God, they're human beings just like us!"[4]

The challenge that comes to us from the prophet Oded is to remember that. "They're human beings just like us."

*   *   *

Here is something else Oded has to tell us: When war breaks out, there is enough responsibility for it to be widely shared. It is very rare indeed when anybody's hands are altogether clean. Oded tells his fellow Israelites: ". . . you intend to subjugate the people of Judah and Jerusalem. . . . But what have you except sins against the Lord your God?"

In this morning's Gospel lesson, Jesus tells us that when we are bringing our gifts to the altar, and we remember someone who has something against us, we are to leave the gift at the altar, go and be reconciled to our brother or sister, and then come back and offer our gift. We are likely to hear such an admonition in very personal terms, I believe, and, if we take it seriously, we probably think of a specific individual, or maybe several, with whom we are estranged. But here is a question. What would it mean if we were to think about this admonition in more corporate terms? What might it mean for us to come to worship God and remember the resentment of those around the world who live in desperate poverty? Or to remember those who are angry with us because they see us going our own way without regard to their interests or their opinions, doing what we want to do because we have the power to do it? Or what if we were to think of those who remember that once upon a time, when we believed it was in our own self-interest to do so, we were allied with the very regimes we now wish to destroy?

Oded reminds us, as Paul does, too, that "all have sinned and fallen short of the glory of God." And Jesus asks us to recognize that others may have grievances that deserve our recognition and our best efforts of reconciliation. Taken together and taken seriously, the result might well be less hubris on our part and more humility, less self righteousness and more penitence.

*   *   *

Here is the third and the most important thing Oded makes me wonder about: whether there might be another way forward other than the age-old response of tit for tat, an eye for an eye, a life for a life.

It is a dangerous and divided world we live in. A "fearsome time," as another puts it, a world "whose wells of kindness seem everywhere to be

running dry."[5] About "the only thing we can think to do to protect ourselves (it seems), is to build bigger and better weapons to hit back harder
those who hate us and hit us."[6]

Oded, a prophet of the Lord, offers a different vision and persuades
his people to undertake magnanimous and generous acts of reconciliation.
I know. I know. You don't have to tell me. I know that these acts occurred
when the war was over. I am reminded of the inscription Winston
Churchill put on the flyleaf of his book about World War II: "In war: resolution, in defeat: defiance, in victory: magnanimity, in peace: good
will."[7] But I am wondering why magnanimous gestures have to wait until
the conflict is over. I am wondering if they were employed earlier on, if
they would not prevent some of our conflicts or, once conflicts have
begun, contribute to their resolution.

It's what Jeffrey Sachs, of Columbia University, has wondered, too.
He suggests that instead of focusing so much on weapons of mass destruction, we should give more of our attention to using what he calls "weapons
of mass salvation": an "arsenal of life-saving vaccines, medicines and
health interventions, emergency food aid and farming technologies that
could," he says, "avert literally millions of deaths each year in the [strug-
gles] against epidemic disease, drought and famine." We spend such vast
sums on the weapons of war, Sachs says, and relatively puny amounts on
humanitarian aid. "One stark result," he says, "is that the world's poor
live, and . . . die, with the awareness that [we are] doing little to mobilize
the weapons of mass salvation that could offer them survival, dignity and
eventually the escape from poverty."[8]

There is so much anger out there, so much hatred, and the normal
response is to fight fire with fire. But one wonders if it doesn't just fuel
the age-old cycles of violence and warfare. In any case, Oded, "a prophet
of the Lord," proposes an alternative vision. One, it strikes me, that seems
to anticipate Paul in his letter to the Romans. "Do not repay anyone evil
for evil . . . , says the apostle. If it is possible, so far as it depends on you,
live peaceably with all. . . . If your enemies are hungry, feed them; if they
are thirsty, give them something to drink. . . . Do not be overcome by evil,
but overcome evil with good."

That phrase "do not repay evil for evil" appears in the benediction I
use rather regularly at the end of our worship, though in the language of
the King James Version: "Render to no one evil for evil." One day, after

I had spoken those words, one worshipper said to me: "I have a lot of trouble with that 'render to no one evil for evil' business. It is what I often want to do." Who doesn't understand that? Who doesn't feel that way, at least sometimes? Our human tendency is to hit back and hit hard. It's why we need the gospel. And the gospel tells us not to be overcome by evil but to overcome evil with good. It's all very different from *realpolitik* isn't it? You may think it is pious nonsense. But if it is, it is Christian nonsense, and as Christians we have to deal with it.

What if we tried it? What if we were to imagine and implement even small, magnanimous gestures? Something equivalent to the clothing of those ancient captives, giving them sandals, providing them with food and drink, putting the feeble among them on donkeys and sending them home. What might it look like to do something of that kind in our world today? Talk about a radical foreign policy!

*   *   *

I close with a story that appeared this past summer in the *Christian Century*. It's the story of a Syrian man who grew up with the typical Muslim attitude toward Christians: to him, Christians represented western religion and the political force that continues its "crusades" against Muslims, blindly supporting the state of Israel despite its injustices against Palestinians. Christians, this man thought, speak of Christ as the "Prince of Peace," yet they resort to war. But then he embarked on a spiritual quest that led to an interest in Gandhi, and through the Hindu Gandhi who was deeply influenced by Christ, this Syrian Muslim discovered the teachings of Jesus and a person who backed up his teachings with his life. Eventually, he had a religious conversion that earned him the wrath of his family and forced him into exile. He thinks of himself now as "a Muslim who follows Jesus." And this is what he says: he believes that if Muslims are ever to see the true nature of Christ, they will have to see his likeness in his followers."[9]

Christ's followers. That's you, me, us.

1. Chris Hedges, *War Is a Force That Gives Us Meaning* (Anchor Books, 2003), p. 13.

2. Ibid., p. 10.

3. Ibid., pp. 13-14.

4. Bruce Catton, *A Stillness at Appomattox* (Garden City, NY: Doubleday & Co., 1953), p. 45.

5. Barbara Kingsolver as quoted by John M. Buchanan in "Small Wonder," a sermon preached in The Fourth Presbyterian Church of Chicago, October 5, 2003.

6. Ibid., John M. Buchanan.

7. In Carroll E. Simcox, *A Treasury of Quotations on Christian Themes* (New York: The Seabury Press, 1975), p. 111.

8. As quoted in *Christian Century*, November 20-December 3, 2002, p. 6.

9. Ibid., August 23, 2003, p. 6.